Reporting Coronavirus

Reporting Coronavirus

*Personal Reflections on a Global Crisis
from ITV News Journalists*

First published in 2020 by ITV Ventures

Editor: Marion Burns
Head of Publishing: Shirley Patton
Production: David Brimble

Typeset by Hewer Text UK Ltd, Edinburgh
Printed and bound in Great Britain by Clays Ltd, Elcograf S.p.A

ISBN 978-1-9103321-6-0 (Hardback edition)
ISBN 978-1-9103321-7-7 (EPUB edition)

10 9 8 7 6 5 4 3 2 1

A catalogue record of this book is available from the British Library

ITV Ventures
2 Waterhouse Square
140 Holborn
London
EC1N 2AE

Contents

CONTENTS

CONTENTS

CONTENTS

CONTENTS

Introduction

Michael Jermey, Director of News and Current Affairs, ITV

In the history of television journalism, which now stretches back well over sixty years, there has never been a news story like the 2020 coronavirus pandemic.

It has affected every populated continent in the world and very directly impacted the life of every person in the UK. It has attracted unprecedented interest from viewers, and because of lockdown, international travel restrictions and the need for social distancing it fundamentally changed the way all news organisations made their programmes.

ITV has been broadcasting news since 1955. Its journalists covered all the major stories of the late twentieth century and the early twenty-first. None of the news stories ITV's journalists covered during those decades quite matched the enormity of coronavirus in 2020. Some stories may arguably have had longer term political and historical significance, some may on a single day have been accompanied by more memorable images and more drama. But none affected every corner of the world and every household in Britain in such an all-encompassing and enduring way. Nor did any have such a profound impact on how news teams made the programmes viewers wanted to watch.

In the first six months of 2020 ITV News' reporters followed the Covid-19 story from the streets of Wuhan in China, to neighbouring countries in Asia, on to Europe and then into communities right across the UK. Nightly news broadcasts tracked the oncoming storm and its arrival in Britain.

When the country went into lockdown in late March ITV News continued to report on life in a transformed Britain. Designated as key workers, journalists and technicians working for ITV News kept the programmes on air and played an important role in conveying vital public health messages, reporting from the frontline on hospitals and care homes and also questioning those in authority about the policies they introduced to tackle the pandemic. Holding power to account is a vital function of the news media in a democracy.

ITV newsrooms and studios across the country, normally busy workplaces with scores of journalists and technicians working closely together, largely emptied. All work was carried out in line with public health guidelines. At the peak of the crisis only about 20 percent of staff were in the newsrooms at the busiest of times. Journalists and technicians routinely worked from home using the latest digital technology and when on location interviewed people with the aid of long microphone poles. Despite the challenges, all ITV's news services, both national and regional, kept broadcasting, bringing information, news and analysis to an audience hungry for accurate information and impartial news. With people living life in lockdown television became a lifeline for many. Viewers wrote to thank our teams for continuing to provide the news. Some said that in such a transformed world it was immensely reassuring to hear from familiar, trusted presenters and reporters.

ITV News staff were affected by the pandemic in all the ways that other citizens were. Some dealt with the challenges of homeschooling, some had to self-isolate, sadly a number, like so many families across Britain, lost close relatives to the disease. Like everyone else in Britain, the people of ITV News admired the work of NHS workers and carers across the country. They joined the weekly Clap for Carers as their neighbours did and helped in their communities where they could. In most ways their lives were the same as those of everyone else.

In one respect, however, the everyday experience of ITV's broadcast journalists was different. By the nature of their work television journalists get to witness events first hand and tell the story to the wider world. The pandemic and its appalling impact was only partially visible in the empty streets of our cities, towns and villages. In lockdown people didn't move far and so relied on television for a picture of the world beyond their immediate locality. ITV's journalists and camera operators did move around, always safely and always within public health rules, and they witnessed scenes others didn't. They were invited by hospitals to observe life on the NHS frontline, they watched communities coming together and in various corners of the world they reported on the international impact of the virus.

The pandemic took an emotional and mental toll on many people in Britain. Journalists were no exception. Covering the story could feel relentless. There was no escape from it. There were stories, especially when the daily death toll was at its highest, that were harrowing to report. No one should underestimate the impact of telling what was so often a heartbreaking story, day after day, for such a long period. As with lots of people across the country, many of those reporting the news found it a testing and challenging time.

All the journalists who worked on the story in the first half of 2020 will never forget the experience. From the first reports of the virus in Wuhan in January, through to lockdown in the UK in March and slowly on to the eventual easing of restrictions in July, it was an extraordinary time. Eighty percent of UK TV viewers saw some of ITV's coverage during that period. The journalists who appeared on the news night after night reported things as they found them. In the months since they've reflected on those experiences. In this book they share those personal memories of how the story unfolded, what they saw and learned and the impact it had on them.

The story of the pandemic clearly has a long way to run and the lessons we need to learn continue to emerge. This book is not intended as a final word nor even a first draft of history, but rather it is the personal reflections of journalists who witnessed a lot, shared it with viewers and now in a series of essays tell the inside story of how reporting coronavirus unfolded over six extraordinary months.

July 2020

Timeline

January

1 A market in Wuhan, China, the suspected centre of an outbreak of pneumonia-like illnesses, is closed

7 Chinese authorities identify the illness as a new type of coronavirus

23 Lockdown begins in Wuhan

24 The first UK Government COBRA emergency meeting is held

30 The World Health Organization says the outbreak is a global public health emergency of international concern

31 The first UK cases are confirmed

Italy declares a national emergency

February

7 Li Wenliang, one of the eight whistleblower doctors in Wuhan, dies from the coronavirus

11 The WHO says the disease caused by the new coronavirus will be called Covid-19

14 The first coronavirus death in Europe – a Chinese tourist in France

21 Lockdowns in small towns in the Italian region of Lombardy begin

29 The first coronavirus death in the United States – a man in Washington state

Flying to the Epicentre

Debi Edward, Asia Correspondent, ITV News

There were no alarm bells ringing, no real sense of foreboding as I got on the plane. I went to Wuhan with the same approach as any other work trip, to get to the source of the story and find out more.

In truth, I was pretty exhausted from the two weeks we had just spent covering the bushfires in Australia. It had looked like that story was going to dominate my Beijing-based bureau's agenda for the coming weeks and months. But when I was still in Sydney, I'd had my first conversation with ITV News' Head of Foreign News Michael Herrod about a mystery virus in China. We agreed I should get back and travel to Wuhan as soon as possible; the story, he told me, was "making its way into and up the running order in programmes."

In the day and 11-hour flight between that conversation and me landing in Beijing on Saturday January 18th, there was growing evidence that something potentially serious was developing. Seventeen new cases had been reported by the Wuhan local health committee, taking the total close to 200, and in the United States they had started screening passengers arriving from China. We booked a flight for Monday.

I had been to Wuhan once before. We filmed there in October 2018 for a report on internet addiction. It is home to one of hundreds of military style addiction clinics where teenagers are sent by parents desperate to cure their offspring of their online obsession.

I didn't get to see much on that occasion, but it had already come to my attention earlier in the year when then Prime Minister Theresa May made it her first stop on her tour of China. It was an unusual choice, not many foreign leaders pass through central China, but the British Government wanted to promote educational links with China and Wuhan has a large student population.

It is an intriguing city and I remember thinking to myself on my first visit that I should come back. The city has an impressive skyline set against the backdrop of the Yangtze River, which has always held a mystical draw for me. My return on January 20th wasn't quite the return trip I had planned.

On the morning we left, Beijing reported its first two cases, and three deaths were confirmed in Wuhan. For the first time I wore a mask on the flight. I took a selfie and sent it to a friend, telling him I was flying to the "epicentre". Of what, we didn't quite know.

Besides the handful of passengers we always see wearing them in China, we were the only ones with masks. Mine was claustrophobic and too tight, but I kept it on.

We'd heard about crowds of patients in hospitals and knew Jinyintan Hospital specialised in infectious diseases and was likely receiving the most cases. It was our first port of call.

But there were no queues or crowds; there was nothing unusual at all as we approached the hospital, its exterior already familiar from newspaper articles and footage I had seen in the preceding days. Our driver managed to drive into the grounds of the hospital, and it was there, at the back of the car park, that we saw half a dozen people in hazmat suits around the entrance to one of the buildings. An ambulance was pulling away, its driver and passenger also wearing protective clothing. I'd seen these kinds of images from Wuhan before we arrived but seeing them there, in front of me, I got my first indication that something serious was spreading in the city. Something from which these healthcare workers clearly required an extreme level of protection. I hadn't experienced anything like this before. It was unsettling. There were several security guards in the grounds so getting out to film was not an option. We filmed what we could from inside the car and drove out.

It's not illegal to film in the street in China, or to film the exterior of a building, but as soon as we started filming the hospital from the road outside, we were surrounded by hospital security staff. We lowered the camera and kept filming as we were asked for our credentials and told to delete our footage. It was hard to tell if they were on edge due to what was unfolding inside, or if this was just another routine and frustrating attempt to prevent us filming.

8

After some arguing and back and forth, eventually someone from the hospital communications team came out to talk to us and we convinced her to let us take some general shots of the building. The footage we took from the outside did not of course reveal the chaos we suspected, and later confirmed, was going on inside.

The Huanan Wet Market was our next stop. It was being described as the source of the outbreak after an initial cluster of cases was linked to workers on some of the stalls. The Chinese Government's move to shut it down on January 1st was also taken as a sign that it was implicated in the spread of the virus.

The security officers were caught off guard by our arrival; we'd started to film the eerily abandoned alleyways when one young officer spotted us, shouted "Oi!" and ran over to block the camera.

What followed were two tedious hours waiting for officials from the local ministry of foreign affairs to come and talk to us. We were being closely watched by the guards but our producer managed to talk to some of the market workers hovering around the sealed entrance. They told her they hoped the market could reopen after the Chinese New Year break. They appeared more concerned about the loss of business than about the virus. None of them were wearing masks.

It didn't add up. The reaction from the authorities, the medics in head to toe protection gear but the people we met at the market, the apparent source of the outbreak, seemingly unconcerned. Our driver told us everyone was mainly upset because the closure of the market meant there wouldn't be any seafood for Chinese New Year dinner celebrations that Friday, January 24th.

We learned that the authorities had started temperature checking people on board flights in China and that checks had been introduced at some of Wuhan's train and bus stations. When we arrived at the main train station there wasn't any sign of the precautions being taken, it was busy and most people were wearing masks. Many also had suitcases, clearly heading off to other parts of the country, and beyond, to join their relatives for the New Year holiday. There were a few groups of school children heading off on trips.

We interviewed some of those entering the station and although they all expressed a general concern about this new "pneumonia", none of them believed it was, or would become, very serious. A few mentioned the SARS outbreak in 2003, and said that the experience of handling that would mean the government would get this under control. Two people remarked that if it was really contagious the authorities would have shut the station down already.

Just a few hours later during an interview on state television evening news, Zhong Nanshan, China's leading virologist, confirmed what had perhaps been glaringly obvious all along – there was human-to-human transmission. He confirmed this new type of coronavirus was very infectious, but said they still weren't sure, and didn't explain exactly, how it was being transmitted.

It was an alarming admission at the start of the world's largest migration, the annual movement of millions of Chinese people going home for the week-long New Year celebrations. At the train station in Wuhan we had seen just a fraction of those already on the move for the holiday. Were temperature checks really going to be enough to control the spread of this thing?

That night I did my first live broadcast from Wuhan. I appeared on the ITV *Lunchtime News*, which was on at 9.30pm our time. The top story that day was Harry and Meghan giving up their royal titles. I confirmed that cases of the coronavirus had been found in Japan, South Korea and Thailand; with New Year celebrations just a few days away in those countries too, that raised the potential of a major outbreak. Even as I spoke those words and reported that President Xi had commented on the situation for the first time, promising every measure to combat the spread, it seemed unthinkable that from 217 cases in China that day it would come to engulf the rest of the world.

We debated whether to stay in Wuhan for a few days. It's a decision I still revisit. Had we stayed we would have been there to see the start of the lockdown, the extreme quarantine of millions of people that wouldn't be lifted until April. But of course, we could well have become trapped there ourselves. Confined to a hotel, or worse.

As it was, we decided to go back to Beijing. It had been difficult to film that first day and it seemed likely to become harder. Our producer Christine Wei was having trouble reaching anyone infected or connected to the confirmed cases; they'd all been told not to talk, and there was obviously a risk in approaching any of those people. The number of cases appeared to be rising in Beijing too and it was there that the National Health Commission had started holding daily briefings. We booked to fly back on Tuesday morning.

When we arrived at the airport on January 21st, we expected to face strict checks. We had used footage in our report the night before of people having their temperatures checked, one by one. We were ready to film that happening to us. But it didn't.

There were more people wearing masks, but it seemed nothing much else had changed since we had flown to Wuhan the previous day. Confirmation that this contagion was spreading from human to human had had little impact, so far.

When I look back at what happened in the next few days it is clear that a juggernaut had been placed in motion. But things were changing so fast, with new cases cropping up in different places every day, it was impossible to see exactly where the juggernaut was heading.

Two days after we had left Wuhan, on January 23rd, it went into lockdown. Deaths there had trebled in as many days, and the virus had reached almost all parts of China. There were also an increasing number of cases with no link back to the market, to anyone who had been there, or indeed to Wuhan. I wrote in my notebook ". . . the danger posed by this pneumonia-like virus may have been underestimated." It still didn't have a name but whatever it was, it was clearly a growing threat.

I think I was perhaps too busy trying to keep track of the case count and the city-wide quarantines being introduced across China to think about the implications of being one of the millions who had been allowed to leave Wuhan before it locked down. As we learned more about the virus it seemed outrageous that the Chinese authorities had allowed so many people to travel out of the city. And I had been among them.

When I got back to Beijing, I of course considered the fact I might have become infected, but I had worn my mask, washed my hands, used sanitiser and I hadn't come into contact with too many people. Then the calls started.

The Beijing health authorities had begun tracing anyone who had travelled to Hubei Province, and specifically Wuhan. They asked when

I left, when I had returned, on which flight, in which seat – all questions they knew the answers to from my passport details – but then they asked if I had any symptoms, did I have a fever, or a cough? I didn't, but it planted a seed of worry.

Beijing had become a ghost town by then. It's usually quiet during Chinese New Year but this was eerily so. Chinese families had retreated into their homes to quarantine and many foreigners had decided to leave the country. There was a palpable fear in the city that this was going to be another SARS. The capital had been among the worst hit during that outbreak.

Among my friends who stayed there was a growing wariness about meeting up. We weren't banned from doing so, but it was becoming more difficult, and we were becoming paranoid about hand-washing and being in public places. I'd started to derive comfort from having my temperature checked as I arrived at the office and again when I returned home to my residential compound.

The few people I encountered on my journeys to and from work and in the supermarket were all wearing masks, but still the tendency was to give one another a wide berth. There were only ever a handful of people in our office, or in the shop at any one time, but if anyone coughed, that sound had come to cause alarm.

The Foreign Office had evacuated Britons from Wuhan and warned against travelling to Hubei Province but on February 4th it upped its warning. British citizens still in China were advised to leave if they could.

I was asked if I wanted to get out. One of my colleagues had already decided it was becoming unsafe and had gone home to the United States. This was a developing story; it had gone from rising up the running order of our programmes to dominating them. I knew what I needed to do to protect myself, I rang my parents in Scotland and told them I would be ignoring the government's advice. I had a job to do. And that is when it really began.

The Hong Kong Story

John Ray, Correspondent, ITV News

Let me start in a different city. Beirut. It's early January 2020 and I'm contemplating the end of the world. As I stand among a crowd of angry Hezbollah supporters sworn to avenge the killing by a US missile of Iranian commander Qasem Soleimani, the prospects for peace look poor, the odds on the war of words between Washington and Tehran turning into the real shooting variety that might engulf us all seem a lot shorter.

It turns out of course I had my money on the wrong Horseman of the Apocalypse. Not war, but pestilence. That was the one to watch.

So, three weeks later, I'm in Hong Kong and something truly awful is galloping towards us. We've glimpsed its work, this silent invisible killer, in the startling images emerging from Wuhan, a city of 11 million people where normal life has been cancelled. Now I'm at the closest of the borders it's beginning to cross. This former British colony is China's gateway to the globe. And where people go, disease follows. As I land on January 30th the World Health Organization declares the coronavirus outbreak a "Public Health Emergency of International Concern". Soon it would have a name: Covid-19.

To be in Hong Kong, I was warned by a friend in the city, "feels like living next door to a volcano". They were expecting the eruption any moment. "Everybody's pretty scared. A lot who can leave have left already," she said. Another friend had packed her husband and children off to the UK "for safety's sake." Within two months, father, son and daughter were making the return journey, again for "safety's sake". But that's to jump ahead of the pandemic.

In January we were following it, like storm chasers I thought. Though what we'd do if we actually caught up . . . caught it . . . well

13

that was a question we didn't dare answer. Still, back then, this new disease felt like a distant threat. A far-off conflict, fought at a safe distance, I remember thinking, long before we heard of the two-metre rule.

But for the people of Hong Kong, it was already on their doorstep and they were braced. That much was clear, though in truth, only in retrospect, on the flight from London. Walking down the aisle between the rows of passengers, I have a clear memory: every Asian face seemed to wear a mask; none of the Westerners on board did. At the time it was unremarkable. As a former China Correspondent I'd lived and worked around the region for four years, and face masks, especially in the winter months, are commonplace.

It's a custom that's been traced back to Japan, a century ago, and the great global flu pandemic; a habit that stuck and spread across the region, as much a barrier to pollutants in rapidly industrialising societies as a potential protection against infection. And then came SARS, an earlier variant of coronavirus that in a few short weeks killed almost 300 people in Hong Kong. They know how little it can take to kill so many.

In 2003, on February 21st, a 64-year-old doctor, Liu Jianlun, checked into room 911 of the Metropole Hotel in Kowloon ahead of his nephew's wedding. He'd been working in a hospital in southern China where SARS patients had been treated. He felt under the weather yet managed to spend the day sightseeing with his family. By the next morning, he was so ill he went to a nearby hospital where he reportedly told doctors to put him into isolation. Within a month, 70 medical staff and almost a score of medical students there had succumbed to the same illness.

Dr Liu was Hong Kong's original "super-spreader". Their SARS index patient, as epidemiologists call case zero. Eighty percent of Hong Kong's cases can be linked to him. Seven guests who stayed on the same floor of the hotel at the same time became infected and in turn carried the disease, unwittingly, to Canada, Singapore and Vietnam. The WHO estimates that getting on for half the world's SARS cases can be connected to his one night at the Metropole. Not that Dr Liu ever knew. And he never made that wedding. He died in intensive care on March 4th. But as we will see, Dr Liu was not forgotten.

The worst of SARS was successfully contained in China and Hong Kong. But the world had been warned and Hong Kong had taken very careful notice. Back to 2020, and we were temperature-checked at the airport, and every time we entered our hotel. Schools were closed and government workers told to stay home. Business was on hold as the Chinese New Year break was extended. But if the streets of this restless city were unusually and eerily quiet, the spectacle that spoke loudest of high anxiety were the long queues for face masks.

They appeared on the mere rumour of fresh supplies. Outside one pharmacy, the line stretched patiently down the road to the end of the block then doubled back on itself and snaked around a far corner. I walked its length and reckoned it was more than a kilometre long. "Hong Kong's in a panic," one young man told me. He'd been waiting for an hour for the shop to open. A woman a few steps back shared the same fear. "It's crazy right now. Everyone's looking for a mask."

There was an irony here. A few months earlier, the Hong Kong Government had imposed a ban on face masks, a measure designed to rob pro-democracy campaigners of their anonymity after the wave of increasingly violent unrest that had crashed across the preceding year. So, add to the virus a toxic political atmosphere. And with it, widespread mistrust of the authorities who were seen by many to be doing the mainland's bidding. We befriended a young student, a sympathiser with the democracy movement. We will call him William, though that's not his real name. He has asked me not to reveal his identity. He has been arrested several times. "The coronavirus is actually a very useful thing for the Hong Kong Government," he told us, in one of many conversations in early February. "At least it has stopped people going out to do the protests."

To her credit, on most days, Hong Kong's beleaguered Chief Executive, Carrie Lam, would brief the media – boisterous encounters that sometimes ended with Ms Lam harangued by antagonistic journalists. The main point of contention: why was the border with China still open? Ms Lam was thought by her critics to lack political clout with Beijing's communist powers.

William said: "Every day thousands of people are coming across the border. Any one of them could bring the virus. But will anyone stop them? Of course not. Beijing is telling our government to keep the border open. The Chinese want people to think this will pass. They do not want to raise the alarm, but this city needs protection."

But the authorities refused to put Hong Kong into total isolation. We sought out Dr Lam Ching-choi, a member of the governing Executive Council. Yes or no, I asked him, is Beijing telling you to keep that border open? "No. It's our decision," he insisted. "Our government message is very simple and clear on this. We will listen to the experts."

That meant ignoring the thousands of medical staff who were striking and forming queues to sign petitions of protest that were even longer than those for face masks. Angry colleagues crowded round Dr Melody Yeung, a speech therapist and member of a local medical union, when she told me: "The government is refusing to block the borders. And we all know it's for political reasons."

Others were taking extraordinary measures to stay safe and to stay at work. Dr Benjamin So was in self-imposed quarantine. He'd been treating coronavirus victims and no longer dared go home. After each long and exhausting shift at the Queen Mary Hospital, the 27-year-old took off his layers of protective clothing, showered and walked a block to a nearby hotel where he cocooned himself in his room. Food arrived by courier. He forbade himself any contact with his family and friends. "I'm worried that I will become the vector who spreads the virus to the rest of the community," he told me in a web call one night. He was remembering Dr Liu and SARS from two decades ago.

Dr So was an earnest and eloquent young man. Dedicated to his job. Scared for the future. "Basically, what has happened to Wuhan now is something that could happen to Hong Kong as well." Even though there were more isolation facilities in Hong Kong since SARS, the population had grown, and grown older too. "Front-line medical staff are very certain that with the current level of resources we wouldn't be able to handle the situation," he said.

By now the authorities were shifting position. The border remained open, but one by one the crossing points had closed. Air links were curtailed, the high speed train link ended. But Hong Kong and its Chinese mirror, the giant city of Shenzhen, are intimately linked through economic, work and family ties.

At one press briefing I asked Carrie Lam to accept that the longer the border stayed open at all, the greater the danger. "This is the balance that one has to strike given Hong Kong's very unique situation," she replied. "But we will take whatever steps are necessary to protect us from this infection."

In the first week of February, a 39-year-old man called an ambulance to his apartment block. A local television camera operator captured the moment the crew, wearing protective suits and masks, lifted him into their vehicle, with security tapes around the scene. Four days later he became the city's first coronavirus fatality. His mother had tested positive and was in quarantine. The atmosphere of dread deepened.

We visited the complex where he'd lived. The entrance was cordoned off but we spoke to neighbours and they were terrified. "We don't know if we also now carry the virus," one woman told me. "We have been sharing the same lift, touching the same buttons, breathing the same air." Another neighbour said: "No one from the government has come to tell us how to protect ourselves."

But the balance that Carrie Lam had spoken about was shifting. The authorities announced that anyone arriving from the mainland would have to go into quarantine for 14 days. Holiday camps and new housing estates were turned into quarantine centres. The daily caseload peaked in March, then it began to fall. Maybe Lam had it right all along. Her government had followed the WHO guidelines to test and isolate suspected cases and to trace all their contacts.

Or perhaps in this want-to-be democracy, this was a triumph of people power. A survey in March showed a huge majority were avoiding crowded places. And an astonishing 99 percent wore face masks when they left their homes. Hong Kong took seriously the threat of coronavirus from the start.

The volcano so feared in Hong Kong did erupt. But not where we expected. It was in Italy, in Spain and then the UK. That's where the sky darkened and the earth shook.

Postscript: UK – late February

Twelve days after I returned to the UK I had begun to feel ill. A really sore throat, as if I'd been gargling shards of glass, a fever and heavy breath. Still, at first, NHS 111 assured me I didn't qualify for a test. "The advice is changing all the time, almost by the hour," an exasperated and apologetic NHS worker told me. "We've had an explosion of suspected cases," said another, who eventually called back to confirm an appointment with the team who would take a sample, send it off to the lab, and determine whether or not I had Covid-19. "We will aim to have the result in seventy-two hours. But we're very busy," warned a third.

In Hong Kong, we'd taken precautions, face masks, hand sanitisers, soap and water. But I still thought of those crowds in the queues and protests. I had a test – a long cotton bud to the back of the throat. Then a long wait. I watched the news as the number of confirmed cases mounted. I remembered the tube and train journeys I'd taken. Might I be a super-spreader. Another Dr Liu?

I've reported from many international crises. Many a war, many a violent uprising. I've been lucky when the bullets are flying and the bombs are landing. Assignment over, like Beirut in early January, I've left all the dangers behind at the airport for the flight home.

But coronavirus is a crisis you might get to keep; to pass on to loved ones, to friends and to colleagues. It could follow you to the office, to your house, to the breakfast table. And you might not know until it's too late.

Three days after my test, the result comes back. Negative. Accurate or not, when weeks later my children succumb to hacking coughs that precisely fit a symptom of coronavirus, I stay well. Hong Kong antibodies in my system? I'll never know.

Hong Kong – June

I've spoken again to my old friend in Hong Kong. How's it going all this time later, I ask. Still a handful of cases, she says. Good news. But this thing isn't beaten. It's biding its time. It's still here.

A View From the Studio

Mary Nightingale, Presenter, ITV News

The first whispers of Covid-19 emerged from China at the end of December; a new "flu-like illness" that was causing concern in the city of Wuhan. But our expert information was reassuring – a slow-moving virus with a low death rate. It didn't sound like much of a story for the UK. Certainly not enough to ruffle the news programme running orders. At the start of 2020 our attention was firmly focused elsewhere.

It's January 31st, Brexit Day, and I'm on a train to Newcastle, to present the *Evening News* from one of the key cities that voted Leave in the 2016 Referendum. The outside broadcast crews are in place, and the guests lined up for special programmes that night. Brexit had dominated the news agenda for the past four years, as the debate raged over Britain's future. This was the day we would formally split from the EU and begin the journey proper to a Brussels-free future. Months of planning, and spending, had gone into the evening's coverage.

Just after Doncaster, as I tucked into my LNER breakfast, the agenda shifted. Britain had identified its first cases of coronavirus, and we suddenly had a far bigger story to tell. I called the editorial team back in London, and we debated the implications for the programme. Nobody wanted to abandon that evening's plans, but there was little real disagreement. It was obvious the pandemic's arrival in Britain should and would lead the ITV *Evening News*. I got off the train at York, crossed the platform, and caught the next train south back to London and our studios in Gray's Inn Road. Coronavirus would be the lead story in almost every programme for the next six months.

Right from the start, it was a challenging story to cover. As soon as lockdown began, we had to adapt to working in ways none of us could ever have imagined. I suspect we may never return to how things were before.

It was essential to maintain the identity and quality of our programmes; communicating with our audiences had never been more important. There was a huge appetite for clear, accurate information, as people turned to a news source they could trust. We've been encouraged by some of our best viewing figures for years. But social distancing and quarantine rules have not made it easy.

The biggest immediate change was to newsroom and studio staffing. News is a noisy collaborative business, and the newsroom's usually full of people arguing and planning. Overnight, the ITV News HQ emptied, as colleagues vacated the office to work from home. The silence and the hand sanitiser have now become familiar – but it all felt very odd in early March.

The programme teams usually work in tight groups, so we can communicate and react quickly to stories. Sitting two metres apart (and logging in from home) have slowed things down considerably. But we have adapted, as have reporters who now conduct interviews via Zoom and edit their reports remotely. Everything just needs to be organised and completed far earlier, to leave enough time before we go on air. Some correspondents like to cut it fine, and that's half the fun of live news, but it can cause real problems when resources are so stretched. There have been a few close shaves, with reports missing their allocated slots or technology failing. With limited staff in the building that was always going to present extra problems, and some programmes have been a bit of a white knuckle ride.

It's the presenter's job to make everything look like it's meant to be, whatever the chaos pouring through your ear-piece. We hear everything that's going on in the production gallery, whether it's the director trying to establish contact with a reporter via a shaky Skype connection, or the programme editor frantically rearranging the running order to make up for a report that's missed a deadline. And, throughout, there's the steadying voice of the production assistant keeping precise track of the timings. The broadcast has to run exactly to time, whatever happens, hitting precisely the moment ITV switches away from our studio output. Every second is crucial and counted.

There's a massive team effort behind every programme, but the presenter is the final link in the production chain and has to take responsibility on screen. We make sure we have spare scripts to fill any gaps and are well enough briefed to ad-lib when needed. Nobody wants to let the team down, but it's self-preservation too. If everything falls apart, the newscaster is the one looking a fool in front of millions. Believe me, we've all been there.

Studio staffing was cut right back to help with social distancing. The role of floor manager disappeared, and we reduced the ambition of our camera shots, so they could be largely operated remotely. As much human contact as possible was removed. I printed my own scripts and grappled with my on screen appearance. Concerned viewers got in touch, worried that I looked ill. I wasn't ill – just doing my own make-up. Turns out it's quite a skill.

Like the rest of the country I didn't see a hairdresser for months, and feared that viewers would be able to track the length of lockdown by the length of my roots. In the end I found a spray that temporarily covered the grey and moved on. It was actually liberating to relax about how I looked. Decades of ensuring I was tidy for television were cast aside as I realised nobody would notice or care. We all had more important things to worry about than the state of my hair.

Early on, journalists were designated key workers, and while clearly we weren't saving lives like those in the NHS or care sector, I think we did have a valuable role to play in keeping people informed; the very essence of public service broadcasting, where the right information, properly delivered, could genuinely help keep people safe.

I felt a huge responsibility towards our viewers. I've been in television news for 30 years, 20 of them presenting ITV's *Evening News*, and there's never been a story like this. Everybody has been affected, tens of thousands in the UK have lost their lives, tens of millions are already feeling the economic and social consequences. I've tried hard to project a calm, reassuring presence on screen. There have been days when the death toll approached 1,000, and that is a tough headline to deliver. I was only too aware of people around the country, glued to their televisions, dreading the next bulletin and yet desperate for news.

I realised early on the way I signed off at the end of the programme would have to evolve from the usual cheery "Have a good evening". I tried "Stay safe – Stay well" and later "Stay at home" too. The viewers seemed to approve; some said they found it comforting. I didn't embrace the government's "Stay alert" message – it never quite made sense to me.

We tried to include at least one point of light, every evening, to pierce the gloom. ITV News is famous for its "And Finally" stories – the uplifting pieces at the end of our programmes that leave the viewer smiling. There had rarely been a greater need for positive news, and we found a rich seam of brave NHS workers and "ordinary" people facing extraordinary challenges. Captain Tom Moore was rightly celebrated, but we found numerous tales of human generosity, kindness and survival against the odds. I think I found them as much of a relief as our viewers.

Coronavirus has presented unique pressures for journalists. We are very well used to dealing with the stuff of death and disaster, and over the years I have learned to put aside the day's horrors as I finish my shift. Some stories linger in the memory, of course, but I am fortunate to have a pretty secure and happy life, and I can largely contain the mental fallout from the tragic news I deliver daily. But with Covid-19 there was no separation. I wrote and read about it all day, and stepped into the story as I left the studio.

The early weeks were exhausting; trying to maintain a professional demeanour amid the uncertainty that gripped us all (as well as the constant effort to remember about social distancing and hand-washing). When I got home I'd find myself craving silence, and would lie staring at the ceiling for a while before engaging with the family. On particularly stressful days I'd even find my voice starting to give up mid-bulletin, which added an extra dimension of pressure. I got through endless cups of tea, and confess I considered a quick swig of something stronger. But slurring my words was never going to be helpful. Colleagues each had their own ways of managing the stresses of broadcasting. I think everyone struggled to find an equilibrium as the pandemic unfolded.

Life and work under lockdown settled into a sort of uneasy routine that would have seemed extraordinary a year before. Gradually the daily death toll steadied and then fell. But nobody felt ready to relax, with the situation still evolving, and the constant threat of a second or even third wave.

This virus keeps challenging us – not least as a reminder of our own mortality. Journalists are used to walking away at the end of a story and resuming our own lives. But coronavirus has demonstrated that every one of us is closer to the precipice than we like to acknowledge. News is no longer something that only happens to other people. We are all vulnerable.

We're Dealing With a Completely New Virus

Tom Clarke, Science Editor, ITV News

I have to be honest here. When reports first arrived of an unknown respiratory disease causing pneumonia-like illness in Wuhan, I didn't run screaming to the newsdesk.

My 20-year-long career as a science reporter had been overshadowed by the potential threat of the next pandemic. For a decade or more, the world of public health had been on alert for "the big one". And while some outbreaks had come close, none had turned out to be the global public health crisis everyone feared. The one that Covid-19 turned out to be.

Nope. Experience had taught me to treat every would-be-pandemic virus with cautious scepticism. I mentioned the Wuhan outbreak to our Head of Foreign News Michael Herrod, suggesting we should keep an eye on it, and he told me our Asia Correspondent Debi Edward in Beijing was already doing just that. Why was I sceptical? Well, that story also begins in China, in January 2003.

People began dying of a mystery respiratory illness, one the Chinese authorities tried to conceal at the time. It wasn't until an American businessman fell ill in Vietnam that the illness came to the attention of the wider world. The patient was treated by an Italian doctor, Carlo Urbani, who realised it was a new virus, notified the World Health Organization and prompted Vietnam to take the first steps to contain it. Severe Acute Respiratory Syndrome, or SARS, as the new coronavirus came to be known, killed 10 percent of those it infected. Before anyone realised the significance of his role, Dr Urbani became infected and died in March 2003.

Once scientists knew what SARS was, they sat up and took notice. It belonged to the coronaviridae family of RNA viruses, a handful of which cause "common cold" illness in humans, with many others infecting animals. But here was a newcomer that caused very severe disease. Seasonal influenza only kills 0.1 percent of people it infects but that means between 300,000 and 650,000 die of it each year. SARS was killing 11 percent. The death toll from a SARS pandemic was unthinkable.

China's initial secrecy gave SARS the chance to spread. It terrified public health experts because it came out of left field. Most experts had been assuming the next killer pandemic would be an influenza virus. Genetic sequence data showed that SARS had recently hopped from bats, living in caves in Thailand, into humans. Based on influenza research, viruses that jump from an animal host into people, called "zoonoses" in the trade, were responsible for dangerous pandemics. Such a virus could be lethal, because it hadn't adapted itself to live in its new human host and humans would have no immunity to it, meaning they were completely susceptible to infection.

SARS ticked all these boxes. And it spread. The advent of rapid genetic testing made this one of the first new viruses to be tracked as it spread from China. But air travel meant the virus was always a few days ahead of the testing. A handful of cases popped up in Europe and Australia, 27 in the United States and, thanks to an ongoing hospital outbreak in Toronto, 251 cases and 44 deaths in Canada. But the grim fact that it was 100 times more deadly than seasonal flu actually helped make it easier to bring under control. People with SARS were only really infectious when they were at their sickest. That made it spread less quickly (since people were too sick to have many contacts) and therefore it was easier to contain outbreaks.

By 2004, the SARS outbreak was over. It had caused around 8,000 cases worldwide and claimed 744 lives. And since the end of the epidemic, the SARS virus has never been seen again and is presumed extinct. The view among public health experts was that we'd got off lightly. SARS could have been much worse, and it made those of us covering science realise that what had been for years a theoretical possibility of a global pandemic on a crowded planet was, in fact, very dangerous and very real.

But the attention spans of television journalists are short, and we soon became distracted by other things. Just before SARS faded into history entirely, bird flu happened. In January 2005, a new strain of avian influenza broke out in Vietnam. Bird flu is common; well known by veterinary experts for its ability to spread like wildfire through poultry flocks. But this strain, a highly pathogenic form of the H5N1 type, was different. It could also infect and kill humans.

And just as the theory predicted, this new virus could kill efficiently. Of those people unlucky enough to be infected, mainly poultry farmers in poor countries with no protective equipment, around 60 percent of them died. That made this strain of bird flu 600 times more deadly than seasonal flu. If SARS hadn't been the virus that jumped the species barrier to become the next pandemic, perhaps it would be bird flu?

What made things all the more terrifying was that research on influenza suggested previous pandemic flu viruses often had their origins in pigs or birds. The world suffers cycles of flu pandemics every 10 to 20 years. Yet we hadn't had a new global flu outbreak since 1968 — a pandemic was long overdue.

Vietnam and then Cambodia culled ducks and chickens to prevent H5N1 spreading through the poultry trade. But they couldn't stop wild birds flying. And starting in January, the world watched as the world's great bird migration routes carried the virus west.

For the second time in as many years, we were on high alert for a pandemic. By October a cluster of Turkish turkey farms near a lake filled with migratory birds were infected. Four local people became infected and died.

And so it was that ITV News' then Science Editor Lawrence McGinty and I, then Science Correspondent for *Channel 4 News*, found ourselves rushing to a lakeside in a remote corner of Turkey. It was a tough assignment for television since there were no birds to film. Whether wild or domesticated, the authorities had culled them all in an attempt to control the virus. But the story was strong: deadly bird flu was on the doorstep of Europe.

By now, H5N1 bird flu was being described by the World Health Organization as a significant pandemic threat. And despite mass culling it was still spreading. More cases were found across continental Europe, though very few in humans. The UK was on high alert for the virus spreading west with the spring bird migration. And in April 2006 it literally washed up on our shores.

A dead swan was found on a slipway in the seaside village of Cellardyke in Scotland. The quiet community had never seen so many journalists. The BBC and Sky had helicopters up looking for dead birds. I scoured the beaches looking for a scoop in the form of something dead covered in feathers. As Britain's miserable poultry industry was put into lockdown, newsrooms went into meltdown. ITV News set up a "bird flu hotline" to receive reports of outbreaks wherever they might occur. But the phones never rang.

Global culling of poultry and improved hygiene on farms meant that by the end of 2007 fewer than 200 people had become infected and died worldwide, none of them in Europe. And while a few cases of human-to-human transmission had been reported it seemed to be the exception, not the norm. The virus clearly wasn't very good at spreading in humans. The chickens and ducks were less lucky. More than 140 million birds were slaughtered worldwide.

Then, just two years later, the long-overdue flu pandemic finally arrived. Worryingly, it was a new strain of the same H1N1 type that caused the 1918–19 flu pandemic that killed millions. Its genetic sequence suggested that just months before it had jumped the species barrier from pigs, being reared intensively on farms in central Mexico, and quickly began spreading from human to human.

Swine flu quickly went global. Efforts to test and trace the virus slowed its spread initially, but soon the virus was in general circulation. It was an unusual flu virus in that it spared elderly people, instead causing more severe illness in younger adults and pregnant women. And while around 250,000 people may have died globally during the pandemic, that was similar to the number that die every year from seasonal flu. While meeting all the criteria for a proper pandemic, swine flu never came close to threatening the collapse of healthcare systems or causing mass mortality; the scenario everyone had feared for so long.

So when reports of a new respiratory illness in Wuhan hit the newswires, can you now forgive my slightly jaded response? Ten years on from swine flu, we'd seen a few bird flu strains come and go with little consequence and no new flu pandemics. And while I'd headed to west Africa in 2014 to cover the most long-lasting, deadly and widespread Ebola outbreak in history, it also didn't spread beyond the epidemic phase.

My indifference didn't last long though. Within days, rather than the weeks it took to isolate SARS, the genetics of the new virus were analysed. It was another coronavirus, clearly deadly, and clearly not as containable as SARS.

The UK's leading experts started to brief us on the virus. And the most astonishing thing we learned was just how little they knew. China had shared the virus's genetic code, but how many people were dying, how many cases were severe, and how it was spreading, could only be inferred from scant reports coming from the WHO and Chinese experts. At the time, Professor Neil Ferguson, a leading disease modelling expert at Imperial College who not long after fell foul of the lockdown rules he helped create, reminded everyone: "We just don't know; we're dealing with a completely new virus."

But it was becoming clear that we didn't need to know very much to conclude Covid-19 was serious. Early estimates by Chinese doctors, which have since been borne out globally, estimated mortality at between one and three percent. That doesn't sound too bad, but when you consider seasonal flu, more than capable of killing a quarter of a million people globally every year, has a fatality rate of 0.1 to 0.2 percent, it's terrifying.

But surely it would be contained? It didn't seem to be spreading as quickly as SARS and, by then, China had implemented the most severe societal lockdown of modern times.

The gravity of the situation finally became clear to me in February when the WHO convened a two-day emergency meeting of leading disease scientists to try to pool the world's knowledge. The first thing they did, on February 11th, was agree on a name for the new disease. The virus would be called SARS-CoV-2; the disease it causes, Covid-19.

Walking through the crowd of scientists at the meeting, which in retrospect was probably allowing the virus to be spread, was like seeing a who's who of pandemic experts. To my left the scientist who had obtained the first genetic sequence of SARS; to my right, the one who'd coordinated Hong Kong's lockdown to prevent its spread; across the hall the discoverer of the Ebola virus speaking to the director of the US Covid response team whose efforts to contain the virus were about to be thwarted by a president who refused to listen to the experts. And all of them looked worried – convinced Covid-19 very much had pandemic potential and that everything possible had to be done to prevent it spreading.

The problem was, it was already too late. The meeting was being held at the WHO's headquarters in Geneva. A 45-minute drive away, a ski chalet in the Alps was being deep cleaned after five British holidaymakers had tested positive for Covid. At the time the UK had just three confirmed cases, two Chinese nationals in isolation in a hospital in Newcastle, and the traveller from Singapore who'd been to the now famous ski chalet before flying home.

But based on an analysis of the various genetic strains of SARS-CoV-2, we now know the virus was already being seeded across the UK. During February and March there were around 1,500 introductions of the virus. Hardly any from China where it originated, nearly all from Italy, Spain and France, which by then had outbreaks too.

By mid-March, cases in the UK were climbing rapidly. Northern Italy was seeing its healthcare system start to be overwhelmed by the virus. Pressure started to mount on the UK Government to lock down the country. Its delay, we now know, possibly led to our outbreak being twice as large as it might have been.

It's not like we didn't see this coming. And many countries learned lessons from the near-misses of SARS, bird flu and swine flu. After the initial stage of our outbreak, the UK was unwilling, and then unable, to test, trace and isolate cases. Countries hit hard by SARS, like Singapore, Vietnam, Hong Kong and South Korea, used tried-and-tested trace and isolate systems, which contained Covid-19. The UK so far has five times more cases than all of those countries combined.

While the UK had stockpiled personal protective equipment and had a pandemic plan in place, it's now clear that the stockpile, and the plan, should have been dusted off and checked more frequently, and checked against the reality of containing a SARS-like virus.

It's not fair to say no lessons were learned. China came in for widespread international criticism for covering up SARS. While there were certainly early delays to its response to Covid-19, most experts credit China with being fast and proactive in sharing genetic and clinical data about the virus that allowed the rest of the world to prepare.

And while the UK's public health response and leadership has been widely criticised, plans put in place for pandemic vaccine and drug research have paid off. A team at the University of Oxford was able to produce a vaccine candidate for Covid-19 in record time because they had an "off-the-shelf" version developed against MERS (another deadly relative of SARS) designed to be modified to work against various types of RNA viruses. Likewise, the clinical trial involving 12,000 NHS patients that discovered that the common anti-inflammatory drug Dexamethasone could save the lives of Covid-19 patients was a drug-testing strategy set up by a network of collaborating scientists following the swine flu pandemic. It was designed to respond to the next pandemic hitting the UK, and it has been praised internationally for its foresight and effectiveness.

But what frustrates epidemiologists and public health experts is that some of the fundamentals that contributed to other recent outbreaks, and most likely to the Covid-19 pandemic, still haven't been addressed globally: risks inherent in the international trade in wild animals, poor hygiene and welfare conditions in livestock farming in some countries, and a consistent lack of investment in public health infrastructure like testing labs and staff training to contain outbreaks when, not if, they occur.

American author David Quammen, perhaps the greatest chronicler of modern plagues, described the global effort to predict where the next pandemic might come from in his 2012 book *Spillover*. The consensus among scientists back then was that it would probably be a virus, most likely a coronavirus, coming out of a bat, and it would likely be linked to the wildlife trade in China. Covid-19 was entirely predictable. And predicted.

If there's anything that we can be thankful for, it is that the virus isn't more deadly. As we now know, the risk of dying from Covid-19 for healthy people under 40 is extremely low. It only starts to become really dangerous for people older than 75. And yet it has still killed more than 60,000 people in the UK (as measured by "excess deaths" recorded by the Office for National Statistics) and done as-yet incalculable damage to the economy. There will be much to learn from this pandemic. Let's hope we remember those lessons for the next one.

Cassandra's 2020 European Tour

James Mates, Europe Editor, ITV News

It's enough to make you weep for Cassandra. She was blessed with the power of prophecy, while being cursed that no one would believe her, and while I'm not claiming any powers of foresight or prediction, I sort of know how she must have felt. What I was reporting in March and April was not a speculative look into the future, just stories about what was happening right here, right now, and what was coming our way, in countries more like ours than we sometimes like to think.

Italy was hit first and hit hardest by the arrival of the coronavirus Covid-19 in Europe, no one quite knows why or how. Whether it was the extensive business links between northern Italy and China, or a single "super-spreader" event, so far there's no definitive explanation of why the virus should have rampaged through Lombardy and Veneto while other regions of the same country escaped almost completely. No one is even sure if the virus arrived first in Italy at all; the French authorities now believe they had their first infection way back in mid-December 2019, and yet it wasn't until large numbers of tourists started to return from the ski-resorts of northern Italy in late February that France began to see its own infection levels spike.

But if there had to be a ground zero for the spread of this infection in Europe, the wealthy north Italian plain should have been as capable of containing it as anywhere on the continent. It didn't turn out that way. The response of the Italian authorities was admirably robust – so strict that civil libertarians were raising eyebrows everywhere. News editors around the world scrambled camera crews to the scene to document a lockdown policy that kept 11 villages and their inhabitants under virtual and indefinite house arrest. On February 23rd, to the east of Milan in Lombardy and on into Veneto, police roadblocks cut access routes in and out of villages like Vo, where reporters could shout across a small river to inhabitants on the other side, trying to get a picture of life inside. It was a weird sort of journalism, but to have gone past the roadblock and into Vo would have meant not coming out again for several weeks.

We have become used now to talking about coronavirus in terms of tens of thousand of deaths, hundreds of thousands of cases. This "nuclear option" of lockdown was being deployed in Italy in response to just a handful of cases (on February 23rd, 159 recorded infections) and just two or three deaths. They knew it was serious, they knew it was spreading, and they were not optimistic that they were doing enough. In the latter days of February and into early March, the stories of Lombardy's overwhelmed hospitals, and of intensive care units unable to cope, were the subject of our reports night after night. As confirmed cases hit 3,000, schools and universities were shut. By the weekend of March 7th/8th, with cases now up to 7,000, it was clear that more and stricter measures were coming. That Sunday morning a lockdown was announced that covered the whole of Lombardy and parts of both Veneto and Piedmont – in other words most of northern Italy. All traffic was to stop, all public gatherings, sports events, bars and restaurants were to shut down, everyone was to stay indoors unless they had an approved reason to go outside.

This was a wartime curfew, only in reality much worse than anything most countries have imposed in wartime. Our Milan hotel told us that night that we'd have to leave in the morning as they were shutting up shop. Heading south to Rome early the next day, before the restrictions came into force, was the only option for us, not least because it would be impossible to work or report under such strict conditions. But just days later, lockdown caught up with us in Rome as the whole country was shut down for at least three weeks (it turned out to be longer). We were lucky to catch one of the very few flights back to the UK.

All of this was meat and drink to a reporter, an extraordinary story about the imposition of the most draconian controls seen anywhere in Europe since 1945. Every night we told of new and breaking developments, but even so the most surprising thing of all was not to be found in Italy, but on our return to the UK. We came back to a country that seemed to consider itself immune to what was happening in Italy. Yes, as returners from Rome, we had been told by the UK Government to go home and self-isolate for 14 days (which we dutifully did), but beyond that there seemed to be no evidence at all of preparations in the UK for what was surely to come.

We passed through Heathrow airport without a check, or a test or even a request for information as to who we were and where we were intending to isolate. Nothing. Nada. We were surely the highest-risk arrivals of all, but beyond being handed a leaflet on the plane, we were left entirely to our own devices. Back in central London nothing had changed since the day we left: the pubs were rammed, restaurants busy, the Liverpool vs Atletico Madrid Champions League match at Anfield was on the television, the Cheltenham Festival was underway. As Italian Health Minister Sandra Zampa had observed, the Italians had studiously ignored what had been happening in China, assuming it could never happen to them. Now the UK was ignoring what had been happening in Italy, and for the same reason.

The data didn't lie; in fact every lesson to be learned could be seen in the graphs that tracked infections and deaths in country after country as the virus spread. The lines showing each nation in turn tracked almost identical paths up until the moment of lockdown, and while Italy was out in front in Europe, others were on the same trajectory. Spain was about a week behind Italy, France 10 days or so, the UK two to two and a half weeks. To anyone following the data, Italy was sounding the alarm and giving everyone else time to react. Few took advantage. London had more time than most but, if anything, did even less. Our reports over previous weeks in Italy weren't predictions. These were real-time reports of the scenes in the hospitals, accounts of patient after patient presenting with double (and often fatal) pneumonia, and evidence of the need to make sure those who needed them the most had access to scarce ventilators. The virus was not very far away and coming towards us rather fast.

Former Health Secretary Jeremy Hunt has been outspoken about the time that was wasted: "The failure to look at what those countries were doing at the outset will rank as one of the biggest failures of scientific advice to ministers in our lifetimes." The failure to use the time we had is, by now, well known and well analysed. What has interested me more is why? What was it about watching the painful experience of a near neighbour that made us think "no, not going to happen here?" Particularly because other countries took the Italian experience extremely seriously, and used the time to spectacularly good effect. Which brings me on to Greece.

Flying to Athens airport was a very different experience to my arrival at Heathrow. Travelling at all had involved a week-long negotiation with the Greek embassy in London, not least to ensure that we would be allowed to move around and report once we arrived. On landing the entire plane was emptied into a holding area where every one of us was swab-tested, and our details taken. Then it was on to a bus, to a government-commandeered hotel downtown and into our rooms, where we were to stay (on pain of a €5,000 fine) until our test results came through. Food was left outside our doors during a quite long and dull day, but by evening we had been given the all clear and allowed to move to an apartment nearby (all the other hotels had long since shut). All our fellow passengers also tested negative, but nonetheless had to go straight into 14-day quarantine at home. Their addresses were in the system, pinpointed alongside their details on a map on a giant screen at the Civil Protection command HQ. Every day they would be contacted by phone to check they were OK and showing no symptoms, and every day either the police or fire-service would visit their address to ensure they were there. The Greeks took this seriously.

The Greek health system had been one of the principal victims of the 10 years of austerity that followed the Euro-crisis. It has still not recovered, and the Greeks know it. If Italian healthcare (rated by the World Health Organization as the second best in the world) was buckling under the onslaught of Covid-19, they believed theirs didn't stand a chance. So if the pandemic was as bad as the scientists were saying, they had to both lock down and prepare.

Back in February, while all the talk in polite circles in London was of "mild flu", the Greek Government was sourcing tests, test-kits and personal protective equipment from China. On finding that others were jumping ahead of them in the scramble for scarce supplies, they sent a team of purchase-agents to Beijing, who eventually brought back 13 plane-loads of the kit their country would need. That meant that at a time when the UK was struggling to test front-line NHS staff, the Greeks had the capacity to test every arriving traveller. It was quite a contrast.

On March 23rd, the day Boris Johnson finally announced a lockdown, the Greeks banned all direct flights from the UK on the grounds of our infection protocols. The only other country put into the same category was Turkey. They had a record to defend with (at the end of June 2020) fewer than 200 deaths *in total*, and a figure for total infections still below 3,500. The country had begun to lock down, with schools, bars, restaurants all closed, before they had a single death. Travel to the Greek islands was banned early, meaning most managed to avoid having any confirmed infections at all. Greek commentators watching the delays and confusion in London were dumbfounded.

It's hard to know to what extent British 'exceptionalism' and a generalised contempt for the organisational abilities of Italians contributed to all this, but both were undoubtedly present. One leading commentator (who I won't name because he has since regretted and retracted) tweeted that "if we are expected to take lessons in disaster management from the Italians, then we know we're in trouble", and he was far from the only one expressing such opinions. The decision to go our own way, first with herd immunity, then with a general but fairly loose lockdown, then with the abandonment of a strategy of widespread 'test and trace' (only to bring it back a few weeks later), smacked of a country that felt it had little to learn from the experience of others. This would be a matter of historical argument if it weren't for the fact that the same pattern is playing itself out over the development and deployment of the tracing app.

The UK was determined to build its own, so it did. It was, of course, going to be 'world-beating'. The only problem was that it didn't work, so now, belatedly, the UK is following the example of others and adopting the off-the-shelf Apple/Google model. But despite that humiliation, no lesser figure than the British Prime Minister was declaring to the House of Commons that "no country on earth has a working app" two weeks after Germany deployed theirs, with 12 million downloads and counting.

It's either a lack of curiosity or an absolute determination that we have nothing to learn from anybody, but whichever it is, it has happened again and again throughout this crisis. One thing it is not is a lack of reporting, either by newspapers or broadcasters, of what is being done in Europe. The German app has had extensive coverage. The testing and quarantine regimes at airports, notably Athens and Vienna, have been the subject of news reports on multiple channels. And that's just the journalists. The Government in Whitehall has, of course, access to a network of embassies across the world who will each have been reporting back on the policies of their host countries, and assessing the relative successes and failures.

Is it all "too early to tell" as ministers keep telling us, that international comparisons are pretty meaningless at the moment, and we would all do well to suspend judgement until the crisis is over and a cool assessment (public enquiry anyone?) can be made? I don't think so. At the time of writing the UK remains the outlier in Europe, not only topping the table for deaths and cases but trailing behind almost everyone in flattening the curve of new infections. The lessons from elsewhere are likely to remain relevant for many months ahead. The German 'test and trace' system, for example, has been functioning in a way its British equivalent simply has not. Declaring, "we're British, we're world-beating" is not going to get the job done.

In the spirit of Cassandra we can do no more than continue to point out what we can see in front of our eyes, in the hope that one day we can escape her curse of never being believed.

My Coronavirus Story

Paul Clark MBE, Presenter, UTV

This time last year I thought that Brexit would be the defining moment of my journalistic career. I was wrong! Until December I had never heard of Wuhan in China, a huge city with a population of 11 million, and certainly not the Province of Hubei. Fast forward to the present and, as I look back, it's been a rollercoaster.

I have been fronting the teatime news in Northern Ireland for just over thirty years. But never in such an environment. When I joined UTV in January 1989, the newsroom was a noisy place. First, there was the never-ending clackety clack of manual typewriters – remember them? Phones ringing, constant conversation. Then there was the pall of cigarette smoke that meant it was only just possible to see the person sitting at the next desk!

Today, that has totally changed. In the lockdown that has accompanied Covid-19, the world is a very different place. As I type this, on my computer, the newsroom is deathly quiet. There is hardly a sound! Why? Because there is almost nobody here. OK, there are a few of us but, these days, all it takes to broadcast *UTV Live*, our main news programme, is eight or nine people.

Not that long ago, there seemed to be an army of us putting the programme on air. Social distancing has re-written the rules of producing the teatime news. Most of my colleagues are working from home – who would have thought? I haven't had a face-to-face conversation with some fellow journalists for weeks. Only people who are technically essential to putting out the programme are physically in the building. We don't know how long this will last nor the long-term effect on how we do our job. But, as a team, we have adapted to this new discipline.

However, that is only part of my coronavirus story. My father had been living with cancer for a number of years. At the beginning of the year, it became acute. As a result my brother Philip, the baby of the family, came home from Italy shortly before Dad was admitted to the Northern Ireland Hospice on St Valentine's Day, February 14th. Essentially, it was to say goodbye. My brother said that his next journey home would be for the funeral. Towards the end of the month he returned to his home in the state of Veneto, in northern Italy.

At the same time, Italian news was reporting that a "flu-like virus" that originated in China had arrived in the Italian state of Lombardy. There were eleven cases. Nothing to worry about, just another flu! Or so he thought.

But Lombardy was next door to Veneto and very quickly the situation in that part of the country deteriorated. It became so acute that within a few days both Lombardy and Veneto were in lockdown. There was no way in, and no way out.

As Italy battled Covid-19 head on, and remember this was before emergency measures were introduced here, flights were cancelled, and airports were shutting down. There was mass confusion, and more than a little panic. Everything, apart from supermarkets and pharmacies, was closed, train stations and bus termini ceased to operate. Everyone was confined to quarters, no exercise, no going out, special permission needed to leave your home. How could my brother travel back home to Northern Ireland?

All the time, Dad's condition continued to deteriorate. And in this country, we were awakening to the possibility that we risked following the pattern seen in Italy and other European countries.

Covid-19 arrived on the island of Ireland at the end of February. Ireland's Six Nations Rugby international against Italy, due to be played in Dublin in early March, was postponed. St Patrick's Day in Ireland is always a good excuse for a hooley. But, not this year! Traditional March 17th parades and parties were cancelled, and the celebration of our patron saint became a much muted affair. People were encouraged to stay at home.

That evening we watched on television as the Irish Prime Minister, Leo Varadkar, told us that this was the calm before the storm. "Not all superheroes," he said, "wear capes. Some wear scrubs and gowns!" It was a harbinger of what was to come. St Patrick's Day is a holiday in both parts of Ireland. Many parents, afraid of what was to come, decided to keep their children from school. Those families were ahead of the government.

Five days before he died, my father contracted Covid-19 in the hospice. We will never know how he caught the virus but, by that stage, his resistance was so low he couldn't fight it. I don't fret over how much it hastened his demise. He was a very weak man, and we were expecting his death.

Quite separately, I had to leave my own home. My wife lives with an extremely rare lung condition called lymphangioleiomyomatosis. As a result, she requires oxygen round the clock. Carol was clearly in the at-risk category. As I was going out to work she had to be exposed to as little danger as possible. So she has been self-isolating successfully with our two sons, while I have been living with my mother (thank you Mum).

As well as fronting *UTV Live*, I also present the weekly politics programme, *View From Stormont*. On Monday March 23rd, just before social distancing really kicked in, I interviewed the First and Deputy First Ministers of Northern Ireland. Owing to our "power sharing" form of government, Arlene Foster and Michelle O'Neill come from opposing political backgrounds. But this night there was to be a rare show of unity from our two most senior politicians. Given the scientific modelling, they must have known what was coming; and they wanted to get the message out there that we were all in this together. It would be the last time I'd interview two guests in the studio at the same time.

The following day, my dad took a turn for the worse. But because he had Covid-19 we were unable to visit him in his room at the hospice. We had to look in from outside the building, literally, and say our goodbyes from there. Dad died in the early hours of Wednesday March 25th. Though it was not the primary cause of death, Covid-19 appeared as the secondary cause on the death certificate. I believe he was listed as the eleventh Covid fatality in Northern Ireland.

Because of coronavirus, the coffin was closed and his body could not be brought home. So he remained in a funeral parlour. In Ireland, we bury more quickly than in England. The funeral was on Saturday March 28th.

Dad was a devout Catholic but we could not have a Requiem Mass. All formal church services had been abandoned. It was a short committal attended by five people, including my mother, followed by cremation. Of course my brother Philip was unable to return from Italy to Ireland. This was distressing for all of us, but particularly for him. The undertakers obliged by streaming live, on two smartphones, directly to my brother in his apartment in Bassano Del Grappa. He says he dressed in a suit and sat in front of the iPad to watch Dad's funeral.

I returned to work two days later, on Monday March 30th, by which time the death toll was rising quickly. By now, Northern Ireland was fully in lockdown. The streets were deserted. Belfast, my home-town, felt like an abandoned city. When I arrived at the office there was no buzz, no sense of anticipation. It, too, was empty. Gone were the "hot-desks" that were shared by journalists on different shifts. Work-stations now resembled a crime scene with red and white tape everywhere, sending out the subliminal message – do not pass!

Each day the news was dominated by the rising number of cases and the growing death toll. Our reporters were talking to families who had been bereaved as a result of Covid-19. With my father having died only a few days previously, I had additional empathy with our viewers in such increasingly uncertain times.

So, what will life look like on the other side of this? Will we go back to the way it was before? I like to think that when this is over, I will be a better, more resilient person. Currently, I just want to get through the day the best I can and try not to give myself too hard a time.

Finally, I am glad that my job necessitates me being in the news-room. Genuinely, I don't know if I have what it would take, to be disciplined enough, to work productively from home. But then, my wife always told me I was more at home in the studio than in the house.

Timeline

March

5 The first coronavirus death in the UK is reported – a woman in her seventies

The airline FlyBe collapses, in part due to the crisis

9 Italy announces an extension of the Lombardy lockdown to the entire country

Ireland cancels St Patrick's Day parades

France bans large events

10 The Health Minister Nadine Dorries tests positive for coronavirus

10–13 The Cheltenham Festival goes ahead

11 The World Health Organization says the virus outbreak is a pandemic

Budget Day in the UK

Liverpool play Atletico Madrid at Anfield

13 The WHO says Europe is now the epicentre of the pandemic

President Trump declares a national state of emergency in the US

14 Spain announces a partial lockdown

The English Premier League suspends the season

UK retailers appeal to the public to stop panic-buying

The Global Shutdown of the Economy

Joel Hills, Business and Economics Editor, ITV News

The chief executive of Ryanair is eccentric, eloquent and opinionated. And he believes that everyone is entitled to his opinions. Michael O'Leary tends to shoot from the hip and is most journalists' idea of a good story.

On March 3rd I travelled to an aviation conference in Brussels to interview O'Leary. The conference was nominally about "sustainability" but delegates there were preoccupied with a new and pressing danger. A virus discovered in China at the start of the year had reached Europe. The number of Covid-19 infections in the Italian state of Lombardy had recently surged and Europe's airlines were being severely impacted. Fully-booked flights to Italy were departing half-empty, ticket sales had slumped and governments were starting to impose restrictions on travel.

Amid the upheaval, Michael O'Leary was characteristically upbeat. "We think things will have calmed down by the time the Easter school holidays arrive," he said. "I struggle to see how [the virus] will prevail for three to six months, as temperatures rise". He laughed at the idea that Ryanair might be forced to stop flying. "That's very unlikely," he insisted. "You're talking about the global shutdown of the economy. That's not possible, nor would it be effective." O'Leary wasn't alone in wildly misjudging the risk that coronavirus posed.

The chief executive of easyJet, Johan Lundgren, said he thought it was "a short-term issue." Willie Walsh, the chief executive of IAG, the group that owns British Airways, agreed. He insisted people could book their summer holidays with confidence. "I don't see in any way that [the virus] will jeopardise airlines that are in a strong position," he told me.

Two days later Flybe, an airline that definitely wasn't in a strong position, went into liquidation. Within three weeks, the skies above Europe were effectively closed to everything apart from repatriation and cargo flights. Ryanair, easyJet, British Airways and Virgin Atlantic grounded their fleets, furloughed staff and applied for emergency taxpayer-backed loans. All four airlines now predict it will take several years for demand for air travel to return to pre-crisis levels. Collectively, they are making more than 20,000 staff redundant.

Walsh now describes coronavirus as "the deepest crisis [British Airways] has ever faced".

The UK's airlines were the first companies to feel the full force of the economic shock that the outbreak of Covid-19 caused. Around the world, governments locked down large parts of their economies in the interests of public health. The restrictions they imposed to slow the spread of the virus triggered recessions of unprecedented scale.

"We've never seen anything like this," Andrew Bailey told me on March 18th. It was his third day in his new job as Governor of the Bank of England. He'd walked straight into a disaster zone.

Bailey sat in the Parlours of the Bank – where the Governor and the Directors have their offices – beneath a fresh oil painting of his predecessor. In his portrait, Mark Carney struck an authoritative pose, his hands clasped behind his back, his face impassive, his eyes fixed calmly on the middle-distance. He should have been smiling; he couldn't have timed his departure better.

The Bank itself was deserted; staff had been told to work from home. The corridors, resplendently carpeted and enthusiastically gold-leafed, echoed to the sound of ticking clocks. On a Chippendale table sat an untouched copy of the *Financial Times*. The front-page headline read: "Global stocks take fresh pummelling". Financial markets were in uproar. Investors had lost their bearings and were trading in the dark. The virus suddenly threatened to sweep all before it. Travel bans, quarantines, factory closures had the potential to bring economic activity to a standstill. Panic had set in. The rampant fear was that companies would fail. Shares in even the most successful were being offloaded.

When I interviewed Bailey, the Bank had already cut interest rates from 0.75 to 0.25 percent, a record low. The next day Bank Rate, the interest rate used by banks and other lenders to set the cost of borrowing money, was cut again to 0.1 percent. The move in Bank Rate grabbed all the attention but the benefits were limited. 5.7 million UK households have fixed rate mortgages so their monthly repayment didn't budge. The 2.2 million people on variable and tracker deals probably saved around £30 a month. That's not nothing, but neither would it keep the wolf from the door.

The other actions the Bank took were less eye-catching, more sophisticated and almost certainly more effective. The Term Funding Scheme, which enables banks to borrow directly from the Bank of England, was dusted down and revived. It was last used during the financial crisis of 2008. The "countercyclical buffer", the amount of capital banks are required to hold to absorb losses, was relaxed to zero. And the Bank announced plans to create an extra £200 billion of new money and to push it out into the economy by purchasing UK government debt. "Quantitative Easing" is another policy dreamed up during the financial crisis in 2008.

The Bank was doing everything it could think of to keep money cheap to borrow and in plentiful supply. It had levers it could pull as we hurtled into recession but its armoury was sparser than it had been when we entered the last downturn. The tried and tested way to deal with an economic emergency is to cut Bank Rate, but it was already set at a very low level because the recovery from the last crisis had been so lacklustre. The Bank was having to be creative.

"We are taking unprecedented action, there is unprecedented support on offer for businesses and therefore people but we'll want to see how it takes effect and how this crisis deepens, and how the situation evolves," Bailey said. "We are not out of what I call 'firepower,'" he insisted.

Like Andrew Bailey, Rishi Sunak was also new in post. He'd become Chancellor after Sajid Javid quit unexpectedly on February 13th. Javid resigned after the Prime Minister ordered him to fire his team of advisors – a Valentine's Eve massacre he was unwilling to accept. It was a dramatic decision and one, I'll wager, Javid rather regrets, given everything that's happened since.

Sunak is, in many ways, straight from Conservative party central-casting. He's the son of a GP and a pharmacist; he was head boy at

Winchester College, an all-boys independent boarding-school; he studied politics, philosophy and economics at Oxford; was a Fulbright scholar at highly-ranked Stanford University in California; he worked for investment banking company Goldman Sachs and then two hedge funds; and he is married to the daughter of a billionaire.

But in other ways, Sunak's background is anything but establishment Tory. His father was born in Kenya, his mother in Tanzania. His grandparents emigrated from India to the UK in the 1960s. He is now unimaginably wealthy and has been extremely successful but, when I met Sunak for the first time, I was surprised by how relaxed and likeable he is – not, perhaps, something a journalist should admit. He also has a strong sense of empathy.

I've interviewed a few Chancellors over the years. I don't recall Alistair Darling, George Osborne, Philip Hammond or Sajid Javid ever introducing themselves to camera crews before an interview. And none of them ever used the word "busted". Perhaps all this demonstrates is that Sunak is from another generation to his predecessors but I also know of gruff, uncompromising union leaders, with a predisposition to dislike Conservative ministers, who have warmed to Sunak and see him as someone they can do business with. Sunak comes across as down to earth and sincere. Those are precious qualities and he'll need them in the months ahead.

As Chancellor, Sunak immediately found himself in an extraordinary position. He was faced with the biggest recession the UK had seen in possibly 300 years and he needed to respond by spending money on an almost unprecedented scale. In his first Budget on March 11th, Sunak served up £12 billion to fund the NHS, companies and workers. It was a mere downpayment. In the following weeks, hundreds of billions more was pledged in the form of tax cuts, cash grants and taxpayer-backed loans. The strategy was simple. The support was designed to limit the number of businesses that failed as the economy was put into a temporary deep freeze, so that a recovery could get out of the traps like a greyhound as soon as lockdown thawed.

The centrepiece of the government's response was the Job Retention Scheme (JRS), which incentivised companies to hold on to their staff as they were forced to close their doors. The scheme proved more popular than the Treasury imagined. At its peak, more than 9 million jobs were "furloughed". One in three private sector employees were not working, instead having their salaries paid by the taxpayer.

In the early stages of lockdown the JRS was successful in avoiding mass redundancies but, as the months wore on, some companies formed the view that their sales weren't likely to abruptly snap back to normal and they began to let people go. Airlines, airports, aerospace manufacturers, cinemas, theatres, gyms, hotels, pubs and restaurants realised that, unless an effective vaccine was suddenly discovered and rolled out, social distancing was here to stay. They would be permanently poorer even when they reopened and they couldn't afford to take back everyone they'd furloughed.

As lockdown lifted, the recovery got underway but unemployment began rising sharply as government furlough support was steadily withdrawn. 650,000 people were removed from company payrolls between March and June. The fear was that the number of people out of work would rise from 1.3 million, pre-crisis, to 4 million by 2021 – a level last seen under Margaret Thatcher's government in the early 1980s. Everything hinged on the strength of the recovery.

This was not a normal recession. It was caused by a government-imposed lockdown, not an oil shock or a financial crisis. As restrictions were removed, the hope was that the economy would bounce back with something like the same velocity with which it had crashed. The downturn had created terrible hardship for some households but the majority actually found themselves better off, unable to get out to spend their money. It was easy to imagine a stampede to spend again, as lockdown lifted, as long as a second wave could be avoided.

But thus far, the bounce-back has lacked bounce. The UK has been slow to emerge from its rabbit hole and has spent cautiously. Unless confidence improves and consumption picks up a gear it could take several years for the economy to return to its pre-crisis size. It's still early days and the true strength and shape of the recovery has yet to be established.

The one thing we most definitely know is that we shall emerge from this crisis deeply indebted. Countries and companies have borrowed money that, in some cases, they will be unable to repay. The consequences will influence politics for decades to come. The UK's stock of national debt will return towards levels last seen after the Second World War. The good news is that investors seem happy to lend the government the money it wants to borrow, but it does leave us highly exposed to future spikes in either interest rates or inflation.

The public finances are self-evidently on an unsustainable path. We can probably run with a higher debt burden but the pound is not a reserve currency, we can't do that forever and a day.

As for Rishi, he's on a roll. He is the only government minister I can think of whose reputation has been enhanced by the crisis. The campfire gossip around Westminster has him as a shoe-in for the next party leader. We'll see.

It's easy to be popular when you're spraying money around; the real test will come when unemployment is heading north and he has to set out how the bills he's run up will be repaid. Sunak is energetic, decisive and highly competent but his fortunes, like all Chancellors', are tied to the performance of the economy. Rishi Sunak will need to be at his most charming going forward because there will be a reckoning, and difficult and unpopular decisions will need to be made. Tax rises are inevitable. Election promises not to raise VAT, income tax or National Insurance look like they will have to be broken.

This downturn has hit the young and those on low incomes in particular. The Chancellor will need to be mindful of this when he thinks about how the deficit is closed and debt repaid. The case for targeting the relatively well-off is compelling but it's politically tricky, for the Conservative party in particular.

Pandemics, like wars, change the world. The way we work, the way we travel, the way we use technology, the way we spend our money have altered and some of those behavioural changes will prove permanent. Our society is in the process of being reshaped. The end-state is impossible to predict but, for better and for worse, we will be transformed.

Reporting on the Virus from Across the United States

Robert Moore, Washington Correspondent, ITV News

Washington DC, May 31st

The police baton charge was sudden and fierce. It was accompanied by stun grenades, tear gas and pepper spray. Hundreds of pellets were fired into the crowd to disperse it, one striking me in my leg. Moments later a second one hit me in the back. For a few perilous minutes, the capital city was on the brink of utter chaos. Protesters were begging the police to stop their assault.

We filmed one activist, Alonzo, on his knees with his hands in the air. A few metres in front of him was a phalanx of riot police. He was begging the officers to switch sides and join the protests. "Treat us like we are American citizens," he implored the officers, "like our lives matter, treat us like you are here to protect and serve." Along with my camera operator, Dickon Mager, I took up a position one block further north, using a lamp post as partial cover, and we continued filming our report, as dozens more riot police struggled to regain control of the streets. Some buildings were now on fire and there were reports reaching us of widespread looting. After spotting the headquarters of an American labour union was now ablaze, I phoned 911 to notify firefighters. The response from the emergency dispatch was that many buildings were on fire, several were inaccessible because of the disturbances, and the firetrucks would reach the building when they could.

At this moment, in the heart of Washington DC, and just 100 metres from the White House, it was difficult to fully comprehend that this turmoil was unfolding amid a pandemic.

Suddenly, the US was facing multiple crises – the worst racial unrest for a generation following the death of George Floyd, a huge spike in

51

unemployment, and a virus sweeping across all fifty states that had already killed over 100,000 Americans.

As we assessed the situation from the corner of 16th and H Street that summer night, with the White House plunged into darkness on the instruction of the Secret Service, it was clear America was in deep trouble. In fact, the scene before us seemed a troubling metaphor for a superpower that had lost its way.

Seattle, Washington state, March 6th

Eleven weeks earlier, in the Pacific Northwest, I was reporting on the very first cases of the coronavirus to have been detected in the US. Seattle is nearly ten thousand kilometres from the Chinese city of Wuhan. They are not only at different ends of the greatest ocean on earth but they could scarcely be more different communities.

Wuhan is a bustling industrial city in central China, far from the coast, and with a now infamous "wet market" that slaughters and sells a variety of exotic animals. Seattle is a famously liberal, environmentally conscious city best known for hosting high-tech companies like Microsoft and Boeing.

So when I arrived at the Kirkland care home on March 6th, in the suburbs of Seattle, I was left to ponder one of the many mysteries of Covid-19: how could the virus have jumped this distance and been seeded here of all places, producing America's first cluster of cases?

My camera operator, Adam Blair, and I witnessed a poignant scene. Outside the care home we met an emotional Bridget Parkhill, who was trying to visit her elderly mother. Bridget was unable to gain entry since the care home was a strict quarantine zone in the aftermath of a dozen mysterious deaths. Her mother was alone and confused inside. Bridget told *News at Ten* viewers that night, "It feels like there's a gun to her head because she can't leave her room. She's in isolation. She's all alone. I'm worried sick. It's like a death sentence."

A short distance away we filmed Dorothy Campbell, 88, waving at her husband through a window. That was the only communication they could have. But for Dorothy it was an uplifting moment. She could at least glimpse the man she loved.

Covid-19 had arrived in America. The question at that time was whether Kirkland was an outlier or a grim glimpse into the future. We didn't have long to wait to find the answer.

New York City

New York City celebrated the arrival of 2020 in its normal ebullient manner. Times Square was packed with people as the famous ball dropped and marked the start of the new year. Couples embraced and kissed; colourful ticker-tape rained down and engulfed the crowd. The year ahead would be exciting – the stock market was booming, a Presidential election lay ahead, New York City had its swagger back.

No one was even remotely aware that a respiratory illness in a Chinese province had emerged a few days earlier; still less that it would bring the City that Never Sleeps to a shuddering halt within a few weeks.

That New Year's Eve, Dr Eric Blutinger was not in Times Square, but on a lonely shift at New York's Mount Sinai hospital. The 33-year-old junior doctor had just completed his residency and was aiming to gain experience in the Emergency Room of a major hospital. Like every New Yorker on that innocent New Year's Eve, his worst nightmare would not have included a major pandemic, mass burial pits, economic paralysis and racial turmoil on the streets. Within ten weeks his world would be turned upside down and those celebrations to mark the start of 2020 would seem like scenes from another universe.

Speaking to ITV's *Tonight* programme at the end of March, once the reality had begun to overwhelm the city, Dr Blutinger spoke of the fears stalking the hospital corridors. He was exhausted and deeply troubled by what he was witnessing. "Every single person in the emergency department – you can see the fear in their faces," he told me. "It's like a war zone, but we are running out of ammo."

New York's first case of Covid-19 was confirmed on March 1st. Three days later, there were ten more cases. On March 14th, the first two fatalities in New York were reported. By March 24th, concern was growing. Governor Andrew Cuomo warned that "the apex is higher than we thought, and the apex is sooner than we thought." By

April 7th, the death toll was 3,000. That was a psychological mile-stone for this battered city. It meant that more New Yorkers had died from Covid-19 than had been killed in the terrorist atrocity of September 11th.

Viruses always find the weakness and the vulnerability in a human society. And so it was in New York. The clue to why New York became the country's horrifying coronavirus hotspot lay not amid the city's famed skyline, but beneath the streets. The super-spreader of the virus wasn't a person, or even a group of infected patients. It was the subway. Mass transit in New York is now seen to have been the primary culprit. The decision not to close it down earlier was one of the great blunders of America's response. The crowded subway carriages hurtling across the city ensured the virus spread from borough to borough like a wildfire.

With the city's morgues full, refrigerated trailer trucks were positioned around the back of hospitals to provide extra space for the storage of bodies. An emergency field hospital was erected in Central Park. And the most dynamic city in the world was suddenly still.

Times Square was now eerily quiet. The great Avenues were largely traffic-free. Millions of residents stayed indoors. The lights had gone out on Broadway. The scale of the New York crisis is captured by this statistic: by mid-June 30,000 New Yorkers had died from Covid, amounting to seven percent of all virus deaths in the world.

Washington DC

On January 23rd Beth Sanner, a seasoned CIA analyst, walked into the Oval Office to give Donald Trump his Presidential daily briefing. For the first time, she would include in her intelligence summary the fact that a respiratory illness was reportedly rapidly spreading in China and was capable of human-to-human transmission.

That briefing failed to capture the President's famously short atten-tion span. At first, despite the growing scientific evidence, Donald Trump played down the gravity of the pandemic, doubting there would be any victims. Then he pivoted and blamed Beijing, repeat-edly calling the pathogen the "Chinese virus".

Finally, on March 13th, forty-nine days after Sanner's intelligence briefing, the President declared a state of emergency across America.

But it didn't appear that his heart was in the lockdown policy. He was deeply worried about the economic impact of the shutdown, its implications for American jobs, the stock market and his own re-election prospects.

On *News at Ten* we reported on every twist and turn of the White House handling of the crisis that was engulfing America. On April 23rd, President Trump turned to his medical advisors at a news conference and mused out loud: "Supposing we hit the body with a tremendous ultraviolet or just a very powerful light . . . Supposing you brought the light inside the body . . . And then I see the disinfectant knocks it out in a minute, one minute, and is there a way we can do something like that, by injection inside, or almost a cleaning? It sounds interesting to me."

Perhaps not surprisingly, those comments led to an uproar. Doctors – and indeed cleaning manufacturers – quickly had to urge people not to swallow or inject disinfectant. The President's bizarre views on the virus extended to his own treatment. He announced that he was taking the anti-malaria drug hydroxychloroquine as a preventative medicine for Covid-19, even though there was no evidence that it works, and some studies suggested that it was dangerous.

But the President's supporters didn't desert him. Many applauded Donald Trump's assault on conventional scientific thinking. They believed he had confronted the political norms of Washington and was now taking on the medical establishment. The great disrupter was causing political turbulence daily, undercutting his advisors, boasting of his own scientific prowess, handing out medical advice, infuriating governors and mayors, and setting his own example – refusing to wear a mask in public.

Harrisburg, Pennsylvania

Americans are not born to be compliant. Deep in their heritage, they are children of the Revolution, and they remain fiercely protective of the rights of the individual. Many are deeply sceptical of central authority, seeing government as the problem, not the solution. In this country, many fear that freedoms lost are rarely regained. A popular slogan in the anti-lockdown protests across America read, "I prefer dangerous freedom to peaceful slavery." Many fear the virus; but plenty of Americans have a greater fear of tyranny.

So when the US Government attempted to enforce social distancing, stay-at-home rules and shelter-in-place orders, the response was unlike anything that unfolded in the UK or Europe. We saw that for ourselves in the city of Harrisburg, the state capital of Pennsylvania. It was startling to witness the depth of the defiance and the anger felt by these libertarian protesters. Gathered here were militiamen, pro-gun activists, science sceptics, angry business owners, pro-Trump voters, bikers, Republicans, evangelical Christians and working Americans who had watched their jobs vanish in the blink of an eye. It was a mosaic of conservative America – and they were not happy.

As one distressed businessman who had lost his job told ITV News at the Harrisburg rally, "This constitutional overreach has destroyed my career. I had a good-paying job, paying bills, earning good money, and now I'm reduced to searching for a job for $20 an hour. I'm very angry."

These protesters were a powerful lobbying group and they leveraged their influence to force governors across the US to weaken the lockdown. One reason they had disproportionate power was because they had an ally in the White House. Donald Trump was also pressuring states to reopen their economies far more rapidly than his health advisors thought was prudent.

The scene in Harrisburg was emblematic to me of the 'Divided States of America' that I have reported on for over a decade. It was the same on the streets of Washington in late May and early June during the unrest following George Floyd's death. A crisis can bring a country together. It can produce solidarity and bridge generational and economic divides. But in America the coronavirus achieved the opposite. The pandemic produced a bungled federal government response, bitter arguments about the science, the highest death toll in the world, and an economy that saw devastating job losses. Covid-19 has killed more Americans than the US wars in Korea, Vietnam, Afghanistan and Iraq combined.

America spends 750 billion dollars a year on defence. It has the most powerful military in the world, by far. The government and its many intelligence agencies have spent decades preparing for disaster. There is a vast surveillance programme in place to identify threats to the homeland.

And yet when the danger arrived on the shores of America in early 2020, it was not a Middle Eastern terrorist who slipped through the net. It was a microscopic pathogen. As ITV News witnessed throughout the first six months of 2020, and in many American cities, the country was hopelessly ill-prepared for its greatest challenge.

We saw it on the streets outside the White House, and in Seattle, Harrisburg, and elsewhere. American exceptionalism – one of the country's founding myths – was exposed by a virus that mysteriously emerged nearly 20,000 kilometres away.

Shutdown, Restarts and an Uncertain Future for Sport

Steve Scott, Sports Editor, ITV News

On March 9th, the day before the Cheltenham Festival, there was a well attended meeting in Whitehall hosted by the Department for Culture, Media and Sport. Decision-makers from all the major sports were there, as were the sports broadcasters who pay many millions to cover the action. They'd all come to get an update on how the government's latest policy on fighting coronavirus might affect them.

I'd been briefed by a government source that the message would be that sport could carry on because the medical advice at the time was mass gatherings were no great risk to public health or the spread of the virus. But the meeting was on the same day that deaths in Italy increased by 50 percent, the UK recorded its fifth fatality and the government's chief medical advisor, Professor Chris Whitty, warned the virus would soon be spreading "really quite fast." Given those developments I expected the tone of the meeting to change. I was wrong.

Shortly after the meeting finished, I called a couple of people who'd been there and their accounts of what happened surprised me. One told me the meeting began with the government "proclaiming very confidently that 'sport goes on as normal'." The audience, I was told, was understandably sceptical. Another described officials as "blasé", convinced the crisis would pass quickly. "They ducked a load of questions and just kept reiterating 'sport goes on as normal'," I was told.

We knew that in private the organisers of Cheltenham had been taking guidance from the government for some time and, acting on that advice, decided the festival would go ahead. Over the next four days, 260,000 people from all over the UK and Ireland crammed onto the racecourse; the only real difference was a number of anti-bacterial hand gel stations. There was a degree of general unease, which grew as the week went on; I spoke to many who were so anxious once they got there, they actually left the course early.

On the second day of the festival, at Anfield, Liverpool Football Club hosted Atletico Madrid in a Champions League match watched by a crowd of 54,000, 3,000 of whom were from Spain. By then Madrid was a Covid-19 hotspot; on that very day schools and universities there were ordered to close and mass gatherings had already been banned, but still Atletico supporters were allowed to travel.

On Thursday the 12th, I received a message from a contact saying Chelsea had closed its training ground for a deep clean after one of the men's squad tested positive for coronavirus. The club would only confirm to me that a clean was underway. The following day, Arsenal revealed their manager Mikel Arteta had returned a positive test and that was the moment everything changed.

Football took it upon itself to effectively shut down, the Premier League suspended all fixtures and everyone else then followed suit. Chelsea eventually confirmed that a sample from Callum Hudson-Odoi had come back positive. Three days after Arteta's test results the government finally introduced social distancing and banned mass gatherings.

That week and those decisions will form a major chapter in an inquiry once Britain emerges from the grip of this terrible disease. In the meantime sport, like everyone else, has had to learn to live with Covid-19 and devise ways of getting back to business even while it is still a significant threat to health.

On that challenge, the Premier League has led the way with "Project Restart", its blueprint to complete the season. From the outset, my job was to find out exactly what that pathway would look like as it was very unlikely to be a smooth ride. Trying to get all 20 clubs to agree on everyday football matters was never straightforward; this was likely to be a minefield of self-interests rising to the surface.

Sport in general, and football in particular, plays a significant role in many people's lives. For both die-hard and armchair fans, not being able to experience matchdays was going to leave quite a vacuum. Football clubs are part of the community, they directly employ many people and local businesses benefit from them too, so it was obvious any detail about the sport's phased return would be interesting to ITV News viewers and those who follow our digital channels.

When exactly did the Premier League aim to start again? Would games be played at a handful of neutral venues? Would players and club staff have to be locked in bio-secure hotels for weeks on end? Would players agree to any of it anyway? What were the financial implications and, if the season had to be abandoned, what method would they use to determine final league positions? Those were just a selection of many questions no one knew the answers to. We had never been here before.

Throughout this period, given the government's rules, it was all about making as many phone calls as possible to those involved in this evolving story. I found that because we were in lockdown, people who were usually difficult to get hold of were suddenly available to chat. Uniquely, everyone had a common concern and, what's more, had more time on their hands!

Support from the government definitely gave the League impetus; the Prime Minister believed that to have the national sport up and running again, albeit without fans, would provide the country with a significant and timely morale boost. Cynics also observed that it would serve as a useful distraction from the criticism the government was getting for its handling of the crisis. The irony was not lost on football because, just a few weeks before Boris Johnson's rallying cry, the Health Secretary Matt Hancock had suggested that by not immediately agreeing to wage cuts, Premier League players were not "playing their part."

I'm no apologist for the Premier League but the criticism from ministers of the players was unwarranted and ill thought through. Hancock had clearly not considered the Chancellor's huge revenue stream courtesy of players' tax contributions or that any wage cut would only benefit their employers (the clubs); nor had he found out that many were actually already working on sizeable donations to NHS and other charities. ITV News spoke to agents who told us how angry the players were that the finger was pointing their way, especially given the generosity so many of them display with private donations and public support of charities.

Manchester United's Marcus Rashford helped raise enough money to provide 3 million meals a week to vulnerable children across the UK. Subsequently of course he also forced the government into a dramatic u-turn on extending its school meals voucher policy. His efforts are perhaps the most eye-catching, but most clubs and most players are involved in one scheme or another to the tune of many millions of pounds. So much for not playing their part.

In addition to encouraging football's return, the government had made it quite clear that it wanted all matches made available to watch live with as many as possible on free-to-air television. The thinking was partly to discourage fans from congregating at grounds where games were being played. There was also much discussion about whether or not matches should be played at neutral grounds.

We landed two key interviews on this issue. The first was with the Mayor of Liverpool, who caused an outcry when he said he did not think Liverpool should be allowed to win the title at Anfield. We also spoke to Deputy Chief Constable Mark Roberts, England's officer in charge of football policing, who said clubs who objected to playing the remaining fixtures at neutral venues needed to "get a grip". That caused quite a backlash too.

Whatever the government's reasoning or demands, the Premier League was more than keen to deliver. With no restart, clubs faced the prospect of paying a rebate to the broadcasters, domestic and overseas, of more than £750 million. Even if the season was completed, they faced handing back more than £300 million. For a business that spends every penny before the cheque has even cleared this was a very serious prospect.

I spoke to a source of mine close to one of the Premier League's key television partners, who laid out the extent of financial pain they were suffering. No live football had led to the suspension of millions of subscribers' monthly payments and there was no way of judging how many would return when it restarted. Broadcasters also rely heavily on advertisers paying a premium to market themselves in and around "live" games and associated programming. Finally, they explained, a relatively significant chunk of Sky and BT's revenue depends on lucrative contracts with upwards of 40,000 pubs and clubs across England. The bigger contracts are worth tens of thousands of pounds a year and they'd been frozen. That's three separate income streams together adding up to major unrecoverable losses. So in strictly business terms, it was in everyone's interest that football returned.

By May, with the virus seemingly under some sort of control, elite sport was given a return date by the government of June 1st, as long as it "was safe to do so". The Premier League's top medics and the club doctors had already been working with government advisors on protocols to get football back, and at the forefront of these was players' safety. They came up with a gradual process spread over several weeks, building from training in isolation, to working in groups, to full contact training and then finally, matches.

Thanks to a player we knew, ITV News was the first to get hold of a draft of the first stage medical protocol that was circulated for consideration. We had been speaking to many players about the prospect of playing again soon. The majority didn't want to go on the record but told us that in the circumstances they were anxious about training and many of their team-mates were too. They felt when it came to consultation, players were at the bottom of the list of priorities.

We discovered that two Covid-19 tests a week, relentless hygiene, social distancing and minimising face to face contact were themes that ran through each stage. If the remaining games were completed that would mean 26,000 tests, costing the league £4 million, but it was important to have the players' support because by now a few were expressing their anxiety publicly.

The protocol was as much common sense as science and had the benefit of learning from Germany's top division, the Bundesliga, which started playing matches several weeks before the Premier League. One of the major differences between the two approaches was that, unlike Germany, players here would be allowed to go home every day in the week before matches, rather than isolating in a hotel.

A leading virologist, who advises UEFA and the Belgian Government, described the Premier League's strategy to me as risky.

The Premier League pushed on with its plans and on Wednesday June 17th, the first game, Aston Villa vs Sheffield United, took place at Villa Park. It was of course memorable for that reason alone but also because the players wore NHS badges on their shirts and their names had been replaced by the words "Black Lives Matter". Before the game there would be a moment of silence for health service workers and then players would take a knee in unison. They were powerful messages.

Those two gestures apart, matchdays inevitably were going to have a very different feel to them, especially for the players. It would be like walking into a dystopian movie, set some time in the future. Clubs playing away from home were encouraged to fly, rather than travel by road. The final part of the journey to the stadium would be by coaches reconfigured for social distancing.

At the ground players would enter a bio-secure environment, or as close to one as the clubs could organise, and follow a sterile route to enlarged dressing rooms. Pre-match warm-ups would be structured to minimise close contact at all times. Teams would walk out separately, ideally from different tunnels and there'd be no handshake before kick-off.

Players were directed to use hand sanitiser when going on or off the pitch, only drink from their own water bottle, not to spit or clear their nose during a game and avoid unnecessary contact during goal celebrations.

The dugout areas were extended to accommodate the extra number of substitutes that FIFA had temporarily allowed, all sitting at least two metres apart, but unlike Germany's Bundesliga, subs were not compelled to use a face covering. To treat injured players, club medical staff were required to wear standard personal protective equipment.

So social distancing was compulsory off the pitch but obviously not on it where close contact is a large part of every match. However, research conducted by the Premier League reveals not as much as you might think. They found that, on average, 98 percent of players spend less than five minutes in close contact during every game. Those statistics represent a surprisingly low risk of infection.

While many thought the Premier League was coming back too soon, record television viewing figures for the first round of matches were proof it had been missed. But the common consensus was it just wasn't the same without fans in the ground. I have spoken to senior sources at the Football Association, the Government and the Premier League and the ambition is to get spectators back into stadia in September once lockdown is eased still further and they've worked through the safety guidelines. Social distancing inside stadia is easy enough; it's the danger of large crowds heading to the grounds and then gathering in the concourses and other meeting areas once they're there that's the harder problem.

The bigger question, and the story that is most likely to dominate my life for the next year or so, will be what permanent change will the pandemic inflict on elite sport?

In football at least, some clubs below the top level could go bust; there is likely to be a correction in players' wages; in the short to medium term sponsors will have less money to throw at the game and the value of the TV rights might drop. The sports broadcasters will have less spare cash and so will their subscribers. Even if the new players like Amazon spot an opportunity to pounce, the price will be driven down by reduced competition.

Many have predicted the Premier League's bubble bursting before and we've yet to see that happen. However, like all of us, they've never faced a challenge quite like this one.

Remembering the Victims

Fred Dimbleby, ITV News trainee

I had only been a journalist in ITV's network newsroom for a few weeks when I first contacted a family who had lost a relative because of coronavirus. As an ITV News trainee, my first job in journalism had begun at one of the most unusual and tragic moments in a generation. I remember my fear at making that first contact. Here was a family who had lost a close relative to a disease that, until that point, must have felt so distant, and I was going to be part of this moment for them. I worried that I could upset them even more and drafted and drafted again the message I would send. I wanted to make sure that every word was perfect, to be as respectful and non-intrusive as possible.

But this was also a family who were angry and wanted to talk about their grandfather and his death. They wanted to talk about who he was and about what had happened. When I called them later that day, I could hear their uncontrollable pain at the end of the phone as they dealt with how this international virus had hit their home. And they were worried too – other members of the family had developed symptoms of the virus but were not able to get a test. This was in early March, and they were one of the first families to go through loss because of Covid-19. By the end of May, tens of thousands of families would have the same experience.

Throughout the crisis ITV News tried to humanise the almost incomprehensible statistics and paint a picture of the people behind them – giving the chance, to those who wished to, to publicly talk about those they had lost. I was constantly struck by these stories and the bravery of those who told them.

Some spoke because they wanted to shine a light on what they saw as a wrong – the families of front-line workers who died told us their relatives had not been given the correct levels of protection while they carried out their essential work. Others spoke because they wanted to highlight the importance of abiding by the lockdown. They knew how damaging the virus could be and, selflessly, talked about their painful experience to warn others to take it seriously. One woman, who had lost her dad, expressed her frustration with some in her community not abiding by the rules. Another spoke of his anger at seeing people gathering together in groups, appearing to break lockdown rules.

But many wanted to speak so that their relatives wouldn't be forgotten or lost in the statistics. Families shared videos of those they had lost singing, dancing, cracking a joke, even flying a kite; snapshots of their lives and the people they were. I heard some touching stories. One husband talked about how he and his wife had fallen in love when they were just children. Speaking only shortly after she died, he described the first moment he met her with such power and tenderness. Another person talked about their dad as a man who had been universally loved in their community. These were stories of lives cut short and it was a privilege that families trusted us to tell them.

We heard about "underlying conditions" as if they could be a caveat to the seriousness of the loss, but for families it did nothing to lessen the pain and the shock. I sensed a nervousness among many families that categorising a range of illnesses, from diabetes to serious lung problems, in the catch-all term of "underlying conditions" could mask the true impact of the virus. When we first had cases in the UK, none of the thousands of families affected by the virus expected that they would lose someone, whether or not they had an existing condition.

Each experience was unique, but there was a common theme of separation. A daughter talked about having to be in full protective equipment to say goodbye to her mum. Cut off from her loved one by a plastic apron, gloves and a mask. Separation continued after death. Families couldn't console each other, cry together, share memories over a drink at a wake. In some cases, funerals had to be conducted over video conference calls. One daughter, mourning her father, described seeing her mother collapse in grief knowing that she could do nothing about it. A man told us he wanted to return his brother's body to their home country, the Philippines, but instead was told that it would only be possible to send ashes. These families had little choice over how they were able to mourn.

There is a Facebook page that became popular during the crisis called "Shine A Light to Fight Coronavirus". It was set up by Lisa Bailey, a 28-year-old customer service advisor from Cannock. She wanted to give people a chance to commemorate those they had lost, and it seemed others shared her desire. Her group grew and grew, reaching almost 400,000 members across the world. There, people talked about their loss and shared pictures, videos and stories of those who had died. When I talked to a daughter who had posted pictures of her father on the group, she said the flood of comments of support had helped her in her worst moment. Her dad's picture had been seen by hundreds of thousands of people – his life remembered and memorialised.

Reflecting on this period, my hope is that ITV News provided a similar space where people could share and grieve. We would show pictures of those who had died and say their names again and again on our programmes – the people behind those daily death totals. These families, by talking publicly, allowed us to reflect and demonstrate the true damage the virus could inflict. I hope in return that we helped them in some way in the midst of so much pain. That we told their story. After each report was broadcast, I would check that everything was OK with the families mentioned in it. They were upset, but I could sense that they felt listened to and were comforted that their story was out there, and that viewers had been given a sense of the person they had lost.

Now, when I look at the government's charts of death statistics, I no longer see numbers but people. Behind each jutting pillar on the chart is a name, a family, a life lived and a life lost. When the history of this extraordinary period is written, there will obviously be a focus on the politics, the science, the health policy. But people should be at the heart of that history because they were at the heart of this story. Their stories will stay with me forever.

Esprit de Corps

David Stanley, Writer, ITV News at Ten

Stating the blindingly obvious, few good things have come out of the coronavirus crisis. It has been unremittingly awful. But in those first few weeks there was something impressive to witness. My younger producer colleagues on the national news programmes had the chance to show just how good they were in those most testing of times. They demonstrated maturity beyond their years, an immense capacity for hard work and huge powers of concentration under enormous pressure as they dealt with the biggest news event any of us has ever had to cover.

Throughout my working life in the newsroom it has been tempting to believe we have reported on the best and worst of times – to claim some kind of ownership of that first draft of history. I have certainly succumbed to that temptation many times over the years. I guess it began for me in the late 1980s when the UK was rocked by a series of disasters: the fires at Bradford City, King's Cross and on the Piper Alpha platform, then there was Lockerbie and Hillsborough. I am not unusual in being able to say where I was when I first heard about them. For three I was at work. I thought there could never be another time like it. But, of course, there was. The Gulf War followed and then in 1997 what I believed, at the time, would be the biggest news story of my life, for me anyway, the death of easily the most famous woman in the world, mother of a future King, in a preventable car crash in a dark Paris underpass. Four years after that came 9/11. Nothing, surely, could eclipse that?

But coronavirus has. Beyond the loss of life, it is difficult to know how our world will change. I hope and pray this is the biggest story any of us has to work on, whether we are experienced journalists or just starting out.

The subject matter is deeply distressing and often relentless. At the beginning, day after day, scarcely believable numbers of deaths were being recorded, involving individual accounts of loss and desperate scenes from inside our hospitals. Inside the newsroom, the environment in which we work has been unsettling, as we skirt around one another at a distance of two metres and look out over row upon row of empty desks. There is little time for office banter, for shared cups of tea – the normal social adhesives of most workplaces. Nor in the early days could I get used to the atmosphere on the tube. It felt surreal. Then there were all the concerns outside work.

Inside work, I'd say that never has the newsroom been under such pressure for so long and yet that pressure is producing incredible teamwork. In normal times, the ITV National News production team is a pretty close-knit bunch. With fewer of us working side by side, we have become even closer; more reliant on one another, more trusting of one another's judgements.

There is an esprit de corps and there are moments of shared achievement. The friendships and mutual support aren't just holding firm, they are strengthening. Because I am working some days at home, I find myself looking forward more to being in the newsroom. It is nice to see those who are there, to immerse my thoughts and energy in work and, unlike many of those who we are reporting on, to know that I still have a job to come to.

It is clear that the younger members of our news teams are accepting and absorbing at least their fair share of the added pressure. In those first few days and evenings, when numbers in the newsroom were suddenly and drastically reduced, before the new routines had taken shape, my young producer colleagues were red-faced and dry-mouthed with concentration, adrenalin and sheer effort, successfully keeping programmes on air.

Then and since, they have been making judgements on sensitive matters, and taking the kind of decisions they would probably not expect to be making at this stage in their careers. And yet they have done so with great skill, accuracy, calmness, patience and good nature.

They have the confidence of young adulthood to carry them through what are shocking events. Some will find it tougher than others. But when, in years to come, they reflect on their part in covering coronavirus, they will, I hope, realise that in the worst of situations their work was among the best.

A Whistleblower's Story

Peter Smith, Scotland Correspondent, ITV News

"We are running out of protective equipment"
That was the message waiting for me on my laptop on March 14th. It was from a hospital doctor who had just started treating her first cases of coronavirus and was already worried. "We need full gowns, not aprons. We need face masks and eye protection – proper personal protective equipment to international standards, not just what's left."

PPE. Those three letters just roll off the tongue, so familiar are we now with stories about shortages. Back in early March, though, PPE was just not on my radar when it came to assessing the UK's preparedness for a pandemic. A few of my colleagues at ITV News had just returned from Italy where they described a health system being overwhelmed because they ran out of ventilators and oxygen. As Scotland Correspondent, my attention was on whether that could happen here.

Daily briefings were now being held by Scotland's First Minister, Nicola Sturgeon, and I was asking how many intensive care beds with ventilators were available, and how quickly this capacity could be increased. There were 190 for the whole of Scotland at the beginning of March, of which only 60 were unoccupied; the Scottish Government said it could be doubled if required. It seemed low.

This, I believed, would be the story I would be covering in the weeks ahead. It never occurred to me to ask if the NHS had enough of the absolute basics like face masks for treating highly contagious coronavirus patients. Then the doctor contacted me anonymously. She had seen the shortage of basic PPE in her hospital and, after speaking to colleagues working around the country, realised it was happening elsewhere.

71

A mutual acquaintance had given her my number, and I vividly remember that call coming in. The number was withheld and the voice at the other end was shaky – she was nervous but also sounded scared. "Talking to a journalist about this could cost me my career, you understand that?" The doctor explained there was a problem with PPE supplies but needed assurances I would protect her identity before we went any further. I also needed to verify that she was who she said she was, but she was not comfortable with meeting face-to-face so we had to think creatively.

I told the doctor about a way of communicating privately that I have used a couple of times before with anonymous sources. The method actually stems from an article I once read about the CIA discovering how Al Qaeda commanders were able to exchange messages without being traced. It is impressively simple: you set up a new email account and only you and your source know the log-in details. Crucially, neither of you ever sends an email: you write your message or upload necessary documents, in this case her identification and proof of employment, and then save it to your drafts folder before logging out. You agree a time of day each of you will log in to read the message the other has left for you, then overwrite it with your own message for them. This leaves no electronic trail and, importantly for this doctor, she could see I was serious about protecting her so her bosses would not be able to trace any messages back to her.

"We are running out of protective equipment." That was how the first message left in my drafts folder began. The doctor went on to explain the situation in detail. She was also able to prove her authenticity to me. I replied with some questions. Most importantly, had she raised her concerns with the NHS and what did they say? I waited for her answers to appear in the draft box.

"I have raised it. The bosses just said it's the same everywhere." This information was enough for me to take the story to my editors. The trouble was, my source was adamant she would not do an interview. "The NHS would not take kindly to a whistleblower in the ranks." In truth, I was confused: surely her bosses would understand she was only trying to protect colleagues in the NHS? I reassured her about how important this information was. I explained it was in the public interest to get it out in the open. Still, it was a no. This PPE story was at a dead end. Or so I thought.

Since receiving that first call, I had also been speaking to doctors and nurses I knew to check if they had heard anything about this apparent PPE shortage. I knew other journalists were now aware of the story but so far nobody in the NHS had been willing to be the first to go on the record. Within an hour of my doctor telling me it was a definite "no", I received a message from another reliable source.

"I have a paramedic. She will go on camera." They sent a follow-up text with a phone number to call. The woman on the other end had a soft Glasgow accent. She told me she had been on shift the night before when she was sent to a suspected Covid-19 patient. "Did you have enough PPE?" I asked, mobile in one hand, pen in the other.

"We didn't even have hand gel," she replied. I asked her to please repeat that.

"We haven't had any hand sanitiser in the ambulance for over a week now."

My plan had been to do our interview on camera the next day, but as soon as the paramedic told me this I asked if she was free even sooner. Like, right now.

We met in my car. This was now March 17th, still in the days before social distancing, but shaking hands was frowned upon so we settled for a nod of the head. The paramedic said she was willing to go in front of a camera on condition that we hid her face. "I could lose my job over this," she explained. I understood – it was a familiar concern.

After verifying the paramedic's credentials, we walked together into the STV studios in Glasgow where I had booked a room for filming. The producer was Reshma Rumsey – she was in Scotland helping me on another story and offered her support with this sensitive interview, taking notes and timings. The camera operator was Marc Smith, whom I had last worked with in Vietnam on a story about human trafficking that also required us to hide the identities of interviewees, so we agreed on a similar set-up. Marc lit the room to ensure our paramedic would appear only as a silhouette. Then he recorded 15 seconds of small talk, which we showed to our paramedic to ensure she was content nobody could identify her. We had to prove we were serious about protecting her and her job.

Then the interview began. "I've been a paramedic with the Scottish Ambulance Service for nine years. I've never seen anything like we're seeing now."

Viewers would not be able to see the conviction in her eyes, but I knew they would understand it from her words. "We're dealing with an increase in calls to possible Covid patients, but we have a complete shortage of protective equipment. We have some face visors but paramedics are being told to share them." She was speaking with impressive courage and clarity, but part of the story that needed to come across now was her motivation for going public. This was the first PPE whistleblower to go on camera and she was doing it at great personal risk.

"You've taken a decision to speak out about this – tell me why?"

"Because something needs to be done and it needs to be done immediately. We want to help people. It's our job to respond and save lives. But we feel let down."

"What are you told when you raise concerns?"

"Essentially to get on with it. That it's the same across the board."

We filmed for around thirty minutes. The details left me cold and, by the time we finished and the lights came back on, I already knew viewers would be outraged at what was being revealed.

For context, it's important to remember this was before lockdown; before some of those who made the rules broke the rules; before anyone considered Covid-19 deaths in the UK could possibly overtake what we were seeing in Italy; before anyone imagined there would soon be calls for a full-scale inquiry into what went wrong.

These were lessons learned slowly and painfully. Back then, though, the daily media briefings were still a little like scientific presentations followed by relatively gentle questions of curiosity. The information given to us by our paramedic was about to change that.

The next briefing with Scotland's First Minister wasn't until the following afternoon – it was one of the last at St Andrew's House in Edinburgh that journalists could attend in person. After delivering the latest statistics and government advice, Nicola Sturgeon looked up. "Now I'm happy to take questions from the media," she said.

As a journalist, this is the moment you wait for at these events. The opening speech is rarely interesting; how a politician responds to a direct question is where the news story will usually be found. When you come to these events already armed with the scoop, though, and have the opportunity to put serious allegations directly to the country's First Minister – well, that is one of the great privileges of being a journalist. It also adds pressure to make sure you get the tone and wording just right. When you confront a senior politician, especially as impressive a communicator as Nicola Sturgeon, you absolutely cannot swing and miss. I wrote my question down, re-worded it until I was happy, and practised it in my head until I was called upon.

"First Minister, there is a whistleblower in the Scottish Ambulance Service who is speaking to ITV News today. She says lives are being put at risk because they are not being given the protective equipment they need. Are you aware paramedics don't even have hand sanitiser and they're being asked to share face visors?"

The First Minister looked a little surprised. I remember her eyes squinting when I said the word "whistleblower", giving me a look that said, "Where are you going with this?" She started her answer by saying anyone with a problem should not feel the need to go to the media and should instead raise their concerns with the NHS or the Scottish Government. "Also, Peter, I would add this is not the time for 'gotcha' journalism."

That answer still frustrates me, though it perfectly sums up the mood at the time. This really wasn't about "getting" a politician, though; the only thing I was interested in getting was appropriate PPE for frontline medics – the very people the country would be relying on in the weeks and months ahead. "But this paramedic has raised concerns," I interrupted. "She's been told to just get on with it."

I believed this was the public service journalism we were expected to deliver, and it didn't have to be meek. The First Minister came back. She was taking the issue seriously. "If somebody is, as you describe them, a whistleblower then no doubt they've done that under conditions of confidentiality but if you're able to provide the detail of that I will ensure it is addressed today."

Of course, I would never give away any details of the paramedic, but what she and her colleagues were going through was now in the public domain. Our report went on the ITV *Evening News* and *News at Ten* and the response was overwhelmingly positive. Within an hour of the broadcast I was sent dozens of private messages from nurses, junior doctors, consultants, carers – all with similar concerns.

The one person I didn't hear from, though, was the paramedic. I was a little worried she thought we hadn't done her story justice. Then two days later she sent a message. "Apologies for the delayed reply, been working. Good news is we finally have PPE arriving and we're being face fitted for proper masks!"

The GMB Union that represents paramedics then posted a Tweet. It was a letter from Scotland's Health Secretary addressed to Scottish Ambulance Service staff and it said, "I am writing to you today to apologise personally for the anxiety and concern you have felt around the supply of personal protective equipment . . . I will do all I can to make sure you have the equipment, the information, and the clinical guidance you need to do the vital job we are asking you to do."

Securing change is the best outcome we can hope for when reporting any story and it was certainly not the last time the media would scrutinise the government's response to this pandemic. I hope when the time comes for that post-coronavirus inquiry, there will be questions asked about the culture of fear and secrecy that made so many NHS workers feel they could not even talk to a journalist without risking their jobs. These are people who save lives for a living, and if they have concerns about people being put at risk they should be supported for raising it, not punished.

Timeline

March

15 Health Secretary Matt Hancock warns over-70s they will need to self-isolate for a long time

16 The first daily Downing Street press briefing is held. The Prime Minister advises against non-essential travel and asks people to work from home if they can. He warns pregnant women, the over-70s and people with some health conditions to take particular notice

17 The Chancellor, Rishi Sunak, announces that £330bn will be made available in loan guarantees for businesses

18 The government announces school closures, and confirms no exams will take place

19 The Bank of England cuts interest rates to just 0.1 percent

20 The last day that schools are fully open

The Chancellor announces the furlough scheme for employees not working

The Prime Minister tells pubs to close

21 UK supermarkets start a recruitment drive

22 Mother's Day

It's announced that thousands of former health staff have volunteered to help the NHS

23 Homeschooling starts

The Prime Minister, in a televised address, announces a three-week national lockdown and says the message is: "Stay at Home, Protect the NHS, Save Lives"

The Barman, the Health Minister and the Nurse

Vicki Hawthorne, Reporter, UTV

On the eve of St Patrick's Day, an exhausted pub manager in Belfast told me that he hadn't slept. Richard Keenan was standing in his empty two-storey bar, which is a hugely popular spot for students in the south of the city. Pubs don't normally smell this clean. The walls were decked with emblems of the annual festivities, and underneath the green shamrock bunting staff worked to sanitise every surface. Richard told me he'd been agonising over how to protect his staff from coronavirus when the pub opened its doors the next day, St Patrick's Day. Synonymous with a pint of the black stuff, it's always the busiest and one of the most lucrative days of the year for bars in Belfast and beyond.

But the bar, like the majority across Belfast and Northern Ireland, didn't open the next day. Families and revellers didn't crowd the streets for parades as normal. There was no "drowning the shamrock". Lockdown proper wasn't announced for a few more days, but March 17th was when the first of the key industries in Northern Ireland, hospitality, closed its doors indefinitely.

Covid-19 claimed its first victim in Northern Ireland the next day, March 18th. That's when the leading politicians at Stormont began giving daily press conferences. These started out in a room close to the offices of the First and Deputy First Ministers. It's a room normally reserved for "big news" days, the announcement of political agreements or to welcome Prime Ministers and Presidents. During one particular afternoon in March, I remember political advisors and press officers lining the walls as we waited for the conference to start. I stood with other reporters, TV camera operators and photographers in the middle of the room. An advisor chastised me for not socially distancing. But it was really difficult; there just wasn't enough room. I was uncomfortable. Everyone was.

Within a few days the briefings moved to the grandly named Long Gallery room at Stormont, in an effort to allow social distancing. Ministers were by now occupied by COBRA meetings with the Prime Minister, coming out in the late afternoon to update the eager local media.

The virus seemed to impact on something new every hour. The last face-to-face press conference was on a Friday afternoon at the end of March. I sat on the far left side of the room, my BBC colleague sat on the far right, waiting for the conference to start. We normally sit close by and chat, but this time we sat awkwardly in silence as we watched microphones and lecterns being wiped down. We both quizzed a sweating and clearly under pressure press officer about why technology wasn't being used to host the conferences remotely. Downing Street was doing it. It's not a perfect solution as it limits the chance for follow-up questions from journalists. But it was beginning to feel very necessary. By the end of the month reporters had moved from a familiar drive to Stormont to dialling into remote briefings with ministers online.

It's worth pointing out that Northern Ireland's devolved government had only been up and running for six weeks when the pandemic hit. Until January, there had been no Stormont Executive or Assembly sitting for three years. It had collapsed in 2017 following controversy, scandal and a lack of trust between the main political parties.

Our new Health Minister Robin Swann knew he faced big challenges ahead: three years of a backlog of decision-making in the health service, the longest waiting lists in the UK, and a nursing workforce only recently back to normal after several days of strike action during December and January.

Rather than tackling those challenges, instead during the week of St Patrick's Day, Mr Swann was warning the public there could be as many as 15,000 coronavirus deaths in Northern Ireland. He spent the following weeks repeating the now well-established maxim – wash your hands and stay two metres apart. Tough questions had to be answered about the lack of personal protective equipment for health workers, orders for ventilators, and deaths in care homes.

In mid-April, when being questioned about the coronavirus response in his department, Mr Swann stood in front of Assembly colleagues and said, "I can assure members there are nights I don't sleep when I think about what we are doing and about what we have to do the next day." His open and honest remarks got a passing mention in the news, but that was also the day the lockdown was extended for another three weeks. That's what everyone really wanted to know about.

Quite rightly, UTV broadcast daily interviews with families who had lost loved ones to the virus. A daughter whose parents died within days of each other, those who didn't have a chance to say goodbye at the end. Their stories were heartbreaking, but also what people needed to hear to grasp the reality of this virus.

The sleepless nights of the barman and the health minister were heard, but they didn't quite register. They were important, but the same anxiety was so widespread. Like so many other people, my time reporting on the pandemic was entangled with a familiar narrative: a husband working from home, homeschooling, care for two children, as well as worry about older relatives. I was also introduced to what is now a well recognised online meeting site. Zoom entered public vocabulary during this crisis. Press conferences and interviews with government ministers were brought to my living room.

The same site offered a lifeline and some light relief when I was part of a gathering of six far flung girlfriends one Friday night during lockdown. But it was a shock seeing the face of one friend pop up. A nurse who had been working in a Covid ward. Pale, drawn, exhausted. I thought she was going to fall asleep during the call. She didn't say much. She didn't have to.

A barman, a health minister and a nurse. They could be characters listed in the opening line of a good Belfast joke. Instead, along with the voices of victims' families, it's their words and their faces that endure during my time reporting on the pandemic.

Your Daily Dinenage

Fred Dinenage MBE, Presenter, ITV News Meridian

Tuesday March 17th. It's a date I will never forget. The government had announced the previous day that all over-70s were to self-isolate, to stay at home because of the coronavirus. Sadly I fall into that category by a number of years!

The inevitable phone call came from my boss and I found myself emptying my desk drawers and taking suits and shirts from my dressing room to my car. That night's ITV News Meridian programmes, in the south and south-east and the Thames Valley, were difficult for me. Was this the end of 10 happy and successful years alongside my dear co-presenter Sangeeta Bhabra?

Was this the end of 36 years co-presenting the six o'clock show? Indeed, was this the end of a career with ITV that had somehow spanned 56 years?

I was depressed and angry. I knew that older people were more at risk, the scientists had told the government so. But I was fit, I was active. I knew many of our older viewers shared my sentiments. These days many so-called elderly folk are incredibly fit and active and often still working into their 80s. For there to be a blanket ban on all over-70s was a clear and simple rule, which of course is a good thing, but for many it did seem unsubtle and unfair. While I sympathise with all of the more vulnerable older folk, I was inclined to agree with one viewer, in her 70s, who told me: "This is age discrimination." And how ridiculous for the presenter of Radio Four's *Woman's Hour* to be 69 and in the studio one day, and aged 70 and having to work from home the next day. Did poor Jenni Murray suddenly become vulnerable overnight? That's a birthday she won't forget!

There was also the pain and mental stress of older folk being unable to see family and friends. Grandparents not allowed to be with grandchildren! I needed to stay involved in this huge story, the biggest, surely, in all of our careers. But, what to do? It was producer Kim Hewitt and ITV Meridian Head of News, Alison Nice, who came up with the idea.

"Fred," said Kim, "you must introduce an uplifting end-of-show item that will cheer our viewers up. They will see a friendly face who's in the same lockdown situation as them." And it was Sangeeta Bhabra who came up with the title: "Your Daily Dinenage".

So that's what we did. Every night, via the wonders of Skype, I told stories of fundraising, fortitude and fun. An antidote to the often desperately sad news that had gone before.

We announced special birthdays and anniversaries for people who weren't able to celebrate with family and friends. It was hugely popular. On occasion, I included my three rescue dogs. One of them, Dave Dinenage, was such a hit he could have had a show of his own!

I had so many letters and emails from viewers . All of them typified by this one from Barbara, an older viewer from Alverstoke in Hampshire: "I always look forward to your Daily Dinenage. You cheer me up when I'm feeling lonely and a bit down. It's very uplifting."

The whole experience was uplifting for me too. Though there were dark moments of depression, of frustration that I couldn't be in the studio helping my colleagues, doing what I should be doing, telling this extraordinary story as it affected our region; talking to the victims, to the survivors and to our wonderful NHS workers and carers. And putting our politicians on the spot. Yes, dark moments and, I'm not ashamed to say, one or two tears.

But then I would start telling the stories of some of our amazing viewers. Their strength, their resilience, their humour in the face of real adversity. And suddenly even though I, like them, had no idea how it was all going to end . . . suddenly, once again, it all became worthwhile.

Finally, my thoughts are with all the victims of the coronavirus and their families. Especially my dear friend and colleague of many years, Chris Barrett, and his family. Chris had been a producer at ITV Meridian, and a very good one. He contracted Covid-19 and died in hospital in April. I miss him terribly.

My Personal Professional Pandemic

Sangeeta Bhabra, Presenter, ITV News Meridian

The email from Fred was the first sign to me that coronavirus was already affecting everything. Fred never misses a show. He told me he wasn't sure when we'd be reunited on screen because he was going into "self-isolation". The jargon was pretty unfamiliar then but because Fred, who has been a legend on our screens for five and a half decades, was over 70 the government advice was to stay at home to prevent exposure to the invisible virus. Fred said it was important he set the right example.

I had been off work that week to dedicate some time to my caring responsibilities. I live at home with my parents and brother. Both my dad and my brother have severe disabilities and my mum, normally their prime carer, was recovering from cataract surgery.

I found time to watch the news – seeing everything unfold. In those days running up to the lockdown announcement on March 23rd, things were changing both at home and at work.

When you're a carer your life is always a delicate balance that relies on others. My brother is 38 with severe autism and cerebral palsy. He can't speak. He can't understand "shut" or global pandemic or coronavirus, so explaining why staff were in tears about his day centre closing was not an option. Confusion and uncertainty about the future was already apparent. Each centre user was given a letter on that last day warning that the charity may not survive a pandemic. This would be the story of every charity in the weeks that followed.

My sister and I tried to plan a new home routine for our brother. The care companies who had been washing and dressing my father each day said they couldn't promise to provide enough staff as many had been impacted by school closures. In any case, we were now hesitant to allow outside carers into the house. The only option was to do it all ourselves – and we weren't the only family in this situation. I'm just grateful for the never-ending support I had from my Head of News, and the wider management at ITV News, which gave me time to find successful solutions.

Being classified as a key worker was a mental life saver. I was fortunate enough to escape the pressures at home to the familiar, but also "not-as-I-knew-it", ITV Meridian newsroom and studio at Whiteley in Hampshire. Our team had been stripped back to just those in critical roles to get the programme to air – always two metres apart. And for the first time in my career I was presenting the news section of the programme on my own until we could check in with Fred, very quickly established as a Skype genius, for his good news section, "the Daily Dinenage".

TV executives often refer to the importance of a "family of faces" on screen and it became apparent from viewers' letters and emails that they valued that familiarity and warmth more than ever.

When you work on an ITV regional news programme, you expect your professional and personal worlds to collide sometimes. After all, we live and work in the region we serve and much of our journalism is dependent on the things we learn and the relationships we build. On April 15th, one such collision affected me deeply.

A new story, late-breaking, had gone into the programme running order, called "RBH death". The Royal Berkshire Hospital in Reading is a place I know far too well because I live in the town and I'm a frequent visitor to its long corridors because of my caring commitments.

I read the script, which was probably around twenty seconds long, and found myself struggling to take in the death of the latest NHS member of staff from coronavirus.

Doctor Peter Tun was 62 years old and a specialist in neuro-rehabilitation at the Reading hospital. Nine years earlier, he had been a key member of the brilliant team who cared for my father after his devastating stroke. What the script didn't say was that Doctor Tun was a regular viewer of our programme. Like most people who watch, I remember him asking affectionately about Fred. The script also didn't mention how Doctor Tun was excellent at his job and genuinely cared for those who passed through his care.

For me, this wasn't just another news update. It was a story about someone I had great professional respect for. The next thing I did was call my dad, wanting to warn him about the news I would be delivering on air.

Dr Tun was a trusted face, like so many wonderful NHS professionals we met, and had helped my family get through the most difficult period of our lives.

As a family we will always be grateful for this NHS hero and all those who sacrificed their lives fighting coronavirus. The one personal regret – that this is the only way I will now get to say "Thank You".

The Royal Family's Story

Chris Ship, Royal Editor, ITV News

On a quiet Thursday morning in March, two cars slipped out of the gates at Buckingham Palace and turned left towards Constitution Hill for the journey west. On the back seat of the second vehicle sat two dogs with their elderly owner. The dogs were Dorgis. The elderly owner was the Queen. And they were all getting out of London.

On that day, March 19th, the country had recorded 158 deaths from Covid-19. But the predictions were for something much, much worse. At that moment, the capital was the most severely affected part of the UK. And the elderly were most at risk.

London was not, therefore, a place deemed safe for a monarch who was just a few weeks from her 94th birthday. She was due to travel to Windsor later that month in any event for the annual Easter court. The Queen would, it was decided, move to Windsor two weeks early. Given the Queen's calendar follows a rigid annual pattern and her movements are watched closely, Buckingham Palace decided that this premature relocation should be accompanied by a statement from the Sovereign.

We are "entering a period of great concern and uncertainty," the Queen wrote, but added with a small measure of hope that "our nation's history has been forged by people and communities coming together to work as one." It would not be the last time during the pandemic that she would refer to the war years when speaking about the national effort.

As the Queen headed along the A4 with her dogs on that March morning, her husband was boarding a helicopter on the Sandringham estate. The Duke of Edinburgh, who was 98 at the time, was also

being transferred to Windsor where both he and the Queen could be better isolated and looked after by a small coterie of staff.

For the foreseeable future, there would be no public visits. No crowds. No royal tours. In fact, the Prince of Wales had been scheduled to be in Bosnia Herzegovina that very week. But that, and all other events, had been scratched from the royal diaries one by one. Suddenly they were all very empty.

The Queen ended her message to the nation that day with these words: "You can be assured that my family and I stand ready to play our part." But how could they? Her family, like all families, had to follow the rules and stay at home. Granted their homes are bigger than most people's but what role could they play as the crisis worsened?

For those of us tasked with covering the royal beat for the nation's television news programmes and newspapers, we were left asking if our workload was about to become very light. We did not have to wait long for an answer.

At 10.31am on the following Wednesday, March 25th, I was at home when my phone buzzed. It was from a senior official in Prince Charles' office. And I read these six words: "Prince has tested positive for coronavirus". I read the message twice. Then wondered if it was a hoax. But an email from Clarence House had also arrived in my inbox, announcing the same thing. I jumped onto social media, called the news editor and prepared myself for a very busy day.

The Prince's symptoms were mild, we were told, and, true to form, the workaholic heir to the throne had continued to do his paperwork from his desk at Birkhall, the home Charles and Camilla have on the Balmoral estate, where they were spending the lockdown. The Duchess of Cornwall had also been tested. But her result was negative.

It was a moment for the country to acknowledge that coronavirus could infect anyone regardless of status, or position, or wealth or hereditary advantage. The 71-year-old Prince of Wales had it, so who else was at risk? And what about his mother?

A conference call for royal correspondents was hastily arranged by Buckingham Palace. "Her Majesty the Queen remains in good health," they told us. But when did she last come into contact with Prince

Charles, we asked. At the Palace on the morning of March 12th, came the answer.

The Royal Family rarely comment on health matters or private family meetings. This, however, was a moment to make an exception to the rule. By our estimation Prince Charles saw his mother about a day before he would have become infectious. The Queen's physicians were satisfied and not alarmed, insisted her press secretary, but it all seemed a little too close for comfort. And this was a virus medics knew very little about.

This all mattered because a Sovereign's role, evolved as it has over many centuries, is largely defined by his or her relationship with the people. At a time when everything seemed to be changing in our own personal lives – work, school, eating, socialising, communicating, families, politics – it might well have sent the country into a collective national breakdown had the Queen herself contracted the virus.

She is someone through whom many identify as British, someone respected worldwide for her dedication to duty, someone whose hand has guided the nation through good times and bad. And this was the reason why, as national life ground to a sudden and dramatic halt, demand started to grow for the Queen to address the country.

In both my work life and my personal one, people were asking me if I thought the Queen would say some words, if she would make a speech, if she could calm an agitated nation. My answer was always the same: "The Queen is not one for rushing to a microphone!" Because she isn't.

Before the coronavirus pandemic, she had spoken on only three occasions at a time of a crisis or significant national event. In 1991, she addressed the nation on the eve of the Gulf War as UK troops embarked on the land offensive in Kuwait and Iraq. In 1997, she broadcast a message live from Buckingham Palace on the evening before the funeral of her daughter-in-law, the much loved Diana, Princess of Wales. In 2002, she spoke fondly of her mother as the nation prepared to say goodbye to Queen Elizabeth, the Queen Mother, who had died at the age of 101.

And in April 2020, the country wanted her to do it again.

Perhaps the demand was, in part, fuelled by an absence of political leadership. Prime Minister Boris Johnson had just announced he had contracted Covid-19. The virus was, by now, striking those who were supposed to be leading the fight against it. Perhaps it was also because people needed to be reminded that some things in their lives were still the same. The Sovereign might seem a remote figure to many people, but she is a visible reminder of stability and continuity – especially at a time when everything else around us was in a state of flux.

And so, as March turned into April, a small television crew was invited into Windsor Castle. The camera operator was told to wear personal protective equipment before being shown to the White Drawing Room. It is one of the semi-state rooms on the east side of the Castle that overlook the manicured East Lawn Terrace.

Thanks to King George IV, who commissioned them, the rooms are large and spacious and it meant the Queen could record her message to the camera without breaking the strict social distancing rules that were in place for everyone except the two dozen courtiers assigned to her care. Approval for the presence of a camera had also been sought and received from the Medical Household, the Queen's team of doctors and surgeons. Everybody else involved in the recording, from the Queen's most senior staff to the other technicians, were watching the recording in a neighbouring room.

The address, broadcast on April 5th, was "deeply personal" according to the Palace, and the Queen, once again, reflected on her experience of living through the Second World War. I recall watching the address in our newsroom and looking up to see that every screen, from every broadcaster was showing the Queen in her green dress, speaking from Windsor Castle. It felt like a national moment. And it was. Twenty-four million people had tuned in to watch. What she said that evening in just four minutes and fifteen seconds was exactly what the country needed to hear.

The Queen acknowledged the disruption, the financial hardship and the grief suffered by so many. She said Britons of the future would call this generation "as strong as any" and she recalled a broadcast she made in 1940, also from Windsor, when the nation had previously felt a "painful sense of separation from their loved ones". And she ended by echoing the words of Dame Vera Lynn: "We will be with our friends again; we will be with our families again; we will meet again." The Queen knew what needed to be said and she appeared to have correctly read the mood of the nation.

Did it change the course of the virus? Absolutely not. How could it? But she did appear to have succeeded in settling the nation's nerves. And yet, by the time we went on air at 10 o'clock that Sunday evening, we had a new lead story. One that was big enough to remove the Queen from the top slot: the Prime Minister's condition had worsened and he had just been moved to hospital.

So where would the rest of the Royal Family go from here? They went digital. Yes, they were locked down, just like the rest of us, but video call software was hastily being installed on Palace laptops and iPads – and it enabled them to do their jobs, albeit in a different kind of way.

So, from the Balmoral estate, Prince Charles completed the first ever virtual royal opening, as he attended the opening ceremony, via a screen, for the new NHS Nightingale Hospital in east London. He had just recovered from his own bout of coronavirus and sounded very hoarse. I was amused by the pictures that emerged afterwards showing his iPad propped up with a stack of books. It was a scene many people working from home would have recognised.

Meanwhile, the Duchess of Cornwall was talking about the lockdown and domestic violence, about osteoporosis, and she chatted merrily to the ballerina and television star, Darcey Bussell, about keeping active in one's advancing years. "We just clatter around," Camilla said of her impromptu ballet sessions with friends.

Over at Sandringham, where William and Kate had relocated to their country home, Anmer Hall, for the duration of the lockdown, Prince George, Princess Charlotte and Prince Louis were shown clapping for our carers, just as the rest of the nation did every Thursday night. New, informal photos of the children, taken by Kate, were released as the young royals painted, played and helped to deliver food parcels. Charlotte and Louis' birthdays were celebrated with more of Kate's photographic work.

The Duke and Duchess themselves went on a video-call frenzy, talking to care workers, nurses, midwives, volunteers, mental health supporters. You name it, they video-called it. And when did you last see a future King and Queen acting as bingo callers for the residents of a care home? Answer: not until the lockdown. "Six and two, tickety boo," Kate called out, via Zoom, holding a number 62 ball as if she played bingo every other night.

Being shut away was unavoidable for the Royal Family. But being out of sight was not an option. "We are making them as visible as they possibly can be in the circumstances," one royal aide told me. As the number of deaths continued to rise, many had started to question the role of our political leaders during the crisis, but few could find bad things to say about the role played by the Royal Family.

As the Queen remarked when she spoke again to mark the 75th anniversary of VE Day, the streets of Britain were not empty. Instead, she said, they were "filled with the love and the care that we have for each other." The royals did eventually come back out onto those streets, as we all did. But it was very different.

I went to the first royal engagement after the restrictions were lifted. We were in Gloucester with Prince Charles and the Duchess of Cornwall, who were thanking the staff and volunteers of the NHS, people who Camilla said were "Britain at its best." Prince Charles said to me after he had met the staff: "they've had to endure an awful lot of stress and strain." We were standing in a quiet corner of the hospital campus, so as not to attract any crowds. Yellow paint marks had been sprayed on the grass to keep everyone two metres apart. My microphone was on a two-metre-long pole. It was nothing like the royal visits I had done so many times before.

Prince William and Kate would also be back out and about in a similar cautious way that week. But not the Queen, who remained at Windsor Castle. She did, however, make her debut on a public video conference. Remarkable as it might have sounded a few months ago, the Queen was introduced to a group of carers on the virtual meeting by her private secretary, Sir Edward Young. He announced to the group: "Her Majesty the Queen is ready to join the call."

"I'm very glad to have been able to join you today," the Queen was recorded saying into the computer screen. But even in lockdown, with the world embracing new technology, some formalities would not be dispensed with. For the engagement with the carers in this virtual room, just as in a room in the real world, protocol was followed: the Queen was the last to enter and the first to leave.

It proved there are some things even coronavirus can't change.

Mam's the Word: Explaining Social Distancing

Rob Osborne, National Correspondent,
ITV News Cymru Wales

It's 9.15am and the editorial morning meeting for *Wales at Six* is about to start. Coronavirus is the only topic on the agenda now. As I head to the conference room my phone rings. It's my mother.

"Can I go to the shop, I need bread?"

"No. Don't leave the house."

"But it's only over the road!"

"No, you've got to stay in."

My mother, June, is 68 and has a heart issue. She's the main carer for her brother, my uncle Neil, who has Down's Syndrome and some of its associated health issues. They live in such close proximity that if one gets coronavirus, the other is likely to catch it. They have underlying health conditions. A term once used solely by doctors and now thrown around by everyone as if we're all experts. Both must self-isolate, but it isn't quite clear, not least to my mother, what that fully means.

"I need my hair done next week!" she adds in frustration as if I can make that happen. At this point I'm in the meeting room, we're about to start and my colleagues are wondering what's going on. The call ends and I explain.

"She's just not getting it," I say. "Social isolation, social distancing, even I'm confused and I'm supposed to know these things." Others share their own stories. "My father is the same, he keeps popping to the pub. He says the virus won't come to west Wales," someone says. "I had the same conversation with my mother last night, the message just isn't getting through," adds another.

My producer Dafydd Jones dispatches me to film this conversation with my mother and, through her, explain to our viewers what terms like self-isolation and social distancing mean. My newly appointed colleague Charanpreet Khaira will be on hand to help.

By now Covid-19 has changed the way we film reports. Radio microphones are no longer attached to contributors. Instead I will hold a two-metre microphone pole to record the sound. It looks ridiculous, as if I'm holding a fishing rod over an imaginary river, but it's essential to keep people apart, even mother and son. Trevor Davies the camera operator is recording and the front door opens.

"Are you coming in?" she asks.

"I can't come in!" I almost shout back with bewilderment in my voice. We've had this discussion on the phone.

"I don't understand. I haven't got it [the virus] at the moment, you haven't got it at the moment," she says, standing on the door-step wondering why her son won't come inside the home he's grown up in.

"You don't know I haven't got it. I may not be showing any symptoms," I reply. Something on her face tells me she doesn't believe it.

She has concerns but they are for my uncle not herself. He's used to regular car trips. I take him out at weekends but that won't be happening for a long time.

"He doesn't understand what's happening, why somebody isn't coming to take him out," she says. That's when it hits me – the most vulnerable will be hit hardest by the pandemic whether they get the virus or not.

Filming finished, I head back to the newsroom to edit my report. I'm not sure what exactly I have, but this is no normal news report. It's almost five minutes long – that's long for a news report – and it features this reporter's family. "It's perfect," says Dafydd, "just what I hoped for."

The report is broadcast on *Wales at Six*. I think no more of it. At the same time, it's uploaded to social media, despite my recommendation not to bother because "nobody will watch it." I couldn't have been more wrong. Hundreds of thousands of people clicked and commented.

"Much needed humanity," said a government minister in a private message.

"Really good piece of broadcast journalism," said award-winning BBC reporter Jeremy Bowen. Even former cabinet minister and amateur dancer Ed Balls tweeted, calling it "brilliant, human, public-service broadcasting."

Most pleasing were the comments from people having similar battles in their own families. Many said they would be sharing the video with their own parents or grandparents in the hope they finally "got it."

Why did it touch a nerve? Because it was simple and authentic. Clarity in messaging had been lacking at that point. No public information adverts, no leaflets through the door. The public were hungry for practical information. Perhaps it took a mam from the Welsh valleys to help give it.

Peston's Pandemic

Vicky Flind, Series Editor, Peston

Just before Christmas 2019, a senior ITV executive offered his thanks to the *Peston* programme team after an exhausting year covering British politics. The Brexit crisis had reached boiling point, there'd been a change of prime minister, and the Conservatives had just won a decisive victory at the general election in early December. There was a suggestion that political life might now settle down, and that the *Peston* programme would have to adapt to this new world. Then the world was hit by coronavirus, causing a deadly pandemic and bringing the global economy to its knees.

Peston is ITV's weekly political flagship show presented by the Political Editor of ITV News, Robert Peston, along with Anushka Asthana, presenter of the *Guardian* podcast *Today in Focus*. *Peston* is broadcast by ITV on Wednesdays at 10.45pm.

The coronavirus crisis rightly dominated our programme from the day lockdown was imposed, but the journey for Team *Peston* – with all the complex editorial, production and technical challenges – had actually started long before lockdown became a reality. In late January, two months before the Prime Minister's announcement, the team was trying to agree on a final guest for that night's show. In hindsight, that discussion would become a useful yardstick for the startling changes to come. Robert was adamant that Sir Jeremy Farrar, director of the Wellcome Trust, should be invited to talk about the worsening health situation in China. The World Health Organization was due that night to make a major announcement about the status of the crisis. Sir Jeremy would join us live from the World Economic Forum in Davos in Switzerland. Robert insisted that this was already shaping up to be the next big story and that Sir Jeremy "would deliver" – by which he meant he would give us an interesting and possibly news-making interview.

We were still getting used to a radically new political landscape: a government with an 80-seat majority, no general election for five years, and the painfully slow withdrawal from an all encompassing Brexit process. Some of the team even feared a big majority could mean a lack of parliamentary excitement after the endless political turbulence sparked by the referendum of 2016. We were trying to familiarise ourselves with this new world, without nightly knife-edge votes and back-room deals, and there was even a dread that politics could actually become a little mundane. I became very aware that I was the only member of the team who had worked through the days of Tony Blair's record Labour majority of 179. To be perfectly honest, the attractions of a quieter news agenda, after years of Brexit turbulence, were not insignificant.

As it happened, Sir Jeremy was unable to deliver, through no fault of his own. We decided a live link from Davos would be too unreliable. He was replaced by a government minister at the last minute – hardly a rare occurrence in this new world. The WHO also delayed their pronouncements for a week, and though the Chinese city of Wuhan went into lockdown the next day, the evolving coronavirus crisis did not dominate the programme that night as it should have done. Robert had been right (as usual, he would say) and any notion of a relatively calm period ahead was rapidly erased.

Two months later, the full terrifying force of the pandemic had become evident. Our focus every week was on the government's handling of the crisis, the quality of its decision-making, the role of scientists, and the deadly impact on society and the economy. These are complex subjects to grapple with in an accessible and straightforward manner.

On a practical level, we were freed from the confines of our dungeon office at Television Centre in west London by the demands of social distancing. There were rigorous new guidelines about the safety of the production and broadcasting processes: we had fewer cameras, we used just one part of the set, we had no guests in studio, we had limits on the number of team members who could attend on programme days, and we even stopped the flow of cheap white wine in the after-show green room. As Theresa May might have said in different circumstances, everything had changed!

Some of the team became ill with Covid-19. Others were self-isolating because of the illness of family members. This also applied to the wider production and technical teams, with the result that the environment in which we worked became extremely tense and marked by persistent anxiety. At one point, Robert himself was having to isolate, leaving us for the first time to create a programme with him at home and Anushka in the studio. The producer's instinctive reluctance to include too many "down-the-line" remote interviews was swept aside by necessity. We found ourselves grateful for even the fuzziest connections on Skype, FaceTime, or Zoom. Indeed, they became the foundation of the programme. Our technical colleagues performed miracles to make it all work on air. Even so there were nights when it all felt rather precarious.

ITV had asked us to stay on air, while most television shows were being shut down, to provide an important forum for public debate and questioning at a time of national crisis. The team responded with exemplary commitment, despite the logistical obstacles thrown in their path. Would we be able to use our usual studio? Would our mostly freelance studio crew be able to work? Would guests even want to take part at such a worrying time? We were eventually allowed access to our usual space at Television Centre, but without the company of our far more glamorous colleagues on the *Jonathan Ross Show*. When we arrived for that first "lockdown *Peston*" in late March, our small team was the only presence in that vast broadcast facility.

The prime focus was, however, unchanged. The *Peston* programme had been born in the months before the referendum of 2016. Robert and I had always wanted to offer a more informal platform for genuine discussion, a departure from the usual "assault-by-interview" and the tedious desire to create more noise than sense. That had proved almost impossible during much of the Brexit storm, but the pandemic offered the opportunity to revisit the original editorial goals.

As the threat grew, there was a palpable public desire for leaders (in politics, science and public health) to do the right thing and overcome the huge challenges posed by the pandemic. Regardless of tribal political loyalties, there was a strong sense of goodwill towards those in charge. Labour sensed this too and offered statements of support and a wish to collaborate in a united national effort. Sir Keir Starmer, whose election as Labour leader had drawn far less attention because of the pandemic headlines, was clearly determined to strike the right note.

Things changed as the pandemic progressed and the number of deaths rose sharply in the UK. The hunger for news and information was notable: audiences for news and other factual programmes reflected the trend, as millions wanted not only to understand the nature of the threat, but also to be kept informed about the latest health advice and guidelines. The new trend of interviewing guests in their bedrooms, offices, kitchens and garden sheds became part of the normal routine, and debates about domestic backdrops, and what they said about the tastes of the interviewee, became both heated and hilarious. Nothing could beat Cherie Blair's office shelves, which for some reason seemed to be showcasing the Wimbledon Ladies' Singles trophy.

Experts were back in vogue, four years after Michael Gove had famously questioned their usefulness in British life. People wanted to listen carefully to the likes of the Chief Medical Officer, Chris Whitty, and the Chief Scientific Adviser, Patrick Vallance, and others as they fielded questions from journalists and members of the public. The scientists' knowledge and advice became essential. At the outset they answered with commendable clarity, but as the politics became increasingly sensitive, they were seen to temper their remarks, sometimes avoiding direct questions or refusing to answer if they considered it too "political" to do so. Their availability for interviews dwindled at the same time.

The Prime Minister's own recovery from Covid-19 marked a turning point in the political and public debate. The public began to think that the government's own messaging became somewhat confused at times. There were changes to advice. There were policy differences with the devolved administrations in Scotland, Wales and Northern Ireland, which fed the political confusion. As the numbers of victims rose, and the UK experience seemed to become one of the most challenging in the world, questions were inevitably asked about the government's decision-making, and the controversial role of a few unelected advisors in the process. The political landscape had changed back to something that resembled the Brexit storm.

The fight over "facts" and "fake news" spilled over into toxic debate on social media, and the mainstream news broadcasters became targets for unremitting hostility. That hostility was very much in evidence again in the wake of the killing of George Floyd in Minneapolis, and the resulting anti-racism protests organised in the UK by the Black Lives Matter movement.

The Covid-19 crisis has taught the *Peston* team that political television can and must be more flexible in future. We need more agility and innovation. So many things deemed unsuitable or unacceptable, or even unachievable, have worked out perfectly well in production and editorial terms. The intense debate about one programme guest on that night in late January seems rather trivial now. We have, in every meaningful sense, entered a different world.

Everything Changed, Changed Utterly

Peter MacMahon, Political Editor, ITV Border

Alex Salmond had just been acquitted on charges of attempted rape and sexual assault. Amid talk of a "conspiracy" against the former First Minister orchestrated by allies and advisors of his successor, Nicola Sturgeon, Mr Salmond was expected to wreak immediate revenge. The media gathered outside Edinburgh's High Court fell into silent anticipation. Mr Salmond spoke: "People are dying, many more are going to die. My strong advice to you is to go home and those who are able, take care of your families. And God help us all."

It was not what was anticipated, but the Former First Minister had captured the moment, as he had often done in the past. Monday March 23rd became the day not when Scotland was shaken by colliding tectonic plates inside the SNP, but when the devastating reality of the impending Covid-19 earthquake struck home. Instead of defending her reputation, Ms Sturgeon announced that Scotland, like the rest of the UK, would go into lockdown. Everything changed, changed utterly, to borrow a W. B. Yeats line much loved by the former First Minister.

And much was to change for the ITV Border team based in Holyrood, charged with reporting Scottish and UK politics for *Representing Border*, our politics programme, and *Lookaround*, our daily half-hour news programme. We turned away from what had been the big stories of the day – Brexit, the constitutional debate, the Salmond trial – to reporting on a disease we initially knew little about, but which was to have a profound impact on our viewers' lives.

Like colleagues across the nations and regions of the UK, we first had to consider whether we could actually do our job while we adhered to the "new normal" of social distancing and lockdown rules. At first the answer was no. *Representing Border* came off air while a member of our team self-isolated, though we began to adjust through reporting for *Lookaround*. We had to master Skype and Zoom, the new tools of our trade. A Skype live into *Lookaround*? Why not. A Zoom media briefing with the First Minister? It could work.

One thing that did not change was what we sought to deliver for our ITV Border audience. The remit of *Representing Border* has always been to report politics in a way that reflects the impact it has on the lives of people in Dumfries and Galloway and the Scottish Borders. And when we report for *Lookaround* we also reflect on how that might affect people who live across the border in Cumbria.

It's said that all politics is local but that does not mean reporting politics has to be parochial. So we set about exploring the enormous impact Covid-19 was having, and would have, on our viewers' lives and livelihoods; and the impact, or lack of it, of decisions made in Edinburgh and London.

There were a lot of questions for which answers were desperately needed. Could GPs and hospitals in our region cope? Might they be overwhelmed, with potentially catastrophic consequences? Did care homes have enough personal protective equipment? Was there enough testing of staff and residents, and was it introduced quickly enough? How effective was lockdown, and what should people who live near the border, who cross it for work, rest and retail, make of differences between Scotland and England? Why should there be one set of rules for people in Langholm, in Scotland, and another for people in Longtown, just a few miles down the road in England? Did that matter?

From Port Patrick in the west to Eyemouth in the east, and everywhere in between, we went out and about as much as we could to find out what was happening. What would the shutting down of much of the economy mean for jobs, for farming, for tourism, for schools and their pupils, for the council services people depend on? What did lockdown and the extraordinary curbs on our civil liberties mean for the sense of community that is particularly strong in our region? Would older people be able to cope with the enforced isolation? Or new parents with young children? Or families who could not see close relatives? What about the effects on the least well-off in our society, in the pockets of often unseen poverty which exist in the south of Scotland?

Above all we listened. We listened to the voices of the people of the south of Scotland, people like our "Peebles panel". Before the election we brought together a farmer, a local GP, a businesswoman, the manager of the local theatre and a representative from the chamber of commerce to discuss the big issues – as they were then.

They all had opinions, often differing opinions, but they spoke for their communities. When we brought them back together in a report – not physically; we interviewed them separately – we found perspectives had completely changed. All they could talk about, all they could think about, was the virus – its impact on their town, their families, their friends, the problems it had caused, and, when they had covered that, their hopes for the future.

There were care homes initially without PPE. The health service did at first have problems coping with this killer in our midst. The tourism industry was devastated after it was forced to close down, with huge job losses, and is still not sure there is a viable future ahead. Farming has a big challenge for the future.

But as well as plenty of problems, we found plenty to celebrate: communities coming together to help and support one another; food banks finding new, socially distanced, ways to continue their work. Big hearts, small acts of kindness.

We'll go back to Peebles to speak to them again, hopefully when we can gather them together, to find out how they, and their town, have fared: television journalism reflecting the hopes and fears of our audience.

Through all of this it was important to hold those in power to account. To tell councillors, MSPs and MPs what we had found and to ask what they were doing about the concerns of the people they represent. This was where the new ways of working came in. It was not without its challenges. As an interviewer not being so close to the interviewee made my task that bit more difficult, but we asked the questions our viewers wanted the answers to and asked again (and again) if the replies were evasive and unsatisfactory.

Politely but firmly I challenged, among others, the First Minister on cross-border differences, the Secretary of State for Scotland on the UK government's role in Scotland, and the leader of Scottish Borders council about deaths in a care home the authority runs. Only the interview with Nicola Sturgeon was done in a room, though with us sitting appropriately far apart and the cameras at a distance too. The other two were done by Skype or Zoom. Not ideal but the fact you are not face to face with a politician does not stop you asking appropriately searching questions.

One other innovation was the First Minister's virtual media conferences at which she personally appeared almost daily – in contrast to Boris Johnson in Downing Street appearing once a week or so. In one way this was a positive development in terms of scrutiny. Nicola Sturgeon answers a question from each of the media organisations who sign up for her Zoom briefing. That gave ITV Border the chance to put the issues that were most important to our viewers to the politician who has the most power over their everyday lives. However, the downside was that Ms Sturgeon rarely took a follow up question and often deploys her formidable political communication skills, leaving the questioner frustrated. We leave it to viewers to make up their mind whether they think she properly answers the question posed to her, or not.

At the time of writing the polls suggest voters in Scotland are impressed with her handling of the crisis, and are unimpressed by Mr Johnson's efforts at Westminster. But Ms Sturgeon still faces what is the toughest part of the coronavirus challenge – leading Scotland out of lockdown, and back to some kind of normality.

If she succeeds, how will the electorate judge her? With gratitude and the reward of a new mandate, including the chance to pursue again her dream of independence? Or, although it's not a precise parallel, will voters treat her like Churchill after the Second World War – perceived as the right leader for a crisis, but deciding there is a need for a new post-corona broom at Bute House?

Lockdown Night

Julie Etchingham, Presenter, ITV News

Since the beginning of the year a new phrase had crept into our programmes as surely as it was charting its deadly mission around the world.

I can't remember the night I first read out the words "Covid-19" on *News at Ten*. But in January and February, our Asia Correspondent Debi Edward had been describing the slow, slow and then urgent total shutdown of Wuhan, the epicentre of a viral earthquake that would shake the world. Covid-19 was fast becoming a phrase that would feature in every news bulletin, around the clock.

By early March, Europe Editor James Mates was telling the story of Bergamo, the Italian town that set all our alarm bells ringing. The hospitals overflowing – makeshift, tented wards where exhausted medics desperately tried to revive those gasping and reeling from Covid-19. Where, all too often, they were failing.

I could barely believe the figures I was reading out. Latest death toll in Italy tonight – 400. It didn't, it couldn't, compute. It surely couldn't happen here.

Look at the streets of the capital and all our big cities. Whatever the warnings, people were out in parks in spring sunshine, ice creams in hand. On the 7th, I'd been to the rugby at Twickenham among tens of thousands. The Prime Minister and his pregnant partner Carrie Symonds were also there, clearly not unduly concerned. The following weekend, notoriously now, similar numbers turned out for the Cheltenham Festival. But on the night of March 23rd it all changed.

The crisis was hitting. Hospitals, whose wards were filling up, were ringing ever louder alarm bells. Closer to home, my sons' school, where they'd just had two cases of Covid, was already closed.

At 8.30pm all the main channels showed the Prime Minister in Downing Street. The Union flag behind him, he made an announcement that made history, that only those who had lived through the blitz might understand. We were about to endure the most extreme limitations on our personal liberty any of us could remember.

His message was stark: "From this evening, I must give the British people a very simple instruction – you must stay at home. If too many people become seriously ill at one time, the NHS will be unable to handle it, which will mean more people will die."

I've been in newsrooms on many occasions when a huge story has broken, but none quite like this. Not only were we putting together one of the most important programmes we've ever produced for our audience, we were all individually piecing together what this would mean for our lives. This would become the defining challenge of journalism in a pandemic: how to tell the story rigorously while, at every turn, living it too.

For that evening, we could all lose ourselves in the mechanics and editorial process of getting *News at Ten* to air. What did people need to know about the new rules for our lives? How well prepared are our hospitals? What about personal protective equipment – could the Health Secretary promise people wouldn't die for lack of it? What was the economic impact going to be? How were parents supposed to work from home and turn themselves into teachers for their kids?

The message from the PM about the "invisible killer", as he called it, was grave enough. An intensive care doctor we interviewed that night underscored it with passion. "This is not a game," he said, his eyes straight to our camera as we interviewed him by Skype. "This is a real and immediate threat to society and to the people we love. It is already affecting your lives. If you don't engage with the need for social distancing, then it is going to hit you longer and harder than you might ever imagine."

How to navigate all this for our audience at ten? It wasn't simply a matter of factual content, it was a matter of language and tone. How not to frighten our audience but give them what they needed and, crucially at this stage, how to show we were "all in this together" – even if later that would be a moot point.

It was on my mind as I took the lift down to our basement studio and to the make-up room, where the make-up artists no longer were.

Social distancing had ruled that out days before. Those few moments where I'm usually fortunate enough to gather my thoughts were now put to daubing on some foundation and sorting my hair. Our offices at Gray's Inn Road in central London were already draining of people.

In the studio, a floor manager was doubling up as autocue operator to keep numbers down. Antiviral hand wash was ready in a dispenser by the door. My scripts churned out next to me, printed remotely, while I wiped down the microphone and keyboard at the presenters' desk. When our Health Correspondent Emily Morgan came in she took a seat two metres away at the far corner of the set. Political Editor Robert Peston reported for us from home where he was self-isolating, his partner upstairs with Covid-19. Everything was already tilted on its axis. Throughout this crisis, while most of your brain was concentrating hard on delivering the news, there was forever a part of it whirring away, guarding against the virus itself.

On a truly big news night there is often a strange air of calm and total focus. On this occasion it also felt utterly surreal and I know everyone on the team felt it too. We could hardly believe what we were sharing with the audience.

The programme went almost without a hitch. But something threw me in the closing moments. On momentous nights, our lead writer and *News at Ten* veteran David Stanley writes some closing thoughts to mark the moment in history. On this occasion, as I read those words, we showed the lights on in Parliament where MPs were still, just about, working. We showed deserted streets, an empty Trafalgar Square, and reflected on how our lives were about to change. Pubs closing, restaurants emptying, theatres falling silent. And then at the end of the sequence of pictures, we cut to helicopter shots showing the city skyline. The top of one building stood out. Several floors had been lit up and out shone an enormous illuminated blue heart emblazoned with three letters: NHS.

Most of us usually work hard to keep our emotions back when delivering the news. But this image made me catch my breath. This single moment, this light in the darkness of a London night, illuminated utterly the sacrifice all those on the frontline of our NHS were about to make for us all.

Timeline

March

24 The first full day of lockdown

25 Prince Charles tests positive for coronavirus

   The first two working NHS doctors die from Covid-19 – a surgeon and a GP

26 Government announces help for some self-employed workers

   First Thursday Clap for Carers is held at 8pm

27 Prime Minister Boris Johnson and Health Secretary Matt Hancock both test positive for coronavirus

28 Italy's coronavirus death toll tops 10,000, three weeks into the country's nationwide lockdown

   New lockdown regulations come into force in Northern Ireland, bringing it into line with the rest of the UK

29 An NHS nurse dies from Covid-19

30 The Tokyo 2020 Olympic Games are postponed

31 An increase in cases of anxiety and depression resulting from the lockdown is reported by researchers at the Universities of Sheffield and Ulster

Where Has Everybody Gone?

Matthew Hudson, Correspondent, ITV News Anglia

"Mate! Mate!" The voice behind me was urgent: "Mate! Mate!" I turned around to find two of Cambridge's many homeless people about ten feet away from me. They looked scared. I motioned to them to stop and they did, although they clearly had no idea why I was doing so. "Mate! Mate!" said one of them, plaintive, almost pleading. "Where has everybody gone?"

It was day one of lockdown and we were going to show our viewers, mostly staying in their homes and gardens with just an hour for exercise, what the city looked like, and try to give them some idea what it felt like. That's what we do of course, show people the things they can't see, ask the questions they can't ask.

It was a beautiful spring morning. We all know now how the wonderful weather helped so many people through lockdown, allowing them to enjoy their gardens and exercise, even queueing outside shops. It helped reporters as well. ITV had advised that all filming should be done outside wherever possible. A largely glorious spring made that far easier.

I'd never driven into Cambridge on such quiet streets, not even early on a Sunday morning. Streets that were normally choked with traffic were, at 10.30am, silent and empty. I parked in Free School Lane, the only car there. Then I performed a ritual that I was to carry out many times a day for months. ITV had given us clear guidelines on how we were to work during the outbreak. I rubbed antibacterial gel into my hands, then I rubbed down my camera and tripod with anti-bac wipes and headed towards the city centre.

I turned onto King's Parade, the city's tourism epicentre, near the mathematical clock that is usually ringed by tourists taking pictures and I stopped dead. There was nobody there. I don't mean there were only a few people, there was literally nobody there. I just gawped at it, wondering how long it would be before I saw someone.

That was when my reverie was broken by the two homeless men. No wonder they looked bewildered. Imagine falling asleep or passing out in a doorway or alley and then waking up or coming round to the fact that everyone had gone. It could be the ultimate practical joke. Wait for someone to fall asleep and then make society disappear.

I asked if they'd heard about the coronavirus and they said they had. But when I said everyone was supposed to stay inside they looked at me blankly. They hadn't heard about lockdown. And how do you go into lockdown in a shop doorway or under a railway arch?

They asked if I had any change so they could get something to eat. I had a few pound coins, which I asked them to catch. I'm not particularly proud of that but I already knew I couldn't go any closer. Thankfully they caught them though I wasn't sure where they would find anything to buy. Everything seemed to be shut. They moved on, clutching their plastic bags of possessions, pleased with the money but still looking disorientated.

As I walked around the city I realised the only people I was seeing were the street people. The addicts, the alcoholics, the lost souls who have always clung to the fringes of Cambridge, attracted by the city's affluence. With everyone else gone, you couldn't miss them and you realised just how many there were, wandering listlessly, unable to go into lockdown because they had nowhere to go.

As it happens the city council did do something for the homeless over the next day or two, finding that there were suddenly a lot of rooms available in hotels that had been forced to close. But on subsequent trips into the city centre I would still see some of them, particularly the older ones who didn't actually want a room. Living their lives on tracks that run parallel to ours but rarely intersect.

I walked down to the market or what now passed for the market. Two fruit and veg merchants amid a sea of skeletal-looking stalls bare of produce. A young woman selling vegetables was looking bored, leaning on the counter and scrolling through her phone. I stopped occasionally to film but no one approached me. Usually it's impossible to film in any town or city without someone coming up to ask what you are doing.

During this crisis, I have reported from hospitals, care homes and hospices. I have met amazing people, scientists, medics and others. I have seen things I never expected to see. But nothing made more of an impression than that first morning in Cambridge. I can close my eyes and see it now just as it was. It was the moment I fully comprehended just how different everything was going to be.

This Time Survival Meant Closure

Judith Hill, Reporter, UTV

Belfast is my city; it's a city with heart and hard-won hope. I've always loved the place and count it as a privilege to get to tell its stories as part of our daily news coverage on UTV.

So to stand, on day one of lockdown, in a quietened city centre was an experience I won't forget. People standing in socially distanced queues looked dazed, not quite knowing yet what this new way of life would bring. Shop owners whose businesses had survived and thrived despite the years of the Troubles were now pulling down their shutters. There was visible emotion on the street for those whose instinct every other time had been to carry on. But this was different. This time survival meant closure. This city, that's been through the mill over the decades, was having to hunker down again.

But it wasn't until I looked into the eyes of a frightened GP that I began to comprehend the courage involved in this emergency. Dr Linda Kelly was going to be one of the first on shift at a new Covid centre in west Belfast and when we began the interview for that night's news, there was fear in her eyes. Her voice trembled as she spoke for so many on the frontline; "I have had sleepless nights and I ask if I have the mental capacity for this," she said. Tears came as she shared how her young daughter had written about her as a hero during a class project; proud of how her mother was bravely doing her job, when her instinct was to run the other way and protect her family. It struck me that Belfast has always been full of people like this, who choose to look painful situations in the eye, to run towards danger, and yet the headlines rarely belong to them.

Across Belfast, community responses to the Covid crisis were swift; this is a city that knows how to handle emergencies. Community

116

workers told me that collaboration was instinctive and crossed the physical divides that still run between us. Some spoke of the hope that this spirit of cooperation on coronavirus would pave the way towards greater long-term reconciliation.

Perhaps what moved me most during this time was speaking to some of those on the complete edges of society. With an escalating number of people being pushed into poverty during the pandemic, we spent a night at St Patrick's soup kitchen in Belfast city centre to see this for ourselves.

We watched people queue for a hot dinner on a back street. There was the paradox of the warmth and camaraderie they found in each other's company – and the desperation in their eyes. One man who visited the soup kitchen had not had a hot meal in five days. And then there was Billy. Aged 36, he had spent more than half of his life living on the street, but at the start of lockdown had secured a place in a hostel. He told me this was brilliant, but also difficult for him to adapt to. I sat on the pavement and chatted to him and thought about how much spirit he had shown in his life. He's younger than me, yet looked older. I reflected on how much strength he had needed to survive on the streets – and wondered what his future would hold.

Like all of those queuing that night, and all who are behind their own closed doors caught in poverty, they have been easy to forget in all of this. We have focused so much on the toll that lockdown has taken on us all that we may have sometimes forgotten those who were already locked out. They shouldn't be forgotten in the recovery.

Belfast is a city that's been trying, and succeeding in many ways, to rejuvenate itself. But it still has its toxic episodes and reconciliation remains a prize not yet won. But, as one community worker put it, lockdown and the generous community responses to it reminded her of Belfast's resilience. Her hope, and surely the hope of so many, is that this spirit of collaboration could guide us towards a city that is free and at ease with itself for all who call it home.

You Have Not Been Forgotten

Richard Pallot, Reporter, ITV News

Tim Pravda licked the back of a first class stamp and sealed that first letter. A brisk walk to the village postbox in West Sussex and it was on its way: *The Right Hon. Rishi Sunak MP, 11 Downing St, Whitehall, London.*

Twenty-four hours earlier, on March 26th, Mr Sunak had told the nation: "Musicians and sound engineers, plumbers and electricians, taxi drivers and many others. To you, I say this, you have not been forgotten."

But when I met Tim he told me he felt entirely forgotten, and also unfairly excluded. As a freelance festival organiser his income had evaporated overnight when the lockdown was announced. So surely the Chancellor was talking directly to him? No. Tim wasn't expecting a penny from the Treasury's self-employed scheme, all because he pays his taxes through PAYE. And the fact he has always dutifully paid his taxes seemed likely to mean nothing.

Estimates vary but between one and three million self-employed workers have not qualified for help from the Chancellor's scheme for various reasons. The furlough scheme doesn't apply to them either, so they are falling through the gaps, with devastating financial implications.

Tim is now relying on food banks. He has written dozens more letters, all to the same Number 11 Downing Street address, or to the address next door. But he is yet to receive a single acknowledgement from number 10 or 11; nor any response to 800 plus emails and 3,000 direct tweets, all falling on seemingly deaf ears.

Julie Wetherell from County Durham also felt forgotten. Imagine you had paid full taxes and National Insurance for 39 years, and then missed the cut-off point for furlough by a single week. And got nothing. Julie had left her old administration job in the second week of March for a better job at a plumbing company. That new role began on March 16th, but she hadn't been put on the payroll when the Chancellor announced the Job Retention Scheme four days later. Crucially, that meant her new employer wasn't allowed to furlough her and her previous company wouldn't reinstate her either. Forced onto Jobseeker's Allowance for the first time, her mental health has deteriorated hugely. She feels she is spiralling down deeper into despair with every week that passes – panic attacks in the day, unable to sleep at night.

The government introduced unprecedented support schemes aimed at keeping people in employment and helping many self-employed. Nine and a half million furloughed workers, more than a quarter of the UK workforce, were paid by the government. More than two million self-employed people applied for similar support.

But as an ITV News reporter assigned to covering the economic side of the coronavirus, I met many people like Tim and Julie who felt they'd slipped through the gaps and received no government support. And it seemed that there were some people, even in this time of "all in it together", who thought the system was there to be abused.

It wasn't why we had gone to interview Danielle in Doncaster. We are not using her surname. We wanted to hear about the problems she faced keeping her beauty business afloat. She had been turned down by 12 different banks for bounce-back loans, being told her credit rating wasn't good enough, even though the government specifically stated such criteria shouldn't be used in these exceptional times.

But it was what she said after the cameras stopped rolling, about people she knew who had received loans, that really stuck with me. "They have been treating the loans as free money, accessing them when they weren't in need at all. Spending on hot tubs, or a gleaming new Range Rover for the drive. Some I know from overseas have already wired the money abroad, back to their home country. They fully intend to be gone within the year before any repayments must be made, knowing it's the business that is liable and not the individual. And in certain instances, they have invented a company and applied on behalf of something that doesn't exist. They have no bad credit marks against them, so get the handout while I don't get anything, can't pay my bills and have to visit food banks," she said.

Robert, not his real name, was so outraged by the behaviour of the IT firm he worked for, he felt compelled to ring the HMRC fraud hotline. When I asked how he would describe the London-based company, he could not have been clearer: "Criminals, pure criminals. I would prefer my family to be struggling rather than compromise my principles. They said they had to save money in difficult times and that they wanted to furlough me but for me to keep on working. I said that's not allowed. They said just do it and don't tell anyone – so fully knew it was illegal. Of course I was then fired."

Robert told me dozens of staff at the company are still illegally and knowingly operating on furlough, but didn't have the inclination to complain. Or perhaps more realistically, simply couldn't afford to. HM Revenue and Customs say they will look into any suspected furlough fraud and, at the time of writing, already had thousands of allegations to wade through.

The anger and helplessness of many of those I spoke to has now given way to a palpable sense of fear of what the future might hold. Mother of three Ebony Seasman in Northumberland left a zero hours contract at a local pub to shield her at-risk daughter. Her job has now disappeared completely with no hope, she says, of finding another in the decimated hospitality sector.

"I will cry when the hoover is on so my children can't hear me – and then I will wash my face, say everything is OK, because I can't bear the thought of them knowing something is wrong, that things are really really bad," she told me.

Jamie Watts lost his job as a quantity surveyor at the end of March, with his redundancy letter stating Covid-19 as the reason. The HR department at his company told the boss there was no word "furlough" in English law, and they didn't want to be held financially liable if it all went wrong. Jamie couldn't believe that after three decades being comfortably off, he might lose his house and have to start all over again.

But there have been some brighter economic stories too. Like the small carpentry firm I visited in Essex that was delighted to get a contract to build perspex booths for disinfecting players as they arrived at Premier League training grounds. Or the trainee doctors at Bristol University graduating three months early to support over-stretched hospitals; they told me they were genuinely pleased to be asked to help, and to start earning a wage earlier than planned.

I was in Havant in Hampshire when Burger King reopened the first of their drive-through restaurants. The huge tailback around the town was something to witness. More impressive was the ingenuity of two teenagers, non-drivers, in the car park. Undeterred when staff refused to let them in on foot, they simply sat on a wall and got on their phones. Twenty minutes later a delivery driver appeared and picked up an order. He then drove all of 30 metres before dropping it in their grateful hands. I asked one of the 14-year-olds why she was so keen to get fast food. She said there was no school, so no school lunches, and with her mum on night shifts, this was the easiest way to be fed.

There are of course millions who have hugely benefited from the generosity of the government, and the paid, enforced career breaks. We should acknowledge that in our storytelling. But as the furlough scheme unwinds, the threat of unemployment looms large especially in the private sector and, in many cases, for careers that only a few months ago seemed rock solid.

Talking of which, Tim the festival organiser is still firing off letters to Downing Street. Unable to afford the rent on his flat anymore, he's now sleeping on the couch in his mum's bungalow. At least the stroll to the postbox is shorter. Handy, he says, given he will never stop writing.

Pandemic Reporting Online

Stephen Hull, Head of Digital, ITV News

Anyone who visited it during the lockdown will tell you the same thing. Central London wasn't designed to be deserted. Leicester Square's iconic digital advertising boards were built to be seen, Carnaby Street was supposed to swing, and photos of postcard settings should have been uploaded to social media platforms and liked.

I was one of those lucky, yes, lucky enough to experience central London in full lockdown hibernation. I generally cycle to work and it was as I pedalled past Downing Street on March 27th that I first received the breaking news on my smartphone that the Prime Minister had contracted the virus. By this time we were only four days into the lockdown and as a country we had already weathered a lot. Like millions of others I was hyper alert to the news, desperate for information and completely dependent on my phone to provide that, be it through notifications, social media, searching for something on Google, directly going to trusted news sources or a message from a friend.

All around the world, digital news organisations were seeing the most frenzied and, crucially, sustained growth in audience that I've witnessed in my career. Digital news was experiencing a boom time. From the moment the lockdown was announced, across the ITV News digital network of regions, nations and national news, we saw in some cases a tripling, but generally a doubling, in audience that held throughout March and April. In June we were still seeing an increase in people coming to our online news pages for information they could trust.

Covid-19 was, in many ways, the first truly global digital news event. According to Ofcom, the UK's communications regulator, internet users in the UK in April spent a record amount of time online. And younger audiences spent nearly an hour longer online a day than their parents.

You might think that the biggest challenge for ITV's online news service would have been the operational business of moving our digital teams out of the office to keep as much social distancing as possible. On reflection, that was the easy part. The hard part was competing for attention on smartphones, which became the battle ground for information. Distributing accurate, truthful content became something of a war.

In the early days I distinctly remember friends sending stories to our shared WhatsApp group from unverified new sources about "secret plans for the army to be deployed". They genuinely believed these reports to be true. These fake stories spread like wildfire. According to Ofcom nearly half of UK adults online were exposed to false or misleading information about the virus. I remember forwarding them links to the ITV News website. One was headlined, "These are some of the coronavirus hoaxes and fake news stories being shared – and what you can do to stop their spread." Looking back at that article now the fake stories gathering attention seem even more ridiculous. The first claim we disproved: "If you can hold your breath for 10 seconds then you don't have the virus." Many people were seeing and believing these stories. It was a source of pride that professional ITV News journalists, one of the world's most trusted news brands, could take time to correct these wrong and potentially life-threatening stories time and time again.

Our digital news service quickly became a place where all the regions and nations of ITV News could combine efforts to make a very confusing world easier to understand. One highlight was an interactive map of new coronavirus cases from across the home nations. It was updated daily and became our single most viewed website page, with millions upon millions of views.

There were five broad areas where digital journalism made its biggest impact during the virus crisis: the first was the impact on young people. There was a surge in desire from social media companies to provide trusted news to their large, generally younger, socially savvy audience. I was being contacted by platforms previously more interested in revenue who now wanted information to drive their brands. We had launched a social media youth news service, *The Rundown*, in September 2019 and we already published on Instagram, Facebook and YouTube, but now Snapchat became an important addition. An edition of *The Rundown* appeared on Snapchat's new "Covid carousel". This was dedicated to news about Covid-19; a single place users could see content about the pandemic from news brands who publish on Snapchat's platform. This was important as Snapchat has a huge reach with young audiences. There are about 13 million daily UK users and almost 40 percent are between 13 and 17, the demographic *The Rundown* is targeted towards.

Digital journalism also made a big impact when it came to live events. Two regular "pop-up" live moments captured the mood of the nation for different reasons: the daily Downing Street news briefing and the weekly Clap for Carers. They both became digitally led news moments. One person said to me of the early daily briefings: "It's the only time of day I watch news now." While the BBC and Sky dedicated their news channels to these events, at ITV we used our social media channels and website to bring viewers the raw, unedited briefings direct to their smartphones. These were hugely popular and gave viewers a rare glimpse under the bonnet of what goes on between the media and government. While these were serious, sombre events, the weekly Clap for Carers, by contrast, became the moment of the week for light relief and release. Often expressed and shared on social media, it was another example of Britain being digitally led.

Breaking news also became digital first. I remember Robert Peston emailing me with his scoop on elderly and vulnerable people being asked to shield for up to three months. The hair on the back of my neck stood up. I instantly thought, "this can't be true." But he was right. That story went to the top of our website.

The vast amount of new information becoming available and being shared made background explanations, explainers as they are known, essential digital content. Our articles and social videos were often headlined in quite literal terms so they were easy to find when searching, headlines such as "what you can and can't do". We launched a daily podcast that went deeper into key subject areas: our Health and Science Correspondents Emily Morgan and Tom Clarke were regular voices on *Coronavirus: What You Need To Know*. And digital platforms offered extended programme experiences by continuing broadcasts online, long after they had finished transmitting on ITV. The weekly *Coronavirus Q&A* programme continued every week online so experts could answer even more questions from viewers. And the ITV News website featured a shelf of content that answered the most-asked questions such as "how do I socially distance?" and "do I need to wear a face mask?"

And finally, as we like to say at ITV News, digital platforms provided a place for some fun. An ITV News Cymru Wales story about a herd of wild goats running through the streets of Llandudno went viral. It was even shared by US talk show host Ellen DeGeneres, who joked the town would be the first place she'd visit after the lockdown ended. It was important to be able to share the lighter, heartwarming and sometimes humorous stories that brought a sense of relief from the scary headlines.

The Right Programme at the Right Time

Nina Hossain, Presenter, ITV News

As the Covid-19 crisis mounted, ITV commissioned a new primetime current affairs programme. *Coronavirus Q&A*, each Monday at 8pm, provided a platform for viewers to get answers to some of their questions during such a bewildering period.

I was asked to host the newly commissioned show. The plan was to get on air in a fortnight, a big ask when so few people were able to come into work in the studios. We needed titles, a set, graphics, we needed staff. Meanwhile, my day job, anchoring the *ITV Lunchtime News*, was more frenetic than usual too, with constant breaking news, and countless interviews conducted over sometimes unpredictable technology, because guests were all in lockdown.

Despite the unparalleled pressure we were all working under, the first Q&A programme made it to air as planned on March 30th, one week after lockdown. Our aim was to put viewers' questions to experts and decision-makers about the impact of the lockdown, and the virus itself.

When I saw the questions the team had been going through all weekend for that first Monday programme, the enormity of the responsibility we had to try to help with the viewers' concerns and confusion really hit me. It cannot have been easy for some of our younger members of staff to deal with such a volume of sometimes heartbreaking questions about funerals, or not being able to see a terminally ill relative. Divorced parents separated from their children; nurses choosing to leave young children with grandparents to avoid the risk of them being infected; fear of the virus itself; the loneliness of those shielding.

In my 20-year-plus career never before had I had such a personal insight into how a story was affecting every aspect of everybody's lives.

At first people wanted information, or a little clarification. So many questions for the peerless Dr Sarah Jarvis about this new virus that even the world's leading experts are still learning about. Viewers wanted guidance and instructions on how to keep themselves, and those around them, safe. They had questions about health conditions other than Covid. So many questions from those who were shielding; concerns about mental health; life after contracting Covid; to wear a mask or not. Their concern for the NHS was also clear. The government's message to protect the NHS had clearly got through.

When it felt like parts of the media had moved on to the economic crisis, the questions we were seeing told us people were still very much focused on the health crisis. In the morning meeting to shortlist the questions, I would cheer at how precise and clear they were; people wanted to know why there was a problem in care homes, with personal protective equipment, with testing. One such question led to the Chief Scientific Adviser Sir Patrick Vallance admitting on the programme that the UK had been too slow to test.

After the revelations about Dominic Cummings, the Prime Minister's special advisor, and his lockdown trip to County Durham, the tone of the questions changed. We started to see frustration and anger in the questions directed at the government. At around the same time Downing Street appeared to rein back on promises to provide us with a government minister for the programme.

It became increasingly frustrating to be promised someone on the Friday, telling viewers to send in their questions to said minister or department, only for them to pull out just hours before we went on air on Monday night. It meant we had to plan for two shows simultaneously, one with and one without someone accountable in government for the decisions being made about our lives during the pandemic.

We had more than enough questions to put to experts rather than politicians, but sometimes it felt like a disservice to our viewers when they were contacting us asking for clarity or explanation or guidance from the government.

The ITV News Consumer Editor Chris Choi and his producer Hannah Kings did a sterling job week in, week out dealing with complex technical queries about everything from social distancing rules in workplaces, to the furlough scheme. There were questions about everything from street parties to paddle boarding, fencing to funerals. Many were heartbreaking. It felt like a huge task to get answers for so many people struggling with so many aspects of their lives. It became much harder when the rules and timetables in England, Scotland, Wales and Northern Ireland started to diverge.

My programme editor Laura Holgate believes we only managed to get to around one percent of the thousands of questions that came in to us every week. At times that was demoralising. How could we help more people? We tried to choose either the most popular themes, or the least popular that weren't getting attention elsewhere. A good example is how hard it is for someone who is partially sighted to navigate all the new signage and queuing regimes in supermarkets. Sometimes we got lovely emails from viewers wanting to thank us for recognising their concerns.

For most of the 12-week run of the programme I worked alone in the basement, in a dressing room with a laptop. The rest of the team were either at home or scattered around the newsroom. Nuanced debate about questions was tricky, as was finding solutions to logistical problems.

Talking of problems, our first show is one I will never forget. Our first guest was to be the Foreign Secretary Dominic Raab, who would be available for a pre-recorded interview sometime between 3pm and 6pm, we were told. In television we always prefer to do such interviews live, but Mr Raab was hosting the government's daily press conference that day, so we were happy to fit in with his schedule.

Then it got complicated. We were told to be ready by 3.30pm. We were. Then he wasn't. A moment of much needed and unexpected levity came when my director Dan Rogers ran into the studio and said, "get your phone and get Raab on Zoom Nina." A month before that I am sure I had never heard of Zoom; now I was considering installing it on my phone and using it to interview the Foreign Secretary, with minutes to spare before our deadline. It soon became clear it wasn't going to work, but top marks to Dan for trying everything at his disposal in such pressurised circumstances.

We all tried not to discuss how this was an 8pm slot on ITV. In television, 8pm is primetime and that is a big deal. But for weeks I had seen doctor and nurse friends working gruelling hours, trying and sometimes failing to save lives, worried enough to write wills. That was real pressure.

There was a final twist to the Dominic Raab story. We eventually did the interview with about twenty minutes to go until the programme. Then there was a change of plan and, after all, we were told the Foreign Secretary would like to do the interview live. We obliged. After a day spent waiting to do a pre-recorded interview we kicked off the *Coronavirus Q&A* programme run with a live conversation with a senior government minister. But I hope never to repeat such a build-up to a programme. I could still start to shake thinking about the experience. As a production team we couldn't even decompress afterwards with a visit to the pub. They were, of course, all closed.

Our second programme the following week also contained high drama; a real "where were you when" moment when I had to cut short an interview with Dr Sarah Jarvis to announce the breaking news that the Prime Minister was in intensive care.

My role at the helm of *Coronavirus Q&A* was challenging, thrilling and rewarding in equal measure and I am proud of our role in ITV's pandemic coverage. On the best programmes with the best guests, we felt like we were at the true heart of the story, giving viewers almost instant access to politicians and experts in the fields of health, education, travel and the economy. As a journalist I had many questions of my own. I still do. I managed to sneak a couple in, but it was right to give the half-hour to those watching. A great example of public service broadcasting. The right programme at the right time.

The Moment Covid Became a Personal Story for Me

Rageh Omaar, International Affairs
Editor and Presenter, ITV News

It was the beginning of the second week of lockdown and like millions around the country, our family was starting to witness how the intimate rituals and small human moments that make one feel part of other people's lives were slowly slipping away. A week earlier, we'd had to abandon plans to help our youngest son celebrate his fourteenth birthday, gathering for Mother's Day in person was suddenly not possible, and the constant stream through our front door of teenage friends of our children was a distant memory.

For nearly a quarter of a century I'd become used to travelling to the farthest corners of the globe to witness how natural disasters, epidemics and conflicts had wrought their devastating effects in the hearts of communities and families. My working life had long revolved around leaving the protection and safety of my life in one of the wealthiest countries in the world, where none of the things I was going to report on would happen to my family, to fly to less protected, less privileged nations to witness and record their stories.

I had told stories of the grief and helplessness of hundreds of families whose relatives had died as a result of deadly diseases – Ebola, cholera, malaria, HIV – never imagining that one day it would be part of my story too; until one night at the end of March. It was the moment that shook me out of the cocoon I'd lived in for so long as a journalist and the moment that Covid-19 became a personal story for my family, much like the stories I had told of dozens of others in Africa and South East Asia.

As I prepared to go to bed, my phone buzzed as a stream of messages came through. My brother, who was in Somaliland, and my sister in

Kenya were simultaneously asking me about our cousin Jirdeh who was living in London. "Just heard Jirdeh taken seriously ill – have you heard about it?" texted my brother, followed by my sister, who wrote: "Hi, got a call from Jirdeh's uncle saying he was taken to hospital – so frightening given Covid situation in London right now."

Jirdeh has acute asthma and was therefore highly vulnerable to the virus. My mind began racing through all the frightening scenarios that were being faced by thousands of other families from Black, Asian and minority ethnic communities; the Somali community in London in particular was one of the worst affected. I eventually managed to get through to Jirdeh's brother Farah, a close cousin. Farah is one of life's natural optimists, his voice always brimming with confidence. To chat to him always felt like having the sun on your face. But that was not the Farah I was speaking to now at this dreadful moment. He sounded utterly hollowed out, his voice flat and deflated as he told me that Jirdeh had been taken into intensive care and had slipped into a coma as a result of contracting coronavirus.

My cousin Jirdeh was admitted to St Thomas's Hospital in London where Prime Minister Boris Johnson was taken a week later on April 5th. Within a day the Prime Minister's condition had worsened and he was moved into the intensive care unit. My cousin, an immigrant from Somaliland, was in the same hospital ward as the Prime Minister of the United Kingdom, both fighting for life against the same deadly virus.

Two days later, on April 8th, as the Prime Minister and my cousin both fought for their lives, I was presenting ITV's *News at Ten*. As I prepared for that night's broadcast, with the whole nation and world gripped by the very real possibility that the leader of our government could die from the virus, I was constantly monitoring my phone to hear news of my cousin.

The following day, on April 9th, I was back in ITV's newsroom, preparing to once again present *News at Ten*, once again checking my phone to hear any further news on Jirdeh. Two hours before we went on air it was announced that Boris Johnson had been moved out of intensive care. I sat down to write the headline story for that evening's broadcast reflecting the sense of relief throughout the country that the Prime Minister was out of danger. But my own cousin was still in the intensive care unit, and he was still in a coma. I paused to reflect for a moment. Fifty minutes before going on air with that night's programme I did something that reporters are never meant to do. For the first time in my career I felt I had to share my own intense personal feelings, because my own personal reflections felt relevant to the story I was trying to tell. I wrote the following words, which I shared with the world on Twitter: "I can find no more moving a testimony to the global miracle @NHSuk is than the fact that my cousin is being treated in the same ICU unit in which @10DowningStreet @BorisJohnson was being treated. British son of African migrants being given exactly the same care by the same doctors as the PM."

For the next two weeks I continued to report on the devastating effects of coronavirus on Black, Asian and minority ethnic communities, especially at that time in London. Socio-economic factors such as deprivation, underlying health conditions and the inter-generational households more common in those communities were leading to a disproportionate increase in the transmission of Covid-19. On April 17th, I spoke to Somali community leader Mohamed Ibrahim, director of the London Somali Youth Forum. He told me that cultural traditions were also a key driver of why BAME communities, like the British Somali one, were being hit so hard. Within the Somali community, he said, many felt the need to visit loved ones who were ill with virus symptoms, or go to a family or friend's house to pay their respects for someone who had died from Covid-19.

I interviewed carer Deeqa Guleed, who told me of the devastation Covid-19 had wrought on her family. Deeqa had lost her brother and said two of her uncles were critically ill from the virus. She knew of many other British Somali families who were witnessing similar losses and grief. "You get to a point where you don't want to pick up the phone," she told me, "you're just constantly worried and you're frightened who's next, or who's been taken to hospital."

On April 19th, Farah called me and for the first time in weeks that familiar sunshine-like voice, that I feared would be gone forever if the worst happened to Jirdeh, was back. "Great news," he said. "Jirdeh has been moved out of intensive care, he's begun to open his eyes slightly. We're hoping and praying that he's going to be safe. He's going to live." Jirdeh had fought off the grip of coronavirus – words we knew we were incredibly lucky to be able to say.

Timeline

April

2 Health Secretary Matt Hancock sets 100,000-tests-a-day target

3 The first temporary Nightingale Hospital opens in east London

5 The Queen, in a rare broadcast, pays tribute to key workers

Prime Minister Boris Johnson is admitted to St Thomas's Hospital in London

6 Boris Johnson is moved to intensive care

Captain Tom Moore, 99, starts walking laps of his garden to raise money for NHS charities

9 Foreign Secretary Dominic Raab, deputising for the Prime Minister, urges people to stay indoors over the Easter weekend

Boris Johnson is moved out of intensive care but stays in hospital

10 980 coronavirus deaths in UK hospitals are reported, higher than the deadliest day in Italy

10–13 Easter weekend. Police and tourist destination bosses urge people to stay at home

11 Home Secretary Priti Patel, speaking at the Downing Street daily briefing, says she is "sorry if people feel there have been failings" in providing PPE for NHS staff

12 Boris Johnson leaves hospital

Inside Intensive Care at the Royal Bournemouth Hospital

Emily Morgan, Health Editor, ITV News

My alarm went off at 4.15am. It was Monday April 6th and although I hadn't thought about anything but this day all weekend, very little could have prepared me for what was about to unfold. I dressed carefully: a washable shirt with buttons, jeans and trainers that could also go in the machine; everything would have to be washed when I got back. A quick cup of tea, then I crept upstairs to kiss my sleeping children goodbye.

The dark, two-hour drive to Bournemouth was therapy of a kind. As the engine hummed and the silent roads stretched ahead of me I thought about what I wanted to achieve that day. With my camera operator and producer, we were about to report from inside a hospital – some of the first journalists to do so since the coronavirus crisis began. Correspondents all know the reasons for going to the frontline: it's our duty to report first hand what is happening, to speak to the very people it affects and act as a window into the lives of those involved. We know all that but we're never quite sure how it will play out, what it will be like or whether there will indeed be a story to tell; that is the challenge. This one though felt different. I knew only too well there was a story to tell, a big one, I just didn't know how bad it would be or whether I would manage to strike the right tone to tell the most challenging story of my career.

And then other demons crept in: would we be safe? Did we have enough personal protective equipment? What if I contracted coronavirus and passed it to my husband, 50 in a couple of months, or indeed my children? As I mulled all of this over I thought about those who had already died of Covid-19 and the families suffering as

137

mothers, fathers, partners and children lay in comas on ventilators. We had heard politicians and scientists telling us about it, now it was time to see for ourselves.

I pulled into the Royal Bournemouth Hospital car park at 6.50am. Before going in I resolved not to touch anything and keep social distancing wherever possible, but after a quick briefing with my team we were swiftly walked to a cramped room where the overnight nursing team were handing over to daytime staff. I suddenly felt foolish for even thinking social distancing would be a priority for staff here. The nurses had spent the night caring for dozens of Covid patients; two had died and seven were still on ventilators. One nurse was moved to tears as she told me the hardest thing was not losing patients, they are used to that, it was the fact they died alone, without family by their side. Whispering inadequate reassurances as their patients passed away is something none of them would ever get used to. I knew scores of patients were on ventilators, I knew scores more were dying each day across the country but hearing it described like that by a front-line nurse struck home like nothing before.

I was conscious that very few broadcast cameras had been allowed inside a UK hospital since the pandemic began so I wanted to see everything, show every aspect of what was happening. The hospital had been divided into green and red areas and we were about to enter the red zone of accident and emergency. We were given our PPE: surgical masks. It felt churlish to question whether that was sufficient when it was all that staff were wearing. All the patients in this area were suspected Covid-19 patients. As we walked over the threshold from the green zone to the red zone we collectively took a deep breath, I could feel the tension, the apprehension among us.

Once in A&E nobody looked up, no one gave us a second glance; we were invisible to the nurses, doctors and care assistants who were running back and forth in teams of two. Trolleys with wheezing, pale patients were being wheeled in from every angle, every cubicle was occupied, each with a door, shutting the patients off from the rest of the department.

Two young nurses stood outside a cubicle, one of them carefully putting on gloves, an apron and a surgical mask, moving slowly and methodically. There was something about her concentration that made me think she was nervous. I watched her go in to treat the patient and asked the consultant why the other nurse was waiting outside. He explained they were working in pairs: the "dirty" one goes in, the other stays "clean" and passes in equipment. The "dirty" nurse came out, took off her PPE and washed her hands, the slow deliberate motion of washing over and over again hypnotic. I asked her if she felt safe, if she had enough protective clothing, and she told me she and her colleagues were happy. But something wasn't right; what she said and how she looked didn't correlate. I pushed her a little harder and she admitted to being frightened that she would get ill. Ami was a year out of training and had bad asthma; she was truly conflicted about treating suspected coronavirus patients. She told me her family worried about her endlessly but her first thought was always for those she cared for. As we chatted I noticed she had terrible eczema on her hands and up her arms, red raw from so much washing. It was such a small thing but it touched me deeply and made me want to hug her, to tell her everything would be OK. But that was not my role.

As I listened to the staff I realised some were desperate to talk, desperate to tell me what it was like treating Covid patients, and desperate to show me how much pressure they were under. They had felt silenced, struck dumb by the volume of patients and the work that entailed but also by the simple fact that no journalists had been allowed into healthcare settings. Their stories were finally going to be told.

We heard about a patient who was about to leave intensive care. Nurses were so relieved she'd survived they clapped her out of the unit. Why? Because Linda New was only in her fifties, she worked at the hospital and had a young family. I watched as she was wheeled towards me. I wasn't quite sure what I expected to feel but as the clapping rang out around me I could barely control my emotions. Linda's body looked broken. She sobbed as she told me her only thoughts, while fighting for her life, were for her children. I hadn't prepared for such an off-the-cuff uninhibited interview and had to fight back my own tears.

Linda's consultant, credited with saving her life, was a fearless young woman who oozed optimism and confidence. In a very candid interview, Dr Michelle Scott told us she worried daily that the hospital would run out of oxygen if their patient numbers increased. She also spoke of the speed at which some of her patients had deteriorated. She and all her colleagues were in new territory. What was most concerning, she said, was how differently each patient responded to treatment; what worked for one made another more ill. They were constantly having to learn, change, adapt what they were doing for each individual case. And it was so hard to predict; a patient could appear to be improving, families were informed, then the patient would die. Or clinicians would begin the process of palliative care, only to find that the patient improved and could leave intensive care within a week. Dr Scott also spoke of "proning" her patients, a common way of trying to get more oxygen into the lungs of ventilated patients by turning them onto their front. But for some Covid patients, it immediately worsened their condition. There were no patterns, no precedents, no real treatment, she said; that was what troubled her the most.

Dr Scott allowed our camera into her unit, the intensive care unit. Groups of clinicians huddled round the seven patients inside. There was a calm, controlled atmosphere. Few of them spoke and it was impossible to tell whether they were male or female, nurses or consultants behind the masks, goggles and hoods, but all had quiet determination in their eyes. They moved around their patients slowly. Quite how they worked under so much pressure in full PPE, I will never know. They spoke of impaired vision from their goggles misting up, numb faces because of the tight straps, and exhaustion from the heat. Yet they carried on without showing a flicker of discomfort.

The patients were all on ventilators and heavily sedated, their bodies slumped back on mattresses with tubes coming out of their mouths and noses. Should I have been surprised at how shocked I was to see how sick these people were? Probably not. We hadn't seen any pictures, any footage from the UK of severely ill Covid patients in intensive care. This was something I had never experienced and it had a huge impact on me. None of the patients looked over 65 and all of them were men. Nurses checked oxygen levels, took blood samples and other than the whir and beep of the machines very little appeared to be happening. But of course it was. Not a moment passed in that unit where a nurse or a consultant wasn't caring for their patients. The devotion, support and tenderness every clinician showed overwhelmed me. It filled me with so much humility, I felt myself holding my breath.

The rest of the day was spent speaking to weary staff and Covid patients who felt lucky to be alive. One was convinced he would die because "everyone else was". As the hours and minutes passed, I too became weary. Being in the red zone meant we were on constant high alert, the mind never stopped, and it was tiring. I was also starting to think about the report I had to compile for the ITV *Evening News*. That was my concern at that moment, nothing compared to what the staff or patients were dealing with.

The programme led on our story from inside the Royal Bournemouth Hospital. It felt like an important moment in the coverage of the pandemic, where we shifted from reporting on what we were being told second hand to showing and hearing precisely how coronavirus was affecting "us" in hospital.

We were working on a longer version of our report for *News at Ten* when the mood in our small, dark edit room changed dramatically. Downing Street announced that Prime Minister Boris Johnson had been moved to intensive care at St Thomas's Hospital in London where he was being treated for coronavirus. Images of the patients we'd just seen in Bournemouth's intensive care unit flashed before my eyes. If there was ever going to be a seminal moment in this dreadful pandemic this was it. The weight of responsibility and emotion pressed down on me and my team that evening as we sent our new report and then prepared to speak live to presenter Tom Bradby in the ITV News studio. The clock ticked towards 10pm and we hunched over our phones, looking for updates on the Prime Minister. As I stood in front of the camera that night, outside Bournemouth Hospital, it took all my resolve, all my emotional strength to report on what we'd seen that day. That, along with the news that Boris Johnson was seriously ill, had profoundly affected me and even now makes me stop in my tracks.

It was 10.40pm and I was back in my car, listening once more to the hum of the engine as I drove back up the empty roads home. That is when I breathed, when I let the tears roll down my face and onto my lap. I had no right to cry – we had only experienced a tiny fraction of what healthcare workers were living through or what patients were dealing with every day – but I cried nonetheless. Correspondents have been to the frontline before, reported from the most dangerous places on earth, as bullets rained down around them. None of us had been in immediate danger that day, and flak jackets had been replaced by face masks, but it still tested us like never before.

At home, I put my clothes in the washing machine, showered and got into bed. It was 1.20am. As I lay there, trying to sleep, I couldn't help but wonder, what will tomorrow bring?

Capturing the Mood of a Crisis

Tom Bradby, Presenter, ITV News

There is a moment that captures the mood of any crisis and in the case of the coronavirus crisis in the United Kingdom, that moment was surely the night when our Prime Minister, Boris Johnson, was admitted to intensive care, and the mood captured was indisputably fear.

For most of us, for much of the time, the news is a far-away business. Moving and tragic as war in Syria or famine in Africa may be, they are happening many leagues from our shores. Rarely do they impinge on the sense of emotional, financial and physical security that is so important for our mental health.

But that night crystallised the idea that the coronavirus was a direct threat to every single one of us, a storm that had blown in from a distant shore and was unlikely to abate any time soon.

Why should the fate of one individual have such an impact? Well, because he was the Prime Minister, I suppose. So much for the idea that this was only a threat to the old and the frail. Was there anyone in the country that night who didn't think; good God, if it can take down the PM, then it really is a threat to all of us.

Many years before, I had been a political correspondent on weekend duty when I got a call in the middle of the night from the news editor, to be told: "get yourself to Downing Street. Princess Diana has been in a car crash." As I watched the nation's agony in the days and weeks that followed, I found myself wondering just why her death had pole-axed us all when the tragic ends of so many others detained us for barely a heartbeat.

Perhaps it was guilt, the sense that our fascination with the Princess had been a factor in her death. But it did seem to me that at least one explanation lay in the sheer improbability of it. If the world's most

143

famous and celebrated woman could fall prey to such a terrible and tragic accident, if such a bright flame could be extinguished in the blink of an eye, it was a reminder that death was only half a step away for each and every one of us.

We experienced something similar with Covid-19. In January, *News at Ten* carried reports from our Asia Correspondent, Debi Edward, on the frankly bizarre events playing out in China. Wuhan, a city of 11 million people, had been entirely shut down. Shut! Who could believe it? I even riffed one night on the possibility of such a scenario playing out in London. It seemed unimaginable.

My wife and I went to Australia in early February to see our daughter, travelling via Hong Kong where our temperatures were taken in the airport about every thirty paces. By the time we got back, it was clear that Italy was in a terrible state and I found it a little hard to understand why we were apparently so calm in the teeth of the approaching storm.

At that time, it seemed the disease was being framed as a threat only to the old and the vulnerable. With a one percent death rate, and possibly much less, the consensus seemed to be that it was only a little bit worse than flu and, if you were fit and healthy and below retirement age, there was not much to worry about. The government seemed to be flirting with the idea of herd immunity and the consensus among a lot of people I spoke to was that this made some sense: protect the elderly and the frail and let it pass through the rest of the population as quickly as possible.

Almost every reference to the early deaths seemed to be accompanied by the phrase "underlying health conditions". This must have been difficult to bear if you happened to have one, but it appeared deliberately designed to persuade the rest of us to carry on more or less as normal.

If that was the public mood, or something like it, sentiment had begun to shift markedly in the early days of the lockdown, but it changed for good on the night the Prime Minister was moved into intensive care. Deemed essential employees by the government, we had been coming into work throughout the crisis, but I still looked out from my corner office most evenings at a more or less empty newsroom. That night, everyone was suddenly running around. I flicked up Twitter and a couple of news websites and established in a few seconds what had happened. The Prime Minister had been admitted to St Thomas's Hospital the night before, apparently only as a precaution, or so we were repeatedly told; it was now confirmed that his condition had taken a serious turn for the worse and he had been admitted to intensive care.

He had looked fairly unwell right from the moment it was confirmed he had the disease. I even tweeted in the early stages of his illness that he should probably be taking it easy, given that the one thing I had been told by a doctor friend who'd had the disease was that it could floor you and it was unwise to attempt to carry on as normal, even if you were self-isolating at home. I was surprised to see officials briefing journalists that the Prime Minister was continuing to run the country while patently under the weather with a disease serious enough to have triggered an almost total shutdown of our national economy. Wouldn't it have been better to have told everyone he was taking a break to recover and advise anyone in a similar position to do the same?

But even the sight of a man plainly struggling in the days before that night didn't quite prepare us for the shock of his admission to intensive care. This was now damned serious. If we had any illusions as to the threat this disease posed, they evaporated for good that night as the many questions crowded in. Was he likely to end up on a ventilator where recovery was even less certain? Who would be running the country while he was ill?

International messages of concern flooded in. The Queen was kept informed and no doubt this was an unexpected twist in this most unusual crisis, even by the standards of her long and varied life as the monarch. I'm not in the habit of saying prayers for anyone, but like so many others I was sure as hell willing him on. Thank God he pulled through, but imagine if he hadn't? Whatever you may think of the man and his politics, the shock of losing your national leader at such a time of national crisis would have been seismic.

I have no doubt his illness altered many people's calculations. It certainly made me reconsider mine. In the days when I was a foreign correspondent, I spent a lot of time thinking about risk. I didn't go to a vast number of war or conflict zones, though I was shot in one in

1999, but every time I headed off somewhere that was known to be dangerous, I inevitably turned it over in my mind in the days before departure, a process that became more and more difficult once I'd had kids. I used to run a slide rule over the odds in the dead of night. Was going to East Timor *actually* any more dangerous than riding a motorbike to work in London?

We can't lead a life without risk, and on so many levels we have to trust to fate, but at the same time, few of us want to take unnecessary gambles. What is a sensible risk and what not?

After the night of the Prime Minister's admission to intensive care, and for the first time in a long while, I found myself consciously weighing the odds and I suspect many of you will have done the same. I flip-flopped a bit. Beforehand, I was pretty chilled out at the prospect of getting the coronavirus. It seemed destined to be with us for a while, it appeared likely most of us would get it and I assumed I would probably be fine. Many of our friends had discussed how we'd be secretly relieved to get it over with.

After that night, I decided I'd really be doing myself a favour if I avoided it and adjusted my behaviour accordingly. I came to work as normal, but I was a lot less cavalier on my journeys in and out.

Like many of us, I will never forget the lockdown. My wife and I were in the middle of the English countryside with the enforced presence of our adult children and some of their other halves. The cooking and the cleaning rota was a bit of a nightmare, but we were all aware this was a simple and precious time together.

So yes, on the national stage, there was death and fear and trauma and loss and loneliness and heartbreak, but there was also the kindness of strangers, not to mention neighbours, and a deep outpouring of love for those who care for our health and wellbeing.

There are some who say that we'll be changed forever by this experience. I doubt it. I sense already us chafing at the bit in our urgency to get back to normality. And when we do, I suspect we will wipe all this from our collective memory and go back to our old lives with renewed vigour.

But I won't ever forget it, for good and ill. And, assuming most of the rest of us do make it through without a scratch, I imagine the event that will encapsulate this strange period is the night Boris Johnson, Prime Minister of Great Britain and Northern Ireland and First Lord of the Treasury, nearly died. It certainly was a dramatic way to prove to us all that this disease was a damned serious business.

The Impact of the Virus on My Community

Charanpreet Khaira, Reporter, ITV News Cymru Wales

When the faces of NHS workers killed by the coronavirus started to hit front pages, an uncomfortable realisation surfaced: they all looked a bit like my dad. Other similarities were uncanny. Like my dad, they were from Black, Asian or minority ethnic backgrounds, in their fifties or sixties, and had devoted their careers to the NHS. Colleagues invariably described how hard-working they were, compassionate, and respected by their colleagues. Often, they left families behind.

I grew up in Birmingham, and the jokes I heard at school about Indian doctors rang true in my family. My mum, dad, sister and brother-in-law are all doctors, and my brother is studying medicine at university. When coronavirus hit the headlines, I went to my family for advice about how to cover the story. I never expected them to become the story.

At first, my mother rolled her eyes at what she saw as the media's "sudden interest" in disease. As a GP, she sees the toll that flu takes on her elderly patients each year. At first, Covid-19 didn't seem too different, except that more people were paying attention to it. Like many doctors, my parents suspected the disease had been in circulation for longer than we realised. Having spent their whole careers in the NHS, they were worried for their vulnerable patients but not for themselves.

But in April, the faces of the first doctors to die from the coronavirus began to hit front pages. I had been working at ITV News Cymru Wales for just two months – a new newsroom, in a new city, and a new job as a reporter. With the privilege of being young and healthy, the coronavirus didn't seem scary to me. Its bark seemed worse than its bite. I had no idea that this was about to become the biggest story of our generation – both on the news, and in our lives.

On April 6th, Jitendra Rathod became the first health worker in Wales to die of the disease. He was 58, two years older than my father. My discomfort gave way to a gnawing anxiety. Phone calls home became more frequent and I noticed my parents' previously blasé attitude towards the pandemic begin to falter.

I remember a family Zoom call when we shared our observations. We'd all noticed that an alarming number of Asian doctors were dying from the disease. We brainstormed why that might be; we knew that a huge percentage of the NHS workforce is from ethnic minority communities and that, so far, the disease had hit big cities hardest, which tend to be more racially diverse. My parents pointed out that Black, Asian and minority ethnic people are more likely to have conditions like diabetes and high blood pressure. But none of this seemed enough to explain the stark picture painted by the faces of those who'd died.

At first, I was nervous to make the leap from my family's personal observations about the frequency of BAME deaths to a news report. Surely it would be insensitive to suggest that this pandemic was hitting some communities disproportionately when lots of people were losing their lives? But on April 7th – my 25th birthday – newspapers began to report that a third of critically ill Covid patients were from Black, Asian and minority ethnic communities. And on April 10th, a representative of the Pakistani community told me that a Black nurse who worked for the Velindre NHS Trust, a specialist cancer trust in Wales, had died.

I spent that weekend contacting members of South Wales's BAME communities to find out what they were thinking. I found my fears reflected in theirs and I heard their insights about the reasons for the disparity, from inadequate information to those who didn't speak English to inequalities in healthcare provision. It was clear that many of them believed structural injustices and inequalities were a part of this story.

On April 14th, I reported for the first time on Covid-19's disproportionate impact on communities of colour. It was an important moment for me, as a new reporter, to take something that started as a hunch, as a very personal fear, and translate it into real journalism.

The response from ethnic minority communities in Wales was overwhelming. They felt represented and acknowledged.

Building that trust with communities of colour allowed me to continue following the evolving story. A moment that stands out for me is when I interviewed Nicola, the widow of Raza Ghulam, the younger of two Abbas brothers. The two brothers died side by side in the Royal Gwent Hospital, minutes apart, from coronavirus. Their deaths came as it was found that men of Pakistani origin were nearly three times more likely to die of Covid-19 than the population as a whole.

Nicola and Raza had been together for 38 years. I interviewed her in her front garden; she stood metres away at the doorstep and her grief was palpable. I couldn't believe the strength and bravery she showed speaking to me about her late partner while it was all so raw. She cried throughout and I found myself crying too. All the usual social norms for empathy, a pat on the shoulder, a squeeze of the hand, were impossible. The only thing I could do was allow myself to reflect her pain. Nicola told me that her two sons, around my age, had buried their grandfather, uncle and father within a week.

The disproportionate effect of the coronavirus on Black, Asian and minority ethnic communities has only been one part of the story, and it's only been one part of my journalism for ITV News Wales, but this is a story that has exposed some of the uncomfortable truths about the ways our society works. It's hit me hard on a personal level, but a part of me thinks that the best journalism always does.

A postscript to my story: My mum had an antibody test and has definitely had the virus, but she was fine and recovered quickly at home. My dad fell ill at the same time as my mum, and also got better – but he still hasn't had an antibody test (because he's been too lazy to queue for it!)

Birmingham: A Day of Dying

Rohit Kachroo, Security Editor, ITV News

The caskets keep arriving. More lives lost, more families grieving. It is April 8th, the sixteenth day of "lockdown", and we are in the car park of a mosque in south Birmingham where a makeshift Muslim mortuary has just opened, housed in a large white tent. It is the start of a day of dying in this city that will help to reveal that coronavirus is a disease that discriminates.

Another black van pulls up outside. The doors are unlocked and the latest wooden box appears. The coffin has no nameplate and there are no personal tributes. There is almost nothing to distinguish this victim from the last or the one before, except for its weight.

"She's very heavy," says one of the funeral directors, straining in the heat to move the coffin into the tent. He and his four colleagues have developed a noisy routine, thinking aloud as they lift and move, lift and move. "This way, that way," "left, left, no to the right," and so on. Their commotion is drowned out by the haunting hum of industrial fridges ready to be filled with victims of the coronavirus.

It has been a busy afternoon for this team of morticians, the busiest of the pandemic so far. They have already brought two bodies to the mortuary and are about to rush back out to collect more, a victim from hospital and another from his home. But before they leave for their next grim journey, one of the funeral directors stops to make an important phone call. It's to his casket supplier. "We're running out, we need more," he pleads. She can offer him a new batch of 24 coffins in four days' time, but he needs them sooner.

"And the order after that, how long's that going to take?" he asks, before his eyes open wide with a look of exasperation. "Two weeks?" Under Islamic tradition, burials must take place as soon as possible and these funeral directors fear they won't be able to keep up.

A glance at social media that afternoon reveals how lockdown feels very different to different people. The loudest voices on my Twitter feed, some of the figures who seem to dominate so much of the national conversation, are complaining they can't secure a slot for their online grocery shop or berating those who aren't abiding by social distancing rules or dissecting the political fallout from the latest Downing Street news conference. However, here in Birmingham the people I am speaking to are not complaining about inconvenience, logistics or politics, but pain, death and heartache.

I am here to find out how the virus is affecting Black, Asian and minority ethnic communities specifically. Everyone I have spoken to in the city this week knows of at least three people who have died with the virus; one man tells me he has lost 18 friends and relatives in the last three weeks. This is a world far from what's being described by some middle-class commentators because poverty and race, where you live, how much you earn, the colour of your skin, help to filter your experience of this outbreak. It is my duty to report and reflect this.

In Birmingham, this has already been the worst day of the pandemic. At a hospital a few miles to the east of the mortuary, a 29-year-old woman becomes the latest victim, one of the youngest people in the city to die with coronavirus. Fozia Hanif's case is all the more heartbreaking because she died six days after giving birth at the same hospital. Baby Ayaan was delivered early after his mother tested positive.

Shortly before losing her fight with the virus, Fozia was granted a few fleeting moments with her newborn baby and was given a picture of him by nurses. She sent her sister, Sophia, a series of text messages describing how excited she was about the prospect of finally meeting her child, once she was well enough to see other people. A few days after Fozia's death Sophia told ITV News: "She was messaging us saying 'oh, I haven't seen the baby yet,' and I said 'don't worry about it, when you come home you're going to come home together.'"

"She was really happy, she got the baby photo they printed out for her," her husband of nearly seven years, Wajid Ali, said. "She was holding the photo and saying 'look it's our baby' and 'we're going to come home soon.' That's the last time I spoke to her."

When the first few cases of Covid-19 were reported in the UK, weeks earlier, Fozia expressed concern that her pregnancy might expose her to extra risk from the pandemic. But she hadn't considered that, in a poor and densely populated district of a busy city, her south Asian heritage might be what pushed her into one of the most vulnerable sections of our society.

It has been a difficult day for the whole country. A record daily rise in the number of Covid-19 patients who died in hospital has been recorded – an increase of 938 to 7,097. The Prime Minister, Boris Johnson, is still in intensive care with the virus, though apparently "sitting up in bed." No one is unaffected by the outbreak. But the worst consequences are not equally spread. It is certain communities, certain towns and cities that are shouldering the burden.

The victims of Covid-19 are disproportionately Black or Asian and from densely populated parts of cities like Birmingham. BAME people are more exposed to health inequalities and are more likely to die for many reasons: deprivation, a raised exposure in front-line professions, a higher prevalence of other health problems. And so, although we are "all in this together," it is people in the neighbourhoods close to the mortuary where we have spent some of the day, people in the community where Fozia Hanif lived, who are "in this" far more than others.

This is my city. The place where I was born, grew up and got my first job as an ITV News trainee. I don't live here anymore, but in a way it's still home. It is a place of resilience, tongue-in-cheek cynicism and optimism. The word "FORWARD" is engraved on its coat of arms and etched on its spirit. But as the Easter holiday weekend approaches, the roads are almost silent. Many people are frightened to go out. Some of the city's neighbourhoods, the districts I know best, are now among the worst-affected places in the country, in the world. At times my mind is taken back to the war zones, the scenes of terrorist atrocities and natural disasters that I have reported from. Perhaps that seems a little excessive, but those are the places where I am more used to writing about "death tolls", "field hospitals" and "emergency morgues." Syria and Somalia, not Sparkhill and Small Heath.

At University Hospital Trust Birmingham, doctors know what war looks like. It is here that many of the injured service personnel returning to the UK from the war in Afghanistan received treatment for their battlefield injuries. The trust's doctors treated Malala Yousafzai, the Pakistani girl shot in the head by the Taliban in 2012, who later made the city her new home. Today the Trust appears to be one of the hardest hit in the country.

That night, at a different Birmingham hospital, the Good Hope in Sutton Coldfield, there is another death that adds to the emerging picture of a disease that affects each town differently. Elsie Sazuze, a 44-year old care home nurse, dies of Covid-19 leaving behind a son aged 22, a daughter aged 16 and her husband Ken. Elsie was born and raised in Malawi but moved to Birmingham to work. It is a familiar story. A key worker who toiled in the care homes of the Midlands, another profession where Black and Asian people are highly represented.

"When they talk about the wartime spirit I cannot listen," Ken tells me. He last saw his wife when she was taken from their home in an ambulance. He believes she caught the virus at work and he says he has heard too many stories of African women in Britain's health and social care sector dying during the pandemic. "They have sent people to war, people like my wife, without the protection they need. People who came here to England to help. It feels like us and them," he says.

From the start of the lockdown we have been challenged to work together to protect our most-loved, most-respected institution, the National Health Service. The approach was proposed by government advisors to avoid tensions between communities and encourage self-policing of lockdown measures. It might have worked. It has certainly helped many people to feel closer to each other. The following day, for the fourth consecutive Thursday, millions will stand at windows and doorsteps to clap and cheer doctors, nurses and other key workers. But Elsie's family do not feel they are part of this shared enterprise.

"I can't clap with everyone else on Thursday nights because it's just a distraction," says Ken. "I cannot go outside and pretend that everything is OK, everyone is happy. A lot of people in Birmingham know the truth because we feel it."

The Story of Captain Tom

Rebecca Haworth, Reporter, ITV News Anglia

I feel honoured to be able to call Captain Sir Thomas Moore my friend. I was the first journalist to meet him and, since then, I have got to know not only a man who has lifted the nation's spirits, but also a much-loved dad and grandad who has been inspiring his family all of his life. Clearly his determination and resilience in the face of adversity is admirable, but what I will treasure the most is the conversations we have had off-camera, and the support and kindness he has shown me during such a worrying time.

The team at ITV News Anglia first found out about Captain Tom's 100th birthday walk on April 7th. His daughter, Hannah Ingram-Moore, had sent out a press release about her 99-year-old dad who didn't want to "just sit still and do nothing about our current epidemic." Later that day I had a phone call to say I was off to meet a soon-to-be centenarian, resolute on doing his bit in the crisis. I knew immediately that it was going to be a lovely local news story; a Second World War veteran who wanted to help the NHS during a pandemic at the age of 99 was always going to appeal. And it couldn't have come at a better time. The strict lockdown measures had recently been introduced, and the British public were keen to get behind something good.

I met Captain Tom, or just Tom to me, on April 8th. That morning, I had spoken to Hannah on the phone to work out the logistics of filming at the home Tom shares with Hannah and her family in Marston Moretaine in Bedfordshire. I immediately warmed to her as she was so friendly and accommodating. The sun was shining as I pulled up on their drive later that afternoon. As soon as I stepped out of my car, I was welcomed by a smiling Hannah and her children,

Georgia and Benjie. They were all so excited we were there. Camera operator Chris Warner and I were getting ready to film in the garden when Tom started to walk out. Suited and booted, medals on show, resolutely stooped over his walking frame, he didn't say a word until he reached his desired position. Then he looked up and gave me the most wonderful smile.

His answers were short at first as he was more interested in how the camera operator and I were doing, but we soon got into the swing of it, and that's when he came out with the golden line: "one little soul like me isn't going to make much difference." I was buzzing after the interview as I knew the story in itself was going to give our viewers a much-needed boost, but his positivity, charm and good humour just added something extra special. And it wasn't long until the rest of the world found out just how special his story really was.

When we finished filming, I chatted to the family about their original target of raising just £1,000 and their new more ambitious target of £5,000. Meanwhile, Tom carried on walking in the background, clearly determined to reach the 100 lengths of his garden that he'd promised to do. We said our goodbyes, and I went home to edit the report. I received several phone calls from a delighted Hannah, who thanked me for coming. The finished report worked brilliantly on the ITV Anglia news programme and just a few days later it was picked up by the national media.

In the days that followed, it was quite surreal watching and hearing Tom and his family on almost every television and radio station. They had no experience with the media and suddenly had to manage hundreds of daily requests from journalists all over the world, yet they did it all with such grace and charm. I was on the phone to Hannah almost every day to help reassure and guide her as it was, at times, overwhelming. In the meantime, as I had developed such a good relationship with the family, I became the unofficial Captain Tom Correspondent – for Anglia and also for my colleagues in other ITV regions and in the network newsroom who wanted to interview him. By now, I was seeing Tom every few days, and we struck up a real rapport. I learned about his beloved hometown of Keighley, how he enjoys doing DIY with his grandson Benjie, his passion for travel, and his fascination with different types of military medals. His optimism about life was inspiring, and every time I saw him, I came away feeling a little lighter.

I have had the privilege of sharing many special moments with Tom; his 100th birthday, the virtual opening of a new Nightingale hospital in Harrogate, and the launch of The Captain Tom Foundation to name but a few. But my favourite has to be his knighthood. I had just come off the phone to a colleague, where we had chatted about the possibility of an announcement, when I received the embargoed press release. Hannah told me she had received a letter that morning from Downing Street, but because she had been so busy, she hadn't had a chance to read it.

So it wasn't until later that evening that Tom even knew about the knighthood. I saw him the following day, and as ever, he was on top form. Ever since our first meeting, his family and I had noticed he had started to look younger, and that day was no exception. He stood tall, and almost had a glow about him. It was another hot day, and so I insisted we sit in the shade in the garden for our interview. He kept making me laugh. He said: "Six weeks ago, what were the chances of me being a Sir? Zippo!" He also told me he was concerned about being in a wheelchair to see the Queen, and not being able to get back up if she asked him to kneel.

Tom's story took off for so many reasons, but it was mainly down to him just being himself. His ability to remain calm during a crisis united people from around the world, and gave us all hope when we needed it most. His grandchildren tell me he is the rock of the family, the one they go to when they have a problem, and he has now become that guiding light for so many others. He has also been unchanged by becoming world famous overnight, and that must say a lot about a person. His motto, "tomorrow will be a good day", is one we should all cherish, because if a 100-year-old can achieve everything he has in less than two months, then it stands us all in good stead for overcoming this crisis.

For me as a journalist, Captain Tom has been an extraordinary gift. To see your story go global, and the man at its heart become a personal friend, has been a wonderful experience. In years to come, what will people remember about the great pandemic of 2020? Meeting Captain Tom, and playing a small part in history, has been an honour. The friendship of this remarkable man is one I will treasure for the rest of my life.

Why Warehouse Workers Wanted Answers

Hannah Miller, Political Correspondent, ITV News Granada

It was early evening on April 8th when I sent a WhatsApp message to Downing Street. I didn't really expect anything to come of it, certainly not so quickly. Regional broadcasters hadn't been taking part in the government's daily press conferences and I assumed there must be a reason why. It turns out no one had really asked.

As a regional political correspondent, most of my time was spent dealing with issues directly connected to the north-west of England and with MPs representing constituencies in the region. I wasn't in the habit of messaging Number 10; I had to ask a colleague for the number. But we were two weeks into lockdown and the desperate messages from warehouse workers who felt they were unsafe at work just kept on coming. A question at the press conference seemed like the best chance of getting a meaningful answer on an issue that was affecting thousands of people in the north-west and beyond. And so it was that less than twenty-four hours later, I was sitting alone in my kitchen, staring at the Downing Street crest on my laptop and waiting to go live on national television. I needed to stop thinking about the myriad of possible technical glitches and focus on the reason I was there.

That reason was Joe Gilchrist. He's registered blind and has worked at JD Sports' warehouse in Rochdale for more than two decades. When lockdown began Joe asked to be furloughed, believing it to be nigh on impossible for him to do his job safely in the new socially distanced world. But the company said he didn't qualify for the Job Retention Scheme. Joe would either have to come in, or take unpaid leave.

Joe's story was the fourth I'd done on warehouse workers in the space of just a fortnight, but the majority were with people whose identities we had disguised. It's a universal rule of television news that reports are more powerful if someone is prepared to put their face and their name to a story, but during our first conversation Joe's wife Donna seemed to think it would be better for her husband to remain anonymous too. That's problematic because there aren't many blind people with 24 years of service at JD Sports, so we couldn't talk with any clarity about Joe's situation without revealing his identity. But it turned out that Joe was no shrinking violet. By the time of our second call his biggest concern appeared to be whether his guide dogs Bilbo and Solo would get to appear on camera alongside him. Joe was willing to speak out, and said he didn't care if he lost his job as a result.

Listening to Joe, I was struck that he didn't want to focus on his own disability but on his fears for his colleagues. "We're only selling trainers," he said of JD Sports, "I don't understand why they want to put lives at risk." A few days earlier a Rochdale Council inspection found the company had put precautions in place and was observing government guidelines. A letter sent by councillors said the company "could go further," urging it to "justify and reconsider" its decision to remain open. JD Sports said in response that the health, safety and wellbeing of colleagues was their "priority", pointing out measures they'd taken such as reducing the number of staff on site, increasing cleaning and putting up reminders about social distancing.

While the specifics of Joe's situation were unique, many of his thoughts and feelings were not. We'd received messages from workers in warehouses run by other companies across the north-west – the majority were scared, some felt angry, one told us she was going home and crying every night. Attached to the emails were photos and videos that flew in the face of everything people had been told to do to keep themselves safe. They showed overcrowding at shift changes, hand sanitiser running out, and aisles that were simply too narrow to make social distancing possible. In the most flagrant breach of the spirit of the rules, staff told us they had been badged as "key workers", despite only handling items like paddling pools and barbecues. As we began to broadcast reports on conditions, some companies did change their practice but at this early stage of lockdown people could see danger at every turn. Some felt even travelling to work was an issue as they made journeys on public transport, which they feared put them at unnecessary risk. It was a cocktail of conditions that people could be forgiven for wanting to avoid.

But many of those who contacted us felt they had no choice. They needed to pay the bills and that required turning up to work in conditions that, no matter how hard employers tried, sometimes seemed to be incompatible with the simple messages that were dominating the national conversation. They were not "key workers", nor could they work from home. They weren't allowed to meet friends or family, but they could stand side by side in a confined space packing parcels. They weren't selling "essential" items; indeed most of the time they were keen to tell us how "non-essential" their work was. Unions had called for the sites to shut down to eliminate the risk entirely, but the government was explicit: online retail was "open and encouraged". More than bread-makers or board games, what the country really needed was these workers to stop the economy grinding to an even more sudden halt.

Local authorities worked with businesses to try to make warehouses safer, while metro mayors wrote public letters to the government raising their concerns about those still having to work in "non-essential" retail. Greater Manchester Mayor Andy Burnham said he received more than 1,600 complaints from across the country. He and Liverpool City Region Mayor Steve Rotheram asked the government to insist on businesses following social distancing rules all the time, not just "where possible" as the guidance stated. They described those two words as a "get-out clause for some employers who are choosing not to follow the rules." It was not an argument they would go on to win, as fears about the economy grew.

Meanwhile, politicians from all parties were growing uncomfortable about MPs and managers working from home, while millions of workers couldn't do the same. Could I, as a journalist sitting comfortably in the kitchen, really know what it was like to work in a warehouse through a pandemic? The best I could do was listen, and report on the concerns that were coming into my inbox almost every day.

April 9th had been a relatively straightforward day. I'd been making calls on long-term stories and wasn't expecting to appear on air when my phone pinged with a message from Downing Street saying I could ask a question at the press conference in just two hours' time. As I cleared the kitchen worktop to make an acceptable video call background, I spoke to my Head of News Lucy West. Together we agreed on what I should ask.

"*The government has previously said that employers should take 'socially responsible decisions' with regard to their staff. Is refusing furlough to a blind man who works in a warehouse a 'socially responsible decision'?*"

That was the question we settled on for the First Secretary of State Dominic Raab, who at the time was de facto Prime Minister while Boris Johnson remained in intensive care. It had been characteristic of the government's response to Covid-19 that much of the guidance was open to interpretation, relying on bosses to listen to the concerns of their staff. So what was Dominic Raab's interpretation of this case? Joe was not the only person in the north-west whose employer was not doing as the employee had asked; what should be the outcome in such a situation?

In the half-hour between a sound check and the start of the briefing, I sat on my own, hoping that I'd be un-muted at the right time (a job that viewers perhaps didn't realise fell to Downing Street, not the journalists themselves). I gave my flatmate advance warning not to come in and boil the kettle while I was on air, and I worked through scenarios as to how I might follow up on my original question. There had been plenty of (often misplaced) criticism of the questions asked at the briefings by "the media". I wanted to get it right. Not just for me, but for other regional journalists who hadn't yet been given a chance.

Dominic Raab responded that Joe sounded like an "extremely vulnerable individual", adding that he "would like employers to think long and hard if they have people like that who they employ who are in their care." I followed up by asking whether the very existence of this battle suggested the guidance needed to be more detailed? He said the government would look at it again. JD Sports did eventually agree to furlough Joe, though they said it was because of his wife's health condition, not his own. He remains on their books at the time of writing.

163

With the press conference over there was no time to relax. I needed to set up on my balcony to report live on *Granada Reports* at 6pm, a slightly precarious set-up that involved using either my phone or laptop (whichever had a better connection on the day), balanced on some books, which were balanced on a chair, which was balanced on a table. Where there's a will there's a way.

At the time, the north-west region had the third highest number of people in hospital with Covid-19 and over the course of a couple of weeks that number would grow. We will never know how many people caught the virus in a warehouse. The data suggests warehouse workers may have had a slightly higher death rate than average, but we can't say that with confidence and there are other factors to consider.

You might then ask why this story matters, if we can't be certain of any link between warehouses and the spread of Covid-19. To that I would say it was important to reflect the tough decisions many low-paid workers were making about whether or not to go to work each day. Later, when the Prime Minister said everyone should go to work if they were unable to work from home, it was widely reported as a significant shift in policy. I couldn't help but think that many of the warehouse workers we had spoken to had been doing that all along.

That night as my neighbours clapped for key workers I wondered how many of them were expecting a parcel or had received one that morning. As they looked out onto a street with shuttered-up shops, had they given any thought to the hive of activity that was going on in warehouses across the country? My phone was buzzing with messages from fellow regional journalists, who were glad to see a story that had become prominent locally getting some national attention. But most importantly of all, I saw some of the people whose stories we had covered in previous weeks celebrating the fact that their voice had been heard. To be able to do that is a privilege.

A Survivor's Story

Ken Goodwin, Reporter, ITV News West Country

Dave Lewins is not a man to get flustered. His training as a former RAF fighter pilot taught him that. He is softly spoken, he considers his words carefully. So it surprised me a little when, near the start of our interview, he broke down in tears.

But as we talked more, I began to understand. Dave's tears were not for himself. Not for having been on a ventilator, in an induced coma in intensive care. Not for how gut-wrenchingly ill he had felt, nor how close to death he had been. They were because, as he recovered back on the ward, he'd listened to a fellow patient being told by a doctor that he ought to phone his loved ones as he may not last the night. Sure enough, when Dave woke up the next morning, the man had gone.

"I heard him shouting out in the night, and then the next morning the bed was empty. I asked where he was and they said that sadly he had passed away," said Dave. "The traumatic side for me was listening to doctors explaining to patients that they probably wouldn't make it through the night. And if they wanted to say goodbye to their family and children, they needed to do it, on the phone, there and then. And that is just . . . you can't imagine."

It's a memory too recent and too raw to be recalled without tears. Dave is 60. He runs his own brewery as well as being a flying instructor. He keeps himself fit and has none of the pre-existing conditions, the so-called "co-morbidities", that can make exposure to Covid-19 more severe. But when the virus hit him, it hit him hard.

"I was at work and I suddenly started feeling dizzy," he said. He also had the classic sore throat that has been reported in so many cases. He left it a day, but then called 111 when his condition worsened. "My chest suddenly started feeling very heavy." An ambulance was called and he was examined, put on a heart monitor, but they decided he was fit enough to stay at home. There was no question of suspecting Covid-19 at the time. This was in mid-March.

But after another day he still didn't feel well, so an ambulance was called and he was taken to the accident and emergency department of his local hospital in Cheltenham. "They gave me a chest x-ray, which was inconsequential. They then gave me some antibiotics and sent me home." Two days later, he was back in hospital. "At that point they did another chest x-ray, which showed pneumonia. They tested me, and confirmed I had Covid."

As his condition deteriorated he was put onto a ventilator. This is a machine that mechanically takes over a patient's breathing. It is an invasive method with a tube inserted into the windpipe, so he had to be put into an induced coma. He says he was not entirely unconscious all the time, with hazy recollections of terrifying dreams, hallucinations, mechanical beeping sounds, and a sense of drifting in and out of reality. "It was very, very scary indeed. I could hear a lot of crying around me and wailing, so the idea of which way I was going was very unsure."

Dave was eventually, after a week, taken off the ventilator. But as he came round, his emotions welled up. "I couldn't stop crying. I was suddenly aware that I had got through . . . got through something that could have gone either way. One of the nurses, called Lizzy, came and held my hand . . ." Dave has to concentrate hard at this point because this memory, a moment of tenderness and compassion from a busy nurse, moves him to tears. "She was very reassuring and said it was not unusual at all to feel that emotional when coming out of a coma."

Dave's overriding reason for wanting to tell his story was to warn people against complacency. "There still seem to be a lot of people out there who simply don't get it, and don't think it will happen to them. People need to realise that they have to self-isolate and stop spreading this damned thing." He also wanted to thank the hospital staff. "All of them, literally, were just fantastic. I can't say thank you enough."

But I also got the feeling that giving an interview had a cathartic effect on Dave. It was his way of dealing with some of the extraordinary emotions he had inside him, just a few days after he had come out of hospital. At the end of it, as we said goodbye, it seemed like a huge weight had been lifted from his shoulders.

I have seen him a couple of times since. He plans to marry his long-term partner Zoe "as quickly as possible" and has been active in seeing others, social distance allowing, he met while in hospital to form, as they call it, a "Covid Survivors Group".

I came away from my interview with Dave considering myself lucky that I had met him and heard his story. And, to be honest, glad that I had not fallen victim to the virus myself. Later on, after Dave had seen his interview broadcast, I received a text from him: "Thank you for helping me get my message out there." That meant a lot.

Timeline

April

14 Several charities express concern that care home deaths are not being included in the daily figures

16 Foreign Secretary Dominic Raab announces a three-week extension to the nationwide lockdown

   Captain Tom Moore completes 100 laps of his garden

   ITV's NHS Day celebrates all those fighting coronavirus

18 Communities Secretary Robert Jenrick says coronavirus appears to affect Black, Asian and minority ethnic communities disproportionately

22 Matt Hancock tells MPs "we are at the peak" of the outbreak but says social distancing measures cannot be relaxed

23 US President Donald Trump suggested exploring disinfectants as a possible treatment for Covid-19 infections

25 Covid tests for key workers are booked up within an hour

27 Prime Minister Boris Johnson returns to work after recovering from Covid-19

28 Health Secretary Matt Hancock announces that care home figures will be included in the daily death toll

   A nationwide one-minute silence is held to remember key workers who have died

30 Captain Tom Moore celebrates his 100th birthday as his appeal to raise money for the NHS reaches £32 million

Celebrating All NHS Heroes

Michael Billington, Reporter, ITV News Calendar

This is Captain Tom country. At least it was 100 years ago when he was born and bred among the rolling hills and dales of the Worth Valley. As I head south-west towards Keighley, he's nearing the end of his journey. The final few steps of his one hundredth lap of his garden are being played out on the radio as his fundraising tops £12 million. The significance isn't lost on me that every step this wartime hero has taken has been for the heroes I'm about to meet.

As I head out of the pretty town of Silsden and start the gentle climb up towards the hospital, this couldn't feel much further removed from the images I've seen of China or Italy. This place is dealing with a global pandemic too? Really? I suppose the clues are there. On a glorious early spring day like today, it should be busy with tourists heading for the Yorkshire Dales. Instead there are mostly closed doors and windows, behind which are paintings of rainbows, no doubt the product of a home-school art class. Still, the whole picture is in contrast with the crisis they're dealing with behind the doors at Airedale General.

This isn't my first time here. Thankfully my previous trips had only been in a professional capacity. Two years ago, I made a film in the operating theatres for ITV's coverage of the NHS at 70. That's how we've managed to secure access to film inside the hospital this time, despite most places being locked down to prevent the spread of the coronavirus. I'm back for ITV NHS Day, celebrating the unsung heroes in our health service across the channel's programmes, from *Good Morning Britain* through to the *Tonight* programme, before we pause at 8pm for the nation to clap for carers for the third week in a row.

171

Camera operator Mike Newton and I from ITV News Calendar in Yorkshire and Lincolnshire are one of the first crews allowed into a hospital during the Covid crisis, to help tell the stories of those trying to defeat this deadly pathogen. It's an eye opener.

Some parts of the building are now no-go zones for all but the most highly protected of staff. "Hot", "warm", and "cold" areas keep "Covid suspected" and "Covid positive" patients segregated from the rest of the hospital population. We're kept at a safe distance, but one "warm" corridor we film, busy with staff, some in masks and gloves, leads to a "hot" ward where the most gravely ill patients are fighting the infection.

Behind the masks are all manner of hospital workers – it's not just the clinical teams that have to protect themselves from this virus. "None of us have learned how to cope with a pandemic, ever had a practice run at this so we're scared, we're anxious, we don't know what we will face each day," says Lead Dietician Lara Rowe. "People put their uniform on when they get to work each day and they don't know what that day is going to bring and that's kind of overwhelming at times."

Everyone here is under pressure. This is undoubtedly one of the biggest challenges of their careers. Some of the 3,000-strong workforce have been seconded to areas of medicine they don't ordinarily practise in order to provide the critical care so many Covid patients need. But I'm keen to learn how the whole team finds working under these circumstances.

"Difficult, very difficult. Being away from family and my little girl is very difficult," Mark Anderton tells me. His cleaning role puts him in as much direct contact with patients as the nurses, sometimes more. Head to toe in personal protective equipment, it's almost a constant process keeping Covid wards disinfected. It's both professionally and personally challenging. Even off shift, he's forced to isolate from his young family. "It's not going to be forever, this is basically how we're doing it. We're generally quite scared, not really knowing what the next step will be. It is quite worrying to see but I have faith that we're doing the right things and we're eventually going to get to a better place," he says.

Outside the laundry room, we bump into Anne Raine collecting her new scrubs. It's probably the first time she'll have worn them in a decade. The former GP and oncologist has come out of retirement to volunteer and will be working with patients to help them stay in touch with friends and family. "I could see that patients that were in hospital without anyone able to visit them, particularly at the end of life, how heartbreaking that was. It's just awful, and if I could just make a difference to a few people, I really wanted to come and do that," she tells me.

"It was a recovery room . . ." a member of the surgical team shouts into her camera phone from behind the virtual anonymity of a plastic visor, ". . . we're now using this as an intensive care unit." The hospital is providing us with a series of video diaries from the intensive care unit, giving us a snapshot of the ward treating the most critically ill, while keeping the virus in, and all but the most essential visitors out. Here, Covid patients are intubated. A machine pumps oxygen into their lungs via a tube inserted into their windpipe. It's one of the riskiest procedures for doctors to perform, as they practically stare the virus in the face.

"Performing that procedure exposes the anesthetist to the virus that the patient is breathing out or coughing out, and in order to look into the patient's mouth you are face to face with the patient," Consultant Anesthetist Frank Swinton tells me. "It is frightening, because you're dealing with patients who are crashingly sick. They are desperately unwell and likely to die very soon unless we intervene, and immediately that turns the stress levels up. As well as wearing gloves and gowns, I've brought my mask here as a demonstration for you to show you just how difficult it is to hear people," his muffled voice explains. "Often we're speaking through a wall or a window or a door, so you're shouting into your mask for two to three hours at a time. It becomes very hot, you end up with a sore throat and it is very easy to have miscommunication."

I'm broadcasting live from here into our *Calendar* programme at 6pm. It's hard to know what I can add – these people's stories speak for themselves. They're doing all they can to defeat this virus, and yet still patients are dying. In a matter of weeks they've built the "hot" area, a hospital within a hospital, to deal with this pandemic alongside the cancer treatments, the coronary care, the babies still being born. It's easy to see how this could become overwhelming.

The last video diary of the day pings through on my phone. Karen Taylor is a senior member of the surgical team. She's got a message for the public. "Thank you very much for all the contributions and all the good wishes, it means the world. We couldn't do it without you all. Thank you." That's it. We're off air. Karen's message of thanks seemed an apt way to finish my report. How can she be thanking everyone else, when she and her colleagues are the ones coming face to face with a deadly pandemic every day?

Before I leave, I'm introduced to Victoria Pickles, one of the directors here at Airedale NHS Foundation Trust, who admits there was some apprehension about having a television crew on site. But she's already received warm words from colleagues at trusts elsewhere. She's particularly pleased about how a range of staff, not just medical, have had their efforts on the frontline acknowledged throughout the day on ITV.

As I head back to the car, I take one final look at the beautiful Worth Valley, which by now is bathed in evening sunshine. It should be a nice night for the third Clap for Carers. I sincerely hope when people turn out tonight, they're clapping for the cleaners, the dieticians and the retired volunteers too.

The Covid Crisis in Care

Paul Brand, Political Correspondent, ITV News

It's 10am on April 28th and I'm parked outside a care home in Peterborough. A video has just pinged through to my phone, and I'm leaning in to listen to it above the sound of the windscreen wipers. The clip shows a carer in her early twenties named Laura, wearing an apron, face mask, goggles and gloves, sitting next to the bed of a resident and gently stroking her arm. "I've got a letter from your granddaughter," says Laura. I realise she is about to read 86-year-old Peggy her family's final words to her.

"Dear Grandma,

You wouldn't believe what's happening in this country at the moment. I can only imagine what Grandad would say about it. If there's one thing that I am happy about, it's that you'll finally find your peace. I'm so extremely proud to call you my grandma. You've fought so hard to stay with us, but now it's time to finally rest and be back with Grandad. We know he's been waiting for you."

Peggy coughs between sentences, and Laura stops to soothe her.

"You have been the most amazing grandma, always making everything perfect for us. You are the most kind and sweet lady we'll ever meet. We have such fond memories of you from childhood, from making dens to feeding the fish. We're so sorry that we can't be with you for your last breaths. But we know that the carers, who have done such an amazing job of looking after you for the past three years, will be there with you, and we're all there next to you in spirit. For now, Grandma, this is goodbye. But I know that you will always be with us in our hearts, which you've made so full of love and happy memories. Goodnight and sleep well."

By the final sentences, Laura is crying. It's a month since the residents have been able to see any family – right now the staff at the home are the closest thing to it. Two days later, Peggy passed away with only the carers for comfort. Her death would be the first of many at Philia Lodge – some with confirmed Covid-19, others suspected. Normally, the home loses two residents a year. By the time I pull up in my car that day, they're losing two a week.

In fact, I've arrived at Philia Lodge just as the true scale of the crisis in care is being revealed. That morning, the data finally told the story ITV News had been reporting for weeks. The Office for National Statistics and the Care Quality Commission issued their first joint figures, which showed that Covid-19 was sweeping through care homes at an alarming rate. Across the UK, a total of 6,000 residents had died by mid-April.

We'd filmed at many of them, though not without challenges. Taking a camera into a care home at any time requires thought – the residents have a right to privacy and dignity. But now that a deadly virus had either invaded their homes or was threatening to, there was no question that our own entry was completely barred. So we captured the crisis in any way that we could, handing over disinfected cameras to carers so that they could film for us, or shooting through windows and doorways, with interviews done outside at a safe two-metre distance.

When I step into the garden at Philia Lodge that morning it's raining heavily. Laura meets me underneath an awning that just about keeps us dry. She's quiet and gentle like many of the carers I've met. She seems nervous, so I try to make some small talk. But I've come to learn by now that the camera itself isn't the problem – all carers' nerves are on edge. After weeks of battling the virus many are emotionally exhausted.

Laura cries again as she tells me that she misses Peggy. "I miss her every day. I'm happy she's at peace. But being here just won't be the same without her," she says. "We're just trying to be strong for the residents we've got left." As broadcasters we always try to keep our personal distance from a story. But two metres feels inhuman. I can't lean in a little closer to Laura or even pass her a tissue. I comfort her with whatever words I can find.

By this point in the pandemic comfort was often hard to come by. While the NHS had understandably been made a top priority, carers repeatedly told me they felt like "second class citizens". From the outset, it was clear that the care sector had been left woefully unprepared.

We'd been following the crisis in care from the very beginning, when there were just a handful of cases of Covid-19 in the UK. We focused not just on care homes, but also domiciliary care, which involves visiting people in their own homes. In early March we aired our first report uncovering the difficulties the sector faced. With personal protective equipment diverted to hospitals, regular supplies for carers had dried up. We filmed as carers at one provider scoured eBay for face masks and hand towels, paying up to four times the usual price.

When we returned to the same domiciliary care company three weeks later, the government had dropped off 300 face masks. But these carers carried out 24,000 visits a week and the manager, Alison, was broken. "We love what we do, we love our clients and we love our team, but it's such a fast-moving situation that we don't feel in control," she said through tears. "People really need to get behind us, not just behind the NHS."

In fact, carers sometimes felt that the NHS was working against them, particularly when it came to discharging hospital patients into care homes. Operating in a disparate sector, with little national representation, care workers found this argument difficult to make at a time when doctors and nurses were rightly being applauded. There is an obvious power imbalance, with carers rarely wishing to question highly qualified consultants or to criticise hard-working NHS staff. When they did raise concerns they sometimes faced a backlash. But many carers felt angry that they had done their bit to relieve pressure on the NHS, only to end up piling it on themselves.

By late March the virus had arrived in care homes and owners began telling us that it had been carried in via hospitals. We filmed at one nursing home near London that had been sent a patient from hospital with no medical notes, only to be told 10 days later that she had Covid-19. Outside on the patio, the manager passed me a floor plan of the home and we mapped out with a marker pen how the virus had spread from room to room. In total, around a dozen residents had caught Covid-19 and three had died.

Later we would uncover evidence that thousands of beds were block-booked in care homes by the NHS and councils in England in preparation for the pandemic. The problem was that patients were being discharged from hospitals without routine testing, with homes sometimes feeling under pressure to accept the admissions regardless. We cannot know for sure whether that is how the virus spread, and both the government and NHS England have insisted that the number of discharges actually fell during the pandemic in England. But 25,000 patients were discharged into English care homes in the month before blanket testing began, and similar concerns have been raised in all four nations of the UK.

By April hundreds, and then thousands, had begun dying in care each week. Early one Tuesday morning I arrived at a home in Lancashire to find what I thought was a cleaner, outside, polishing a window. But it was the daughter of a resident, wiping the glass to have a clearer, final look at her mother. The windows would only open a short way, so her calming words had to be shouted through a two-inch gap. Inside, I could hear the cough that often accompanies Covid-19.

As we were about to do an interview, the daughter of another resident approached me in total distress. She too had arrived to say her goodbyes. I will never forget the reflections in the windowpanes as both women wept for their mothers.

But while every death was felt deeply by family, friends and by the carers themselves, for weeks the statistics didn't count them. Deaths in hospitals were being announced daily but deaths in care homes were not included. At a home in Gateshead in April one carer told me, "our residents are still part of the population, they shouldn't be forgotten about because they've died under our care." Later that day I sat in the back of an edit van at a service station car park, and prepared to take part in the daily Downing Street press conference. I asked the Chancellor why deaths in care should matter any less. A few weeks later the government finally began including them in the daily figures.

By then, dozens of carers themselves had been added to the statistics. Having battled to stop the spread of Covid-19, many were now facing their own fight with the virus. At a care home in Newcastle we met staff who were desperately holding out hope for their manager, Christine. After a lifetime providing care she was now the one in desperate need of it. As she was deteriorating on a ventilator in hospital, Christine's family were deciding whether or not to switch off life support. That afternoon my producer, camera operator and I sat editing our report, checking our phones every five minutes for updates. At 4pm we cheered as a message came through saying Christine was showing signs of improvement. That was one death we wouldn't have to report that night.

The lives of other carers were still at risk, sometimes unnecessarily. One night I drove to a park in Dagenham where a carer we called Charlene had agreed to meet me anonymously. I spotted her through the darkness, approaching in a headscarf and sunglasses. I never got to see her face but I could hear in her voice the fear she felt each day caring for multiple residents with Covid-19. With PPE still in short supply, her only protection was one paper face mask per shift. The masks were designed to be changed every few hours, but Charlene was forced to shake hers out to let it dry during her lunch break before putting it back on. It is perhaps no surprise that she too would catch Covid-19.

Around six weeks into the pandemic the crisis in care was so apparent that the government announced an action plan. It included blanket testing of all patients discharged from hospital and billions of pounds of additional funding to help homes with costs such as PPE. But by that point so many residents had lost their lives that others now faced the prospect of losing their homes.

In early May care home managers began telling us they could no longer cope financially. The virus had been costly to control with the expense of staffing and equipment soaring. But there was also another brutal reality – by emptying beds, the virus had emptied bank balances too.

Rising vacancies, or voids as homes call them, meant that care companies were having to take out loans to survive. And in the second week of May we reported on the first home to close. Friary Lodge in north London asked all residents to move out by the end of the month, having been crippled by the costs of Covid-19. It hoped at the time that it might be able to reopen. Many others faced the same fate. At a home in Nottingham, the owner sobbed as she told us that the family business set up by her parents would have to close within eight weeks. It is a common misconception that care companies make millions. A handful of the big operators do, but most homes are small businesses on incredibly tight margins. Their finances cannot withstand a global pandemic.

Many of those economic problems will persist beyond the pandemic and of course many of them began long before it. The Covid-19 crisis in care has highlighted the urgent need to reform a sector that has been neglected for decades. Successive governments have tried and failed to find a sustainable funding model. Often they have been timid to tackle the issue. Talk of a "dementia tax" almost certainly helped cost Theresa May her majority. But while carers wish this virus had never swept through their homes, perhaps it has brought with it a momentum to finally put social care centre stage.

Indeed, the current Prime Minister has promised cross-party talks to agree a long-term plan. If that is to be delivered then we in the media have our own responsibility not to turn a blind eye once this crisis is over. For too long social care has been neglected in the national conversation, often only making headlines when a home mistreats residents or is shut down by inspectors. But this pandemic has created thousands of witnesses to the struggles of the sector – the grieving families and friends who have seen how precious and yet how fragile care can be. They surely won't let us forget their stories, while the tears of carers like Laura will long tell a tale of their own.

Unthinkable Choices for Hospices

Daniel Hewitt, Political Correspondent, ITV News

Liz and her granddaughter Lisa are close. "My favourite, but don't tell the others I said that," Liz tells me, a television reporter, standing next to a camera that's recording her words. Liz is 81. A mother of two, a grandmother of seven and a great-grandmother of eleven. Despite having four children of her own, Lisa visited her grandma almost every day – dropping off food, staying for a cup of tea, and another, and then one more. "We put the world to rights," says Lisa. "We chatted for hours."

One of the particularly cruel consequences of coronavirus has been the separation of young and old; that cruelty felt even more by those for whom time was already especially precious. Liz has terminal breast cancer. When we meet at the Heart of Kent Hospice in Aylesford she is FaceTiming Lisa on her iPad. This is how they chat now, at least twice a day. They haven't been able to meet in person for six weeks.

The Heart of Kent, like the vast majority of hospices, has banned visitors. When I filmed there in April, hospice policy allowed just one family member or friend to be with their loved one "at the end of life". Each family has been contacted and asked to provide the name of a designated visitor for when the time comes.

But Liz still worries. "I don't know who will go first – the virus or me," she tells us. "It's not a very nice feeling, to know that you could die alone. That's the worst part about it. I know I'll have a nurse, but it's not quite the same as your own family. I think about that a lot."

Children unable to say goodbye to their mother, siblings forced to decide who sits with their dying father and, tragically, who doesn't. "It's one of the hardest things we've ever had to do," one member of staff tells me, "and we're used to having hard conversations."

Hospices face death every day. They are experts in it – clinically, mentally, emotionally. Yet providers of end-of-life care entered the coronavirus crisis facing a crisis of their own and within hours of lockdown they were suddenly facing their own unthinkable choices.

Britain's modern hospice movement is one of the UK's great success stories. In 1948 Dame Cicely Saunders, then a nurse in a London hospital, watched a dying patient in her care spend the last two months of his life on a busy surgical ward because there was nowhere else for him to go. She retrained as a doctor and raised hundreds of thousands of pounds to open St Christopher's in London; the first modern hospice, a place that would pioneer palliative care, outside the sphere of the National Health Service. "You matter because you are you and you matter until the last moment of your life," she said. "We will do all we can, not only to help you die peacefully, but to live until you die."

The founding of many local, charitable hospices followed and today more than 200 hospices care for over 225,000 terminally ill patients every year. Most are largely funded through donations with some support from the state. The average children's hospice receives around 17 percent of its funding from government; for adult hospices it's a third. Some receive more, others receive much less, but it means hospices in the UK have to raise more than £1 billion each year themselves.

It costs £11 million a year to run Shooting Stars children's hospice in Guildford. They receive just under £1 million from the NHS, and it is a gargantuan task to raise the rest to ensure local children with incurable and often complex conditions receive care that keeps them as well as possible for as long as they need it.

Even before coronavirus many hospices were finding the funding model increasingly unsustainable. In May 2019 an ITV News investigation uncovered a funding crisis in the sector: one in three hospices had been forced to cut services, 55 percent had either cancelled or delayed the roll-out of future plans to provide end-of-life care and 90 percent said they did not believe they had the resources to meet rising demand. For 89 percent of hospices the cost of providing end-of-life care had risen in the past two years but had not been matched by more government funding. 73 percent had seen their funding from their local Clinical Commissioning Group (CCG) frozen or cut.

A month later, the Acorn children's hospice warned that its centre in Walsall would have to close because "the costs of providing high quality children's hospice care are rising every year and are outstripping our ability to raise all the funds we need." In July, children's hospice Grace's Place in Bury closed its doors permanently, blaming "rising costs of providing high-quality care, an uncertain climate for fundraising . . . and a challenging statutory funding environment."

By October eight out of ten charitable hospices were running at a loss. "We are gravely concerned about the financial situation of many charitable hospices," said Tracey Bleakley, Hospice UK Chief Executive. "This is symptomatic of how the funding model for end-of-life care as a whole is broken. It no longer reflects the complexity of modern end-of-life care and what people actually need, nor the immense growing demand for this care."

This was the backdrop to the Covid crisis for hospices; their work paid for predominantly by jumble sales and fun runs, dying people cared for thanks to the generosity of strangers whose donations increasingly couldn't keep up. Then the donations all but stopped. In March lockdown shut down the way in which hospices make most of their money. Overnight their charity shops closed and all fundraising events, large and small, were cancelled, including the lucrative London Marathon.

Hospices lost £70 million in less than four weeks. The Sue Ryder charity, whose hospices care for 5,000 people each year, was one of many providers to warn it would have to shut down services at the exact moment when they were about to be needed the most.

Shooting Stars children's hospice in Guildford was facing a 90 percent loss in funding by September. They immediately closed one of their homes and cut back on respite care for some of their families. For those families it is simply unthinkable to imagine life without the hospice. Nine-year-old Sam has a severe, life-limiting form of epilepsy. He needs round-the-clock care, and regularly visits Shooting Stars for respite. His parents Sarah and John don't know how long Sam will live for, but they know that when the time comes, they want the hospice to be there for their son. "How would we feel if the hospice wasn't there, supporting us? Pretty terrified," Sarah tells me. "It doesn't bear thinking about," adds John.

The financial situation for hospices was dire. Hospice UK, the sector's leading body, raised the alarm with the Department for Health and Social Care, and while talks began on a short-term, £200m emergency cash injection to see them through the coming weeks, another crisis was quickly emerging.

In March, as coronavirus began to take hold in the UK, one of the great challenges for the government was ensuring there were enough supplies of personal protective equipment for health workers. Masks, aprons, gloves and gowns – essential barriers for those on the frontline dealing with wave after wave of infected patients. The majority of hospices in England usually get PPE through NHS supply chains, managed by Supply Chain Coordination Limited (SCCL) – a company owned by the government. However, at the start of the crisis hospices were removed from the company's supply chain list in order to prioritise hospitals. Hospices soon started running out, despite treating patients with coronavirus in their centres, in care homes and in people's own houses.

Most hospices put out public appeals for donations of masks, aprons and gloves but also basic essentials like soap. St Clare Hospice in Harrow was running low on hand sanitiser, hand wash and washing up liquid. They weren't alone. St Joseph's Hospice in Hackney said its front-line staff were working 24 hours a day "without any PPE." In a Twitter post they pleaded: "Please, please provide us with SFP3 (medical grade) masks, long gowns, gloves, plastic aprons and sanitiser gel so that we can work safely."

We saw evidence of hospices being quoted £480 for a box of surgical face masks that were costing the NHS £18. A pack of 100 gloves from one supplier was £120, rather than £22.50. For higher-spec respiratory masks, the cost to the NHS was £91.70 per box, but £696.50 for hospices. Some items were almost 30 times more expensive. In mid-April, Hospice UK was given assurances that hospices in England would be readmitted to the NHS supply chain by members of SCCL, but by the end of the month they were still being denied access and were not receiving PPE from the government.

Hospices were now days away from running out altogether, despite caring for 24,000 patients each day, three times more than the same period last year, a result of more people dying because of coronavirus, but also because more people were choosing to die at home rather than go into hospital.

"I don't think people really understand what hospices do," said Hospice UK's Tracey Bleakley. "We carry out medical procedures every single day, we employ doctors and nurses who are putting themselves at risk just as people are in acute hospitals."

In the first week of May, we visited Bolton Hospice. As you walk through the automatic doors into the reception area, one of the first things you notice is the decorative memorial tree covering the right-hand wall. The large steel construction is painted silver and gold, and each branch weaves and winds to a petal-shaped plaque at its tip, bearing the name of a patient who had been cared for by the hospice.

They are used to goodbyes, but so rarely to one of their own. Gill Oakes was a senior nurse at Bolton Hospice for 24 years. The weekend before our arrival she died after contracting coronavirus. She was 53.

While her colleagues mourned the loss of a woman "who gave her life to this place," the hospice's Chief Executive Leigh Vallance was desperately trying to source PPE. In 48 hours they would run out of protective gowns. "I haven't been able to get a consistent supply at all, for two months," Leigh told us. "I know there is a national shortage, but what do I tell my staff on Friday when we run out of gowns and we have a Covid-positive patient? What do I do on Friday? There is no supply in Bolton, and there isn't a supply on its way."

Even Marie Curie, Britain's biggest provider of end-of-life care, couldn't access the PPE they needed, despite successfully lobbying to eventually get back on to the NHS supply chain. When I spoke to them on the same day we visited Bolton, they hadn't received any face masks for almost two weeks, and staff were having to drive the length and breadth of the country to move PPE from hospice to hospice as some began to run out.

The government repeatedly pointed to a global shortage of personal protective equipment and the Health Secretary Matt Hancock told me the government was doing "as much as we possibly can" to supply hospices with what they needed.

On May 8th, the day Bolton Hospice was due to run out of gowns, the UK government agreed to supply hospices in England with a weekly drop-off. They were not being readmitted onto the official supply chain yet, but supplies would be found and delivered to ensure hospices could carry on treating coronavirus patients, which in turn alleviated pressure on the NHS. It had been a six-week fight just to be treated the same as hospitals and care homes, to access the same life-saving equipment.

The "forgotten frontline" is a phrase used a lot in coverage of the coronavirus crisis. It has been used to describe care home workers and cleaners, food delivery drivers and supermarket staff. Hospices have at times felt that way – as they begged and borrowed PPE and lobbied the government for enough money to stay afloat. They have spent years campaigning for state funding that would allow them just to keep up with a demand that fundraising increasingly can't.

My mum Diane was 51 when she was diagnosed with breast cancer in 2014. She lived with it for five years. For much of that time her condition was managed through the marvels of modern medicine that gave her precious years with my dad, my sister and me.

She had what some hospice staff I've met call "a good death", an odd phrase that may jar when you first hear it, but one I understand having sat with my mum in her final days. "She lived until she died" as Dame Cicely Saunders put it. There was a short window of about a week, between Mum being told the cancer had spread uncontrollably, and her death. She was sent home from hospital but soon began to experience great discomfort. It was horrible to watch. To this day I can't really think about it. The district nurse referred us to a local hospice, which swiftly dispatched a specialist cancer nurse who adjusted my mum's medication and made her much, much more comfortable.

She died a couple of days later surrounded by her family, holding my dad's hand. It remains an unbearable loss to us, but her pain was bearable, she didn't have to go back into hospital, and she died at home in her bed as she'd wished. Without hospice care, this would not have happened. It is a debt we can never repay.

Our experience with the hospice was short. Other people rely on them for many years, their conditions incurable but manageable through physiotherapy, adjustments to medication, psychological support and much more. As a result, their lives are "lived" right up until they die.

The cost of such comprehensive care is rising and rising, and as we live for longer with more complex conditions, the money isn't keeping up. Most hospices are fiercely independent organisations; they were born that way, and wish to stay as such. They do not want to be fully incorporated into the National Health Service or become wholly state-run and state-funded. They want to remain charitable organisations, their work partly funded by the community they care for whose members are inspired to run marathons and climb mountains and bake cakes and donate to their shops.

But fundraising can only go so far and most hospices are finding it harder and harder to raise what they need. They have been there for tens of thousands of families during this crisis thanks in part to emergency and, at times, last-ditch state intervention. What they need now is a serious plan for long-term sustainable funding, to address a problem that will be with us long after this present crisis.

Policing the Lockdown

Rachel Younger, Correspondent, ITV News

It is week six of lockdown and the UK is beginning to swelter. The last week of April is unseasonably warm and we are in Liverpool, one of the country's most hospitable cities. Normally, the first hint of sun is enough to fill up the parks and beer gardens. But now no one is allowed to linger outside for more than the time needed for one form of exercise. That's the theory anyway, only it's increasingly clear that things are beginning to fray round the edges.

We are spending a week with the men and women of Merseyside Police, tasked with keeping us safe in these unprecedented times. It's their job to challenge the surly teenagers gathered by the football pitch and the families picnicking in the park. We watch them send home the freckled kids who say they've only been at the skate park for ten minutes but whose sunburnt faces tell another story.

Most people take being moved on well but it's a strange process to witness. Just a few months ago, none of us could have dreamt that the small freedoms we've always taken for granted would be taken away so abruptly. But imagine being the ones to police it. Coronavirus has caught the UK unawares and officers are having to enforce the lockdown with no rulebook, no training and no choice.

We are out on patrol with PC Gemma Doyle and her partner PC Mollie Ryder, who are part of the city's Response team. Like the great majority of the force here, they are Merseyside born and bred. Policing the restrictions isn't easy. But in this tight-knit city they're motivated by the knowledge that it is their friends, neighbours and families who they are protecting by trying to contain the virus.

As the sun starts to set over the roofs of tightly terraced houses we are called to a street not far from Anfield. The front doors of the homes here open directly onto the pavement, so there isn't much privacy. We see big families crammed into small rooms watching early-evening television.

A neighbour has dialled 999 to report a barbecue being held in front of one of the houses. The unmistakable smell of grilled chicken fills the air, smoke spiralling up into the cloudless sky. "You can't be having a barbecue in the street," says Gemma but the family aren't particularly apologetic. They have a four-year-old and want to celebrate his birthday. "I understand that," Mollie tells them, "but everyone is having to do the same."

Gemma and Mollie quickly establish the family has invited cousins over who don't live in the house. You can be fined up to 1,000 pounds for breaching Covid rules and already, six weeks into lockdown, around 9,000 fines have been issued. But unlike some other forces, Merseyside has decided to take a gentle approach, encouraging people to do the right thing rather than using more draconian measures. As neighbours peer around net curtains, the five extra party-goers cram themselves into a car parked outside and leave.

I ask Gemma if she feels any sympathy for them. "We are all in the same boat," she says. "We've all got families we can't celebrate with. If people are just going to go out and crack on with their plans it's just going to have massive, massive implications."

The force has seen some remarkable breaches including someone operating a hair salon from their garden. It's just a few days since they had to disperse a crowd of 45 people holding a party in the Albert Dock.

Overall, crime is down 20 percent. Mollie and Gemma now have far fewer burglaries, muggings and shoplifters to deal with. But there are signs here of a small increase in organised violence. Criminal activity doesn't stop for lockdown and with the ports all but silent, the city's gangs are tussling over a diminishing supply of drugs. Equally worrying are the clear signs that domestic abuse is on the rise too.

In between calls Gemma tells me it's barely a month since she completed her training. Like many other new constables, she finished early to help plug the gaps in a police force expecting to be stretched to its limits. But what she does on a nightly basis now, persuading people to stay in their homes, is a long way from the job she signed up for.

Like every other officer she's having to adopt a new way of working, at the same time as policing our new way of living. Most of the public seem to appreciate that. But others have tried to use Covid-19 as a weapon against the very people trying to stop its spread.

I meet one of Gemma's colleagues, a young police constable called Markluke Hanson, whose initial training also came to an abrupt end when the crisis peaked. At the beginning of lockdown, during his first fortnight on the job, a suspect he was trying to arrest spat in his face shouting, "have some of my corona."

The man didn't have the virus but there were a few sleepless nights for Markluke before a test result could prove it. His assailant got an eight-month sentence for assault, while Markluke simply got on with his job.

It's a reminder that despite the protective equipment officers are given, they are regularly exposed to the virus. By the end of our week in Liverpool it's well on the way to becoming one of the country's Covid hotspots. Although a number of Merseyside officers have gone down with the virus, remarkably no one we talk to knows of anyone on the force who's been seriously ill with it.

By the end of Gemma's shift she and Mollie have been in and out of four different houses. Some of the calls have been domestic abuse emergencies and although the 999 call handler asks if the virus is present, it's not something either woman pauses to check before rushing in. Their first instinct is to make sure everyone is safe before they consider any danger to themselves.

Gemma tells me how she now showers at the end of every shift before hugging her young daughter. But as many of her colleagues point out over the week we are with them, they regularly deal with worse. Gang members high on drugs, dealers all too ready to pull a knife – heading towards danger, rather than shying away from it, is part of the job description. It occurs to me later that police officers, used to living with a far higher level of risk than the rest of us, have in many ways been the best prepared of all for this virus emergency.

But enforcing lockdown is a balancing act. The week before we arrive in Liverpool another force is ridiculed for threatening to check shoppers' trolleys for non-essential items. If the police get this wrong, they risk undermining their own authority and destroying the public's trust.

At Merseyside's Police Headquarters Chief Constable Andy Cook tells me getting it right is tough. "We police with the consent of the public," he says. "When this crisis is over, we will still have to police the same public. We have to do it the right way now to ensure we hold onto public support." He fears that the real challenge lies ahead, when lockdown begins to loosen and the rules become less black and white.

Spending time with his officers reminds me how thankless the job can be. Over the past few weeks, we've grown used to applauding NHS staff for their heroic efforts and rightly so. But policing a national emergency while keeping the nation onside is a more complicated matter.

What we have witnessed over these unseasonably warm days is a force having to quickly adapt to a different kind of law and order. Learning as they go how to fight a virus that threatens not only their health, but also their reputation.

How a Crisis Affects Those Already in Hardship

Ria Chatterjee, Reporter, ITV News London

I had just finished a video interview with Azi and now she is using her phone to show me her temporary accommodation. A long, bare corridor stretches ahead. It leads to the lounge. "But, we're not allowed to use it," she tells me. The warmth in her voice fosters connection, it surmounts the inevitable detachment of video calls. Interviews with people in desperate situations aren't meant to happen like this, but we are in the middle of a pandemic. For now, it's the only way. A few seconds earlier, her phone had dipped towards the open bedroom door. I caught a glimpse of a small head, determinedly focused, bowed over a colouring book. "Is that your son?" I asked quietly. "Yes, it is." Her voice softened and she chuckled inwardly, in the way parents do when they're proud of their children. I waved down the phone, energised my voice to greet the child and he looked back at me with wide eyes and a big grin. This is a child who has to go to school for a full meal, who lives in a small room with his mother with boxes, clothes, books and everything in-between stacked up around him like a fortress that both protects and stifles. Neither Azi (an alias used to protect her identity) nor her son are aware that seeing him like this has startled me. I had no idea that, during my 20-minute interview with Azi, her son was quietly drawing out of shot. Of course he was. He has nowhere else to go.

Azi left Sierra Leone eight years ago. She gave birth to her son in London and has moved 12 times. She is classed by the government as a person who has no recourse to public funds (NRPF). Under section 115 of the Immigration and Asylum Act 1999 "a person subject to immigration control" "does not have recourse to public funds." According to the Gov.uk website, people with NRPF will "not be able to claim most benefits, tax credits or housing assistance that are paid by the state." The government says the NRPF rule is in the public interest and exists to protect public funds. The policy affects tens of thousands of people in London alone. They may, like Azi, be working under limited leave to remain, be on student or spousal visas, or seeking asylum. The policy's net is far-reaching, so what happens to those people caught in it when an infectious disease brings the capital to a standstill? For Azi the lockdown means her son can't go to school, which means she must stay at home to look after him, which means she can't work as much, which means she has less income, which means she must rely on food banks and charity to survive because her savings are running out.

As a carer for adults with epilepsy Azi is a key worker but school closures have hit her hard. She would normally work between 25 and 40 hours a week on a zero hours contract. Now, without the means to pay for childcare, she finds herself indoors with her son and her mental health is suffering. During the interview Azi perches on the edge of the bed. "We are confined to just one bedroom," Azi tells me. "It's really choked in here. This is where we eat, this is where we sleep. It's really demeaning." It's hard to know how Azi and her son find space to breathe and flourish when their bed is also their dining table and sofa. But signs of success and determination stand out. The wall is lined with certificates of excellence from the boy's school and, elevated on a small cardboard box, trophies twinkle alongside medals attached to colourful ribbons. I notice the colours of the rainbow gushing across a piece of A4 paper with the letters "NHS" bold and centre.

A month or so after meeting Azi online I find myself in the wild and blooming gardens of The Magpie Project to tell another woman's story. The Project is a charity that supports mothers and children in temporary accommodation – many with NRPF. Research shows that women make up 85 percent of those trying to get the NRPF condition lifted. "I just feel like I was rendered useless," Maya tells me. Maya (not her real name) is softly spoken and keeps a tissue at hand for her watering and itchy eyes. Hayfever tablets aren't an option because she's a new mum. We glance over at her son being wheeled around in a pushchair by Jane Williams, the founder of The Magpie

Project, a person Maya describes as a lifeline. It's a hot day, the grass is dry, the pollen count high and huge insects flutter around us. It feels like a suburban wilderness but we are in the London Borough of Newham where 52 percent of children live in poverty, compared to the London borough average of 38 percent.

The camera operator busies himself around us, setting up lights and microphone stands. It's more technically challenging to shoot an anonymous interview but small and inconsequential compared to the reasons Maya feels she must hide her identity. She's spent years waiting to be recognised by the government and cannot risk jeopardising the recent decision to lift her NRPF status and grant her five years leave to remain. But, in the midst of a crisis those in perennial hardship find themselves sinking further into trouble and that's why Maya, box braids pulled back into a pony-tail, wants to tell her story. She's living in a four-bedroom house with five other families. There is no living room, no dining room and they must share the kitchen and bathroom facilities. Eleven strangers under one roof in the midst of a pandemic. I ask if everyone is following the quarantine rules? The answer is no. It's government accommodation, so has she heard from the Home Office with advice on how to stay safe? "No, we haven't. No one's contacted us about anything about staying safe." Evidently, this baffles her. The rhythm in her voice accelerates and her words tumble into one another as she explains the precariousness of her household's collective health. What are we meant to do, she asks, wipe everything down in the bathroom *every single time* we use it? And in the kitchen too? Why haven't they *at least* put posters up in the house with some simple instructions – with illustrations – on hand-washing? She tells me most of the people she and her baby boy live with don't speak English.

Both Azi and Maya spoke the language of invisibility and abandonment. They told me they felt rejected and unwanted. Both described feeling trapped; at first by the system but, as a consequence, by their own minds. Depression has affected them both, further exacerbated by lockdown.

Jane Williams from The Magpie Project told me: "There's a saying, 'It takes a village to raise a child.' But there's a corollary to that, which is, 'If the child doesn't feel the embrace of the village they'll burn it down to feel its warmth', and we're in danger of creating a generation of disenfranchised young adults if we're not careful. It's so important that we include every child in our wish to create a community." During the pandemic The Magpie Project was delivering food parcels to 145 families. The Mayor of Newham, Rokhsana Fiaz, told me there was a 300 percent increase in the need for help from families with NRPF during the pandemic. And research showed the policy disproportionately affects Black and minority ethnic children.

There is a postscript to this story. A week after my report on Azi was broadcast, the High Court ruled NRPF to be unlawful. About a month later, Azi texted to say she'd finally been granted recourse to public funds. For her, the possibility of structure and opportunity is within reach.

Telling a Bangladeshi Story From an English Garage

Mahatir Pasha, Assistant News Editor, ITV News

As a British Bangladeshi, when I learned that ethnic minority communities were being disproportionately impacted by Covid-19, I had to take precautions to minimise interaction with my parents. An inflatable mattress was put to use and I moved into the garage as I continued to go out to work – producing location stories, or at Westminster working with the ITV News politics team. I was reluctant to stop going but my father has a number of health conditions and it eventually became obvious that I could not leave the house and risk bringing the virus home. Working from the garage would become my new normal.

ITV News learned that Bangladeshis were not just suffering disproportionately from the virus in the UK. In Bangladesh, garment workers were being directly impacted by the UK lockdown as companies here cancelled contracts because their sales had slumped. I was part of the team assigned to report on the story. Being able to shine a light on how lockdown in the UK was leading to tribulation for some of the poorest people in the world felt like a very important story to share with our viewers.

I am still very much in touch with my Bangladeshi roots. I have family and friends there and am confident speaking the language. I have visited the country a number of times, most recently in December 2019 when I cultivated a number of relationships that would be beneficial for work. The connected digital world makes it easier to communicate with contacts regularly and some of these would prove to be very helpful for our story.

The president of the body that represents garment manufacturers in Bangladesh (BGMEA) told me the contract cancellations were decimating the industry that the country so heavily depends on, with millions of garment workers across the country, earning on average just £88 a month, being put out of work. A Bangladeshi Government minister urged the UK Government to intervene and help prevent mass factory closures.

But to really tell the story, I needed to find people in Bangladesh, garment workers, who had lost their jobs. I needed to find a camera operator who could film them as they told their stories. And I had to arrange to get those pictures back to London – all during Ramadan. My contacts led me to a camera operator who was up for the job. Because of the five-hour time difference, I started work at 4am, guiding him through his tasks for the day. We were able to interview two garment workers, translate what they said, and film a small protest as well as more general shots of Dhaka, including shots of the Rana Plaza memorial, which marks the tragedy of the 2013 garment factory collapse in which over 1,100 workers lost their lives.

The footage was needed for a report on our 6.30pm *Evening News* programme. It had already been an intense day for both myself and the camera operator in Bangladesh – especially since we were both fasting. So you might imagine just how high my heart rate spiked when at around 2pm UK time, with four and a half hours before we were on air, the camera operator told me that, with his current internet connection, it would take eight hours to complete the feed of the material. Thankfully, we managed to work out a system where he just sent clips of the most urgent footage so it arrived in London in time for our report.

In the end, ITV News ran two reports on two consecutive days. We heard from factory worker Kulsum Begum. She and her husband had been working at the same garment factory and both lost their jobs. They had earned £160 a month between them. She said she now worried about her daughter's education and looking after her parents. We also heard from Jannat Akhter, who worked for a factory that supplied UK supermarkets. Her factory closed on March 16th, leaving her out of work. Jannat's family of five depends on her income of £78 a month. She told ITV News, "if we don't have jobs we won't be able to pay the rent or feed ourselves."

I wanted to become a journalist to bring to the forefront under-represented voices, hold the powerful to account and have an impact. It felt like we were able to do all three things with these reports. To me, it still feels remarkable that we were able to speak to a government minister and other key stakeholders, find and film workers who had lost their jobs, film around the Bangladeshi capital and inside factories, all during a worldwide lockdown, all in such a quick time frame, and all directed from my garage.

Sweden: The Country that Kept Calm and Carried On

John Ray, Correspondent, ITV News

It was so quiet, I could hear my own footsteps echo round the cavern-ous hall. A few fellow travellers perched on otherwise empty rows of chairs. Like lost souls in a cathedral's pews, I thought, deep in silent contemplation long after the last benediction. Dearly beloved, why are we gathered here today?

Yes, Heathrow at the height of lockdown was a lonely place. Then again, this was how much of the world looked in late April. One exception was my destination. Sweden – the country that kept calm and carried on.

I found a strange land where the bars were open and couples smooched in parks bathed in early spring sunshine. There were chil-dren playing football and groups of young friends chatting on picnic blankets on the grass. If I make it sound like paradise, then that's sort of how it felt. Or maybe it was just the glow of a warmly remembered past. But it was also oddly unsettling. I was reminded how quickly we had all adapted to the new abnormal back home.

The journey out, my first foreign assignment since the lockdown, saw me in a nearly deserted plane from London to Helsinki. And then to Stockholm in an economy cabin so crowded I was almost sitting on the lap of the large man in the next seat while a crying baby in the row behind coughed intermittently down my neck.

Then, at my hotel, I shrank back when a waiter delivered dinner to my table. He felt uncomfortably close. And it was strange to stroll down a street full of shops that were actually open. With actual customers. I bought some clippers for my unkempt hair.

Sweden was an out-rider. No lockdown here. Instead, light touch regulation. Schools and businesses were open. Citizens were asked to keep a safe distance; but the police weren't rounding up those picnickers in the park. Really big mass gatherings were banned; but you could have a birthday party and invite up to 49 guests, if you had that many friends.

This grand design was the work of State Epidemiologist Anders Tegnell. At the time of our meeting, he'd become a bit of a celebrity. You could buy tee-shirts with his face emblazoned on the front. The idea, though never explicitly stated, was to aim for something like herd immunity. Without a vaccine, the disease was unstoppable. Better then to slow its progress while ensuring the economy lived to tell the tale. I asked Tegnell whether, as his critics claimed, this approach was a gamble.

"Definitely not," he replied. "We're trying to do the best we can with the knowledge we have. And so far, if you look at the projections done by a number of modellers, the Swedish model has worked a lot better than people would have believed. They said the Swedish healthcare system would collapse already a month ago. It did not. It keeps on working." But there was a price. And like the UK, it was being paid by the oldest and most vulnerable. Sweden's care homes were suffering an appalling rate of attrition. Even Tegnell admitted this was an area of failure.

Twenty-two leading academics had written an open letter lambasting what they called the "officials without talent" in charge of policy. One of the signatories was Dr Stefan Hanson, an infectious disease specialist. I met him on a day the spring sunshine and clear skies gave way to rain clouds and a blast of cold air. It fitted his mood. "When you look at the shops and the bars that are open, what is it you feel?" I asked. "I see the infection spreading," he said. "There's no doubt. And we're talking about human life, not just numbers. A lot of grandmothers and grandfathers have died and we think that should not have been necessary."

Compared to the UK, Sweden's death rate was low. But it was much higher than its Nordic neighbours. The odd Scandinavian out, and the only EU country not to impose wide-ranging and mandatory lockdowns. By contrast, Denmark, Finland and Norway went hard and early. The ironic reward for this paragon of social democratic virtue was to win the praise of conservative commentators in the UK and beyond.

Still, it wasn't entirely business as usual. The shops were open, but far from busy. And the news from the economic front was mixed. I met Carina McLane and her British husband, Mally, as they picked up their two young children from school. The family had recently relocated back to Carina's homeland. But like so many of the friends they'd left back in the UK, they'd been furloughed from their jobs. Yet Mally had no doubt where he'd prefer to be.

"Sweden is the better country to be in for the coronavirus crisis because life is going on pretty much as normal," he said. "It makes existing as a family and getting through this crisis just a little bit easier than it would be otherwise." Carina, though, was fretting about her grandfather. "He's eighty-nine years old and isolating at home. He doesn't have a lot of help around him. He's essentially on his own."

And so the debate raged. Were the famously risk-averse Swedes taking too great a chance? Professor Johan Giesecke is the former chief scientist for the European Centre for Disease Prevention and Control and a current advisor to the World Health Organization and the Swedish Government. We met after the regular morning meeting of experts at the medical university, the Karolinska Institute in Stockholm.

Coronavirus, he agreed, was a shape-shifting monster. "We now count more than 20 symptoms of the disease." And it was, he insisted, impossible to stop. Those countries who had minimised fatalities would inevitably find those numbers rising again once their lockdowns were lifted. "And you can't keep a democratic country in strict lockdown forever," he said. "Nor should you count the casualties until the battle is over." And that, he warned, would be a long time coming.

It's Good to Talk: Calls in a Crisis

Emily Kerr, Content Editor, ITV News Calendar

The soundtrack of the ITV Calendar newsroom is generally the constant ringing of telephones; landlines trilling on the desks, at least one mobile phone per journalist buzzing away, plus what we call the "bat line" with its piercingly urgent tone demanding instant communication between the newsdesk and the studio gallery when the programme is on air. On any one day working as news editor or programme editor, I will answer dozens of calls; the greeting, "Hello, *Calendar*," now so second-nature that I've been known to answer my home phone with the same phrase.

In a world of emails and social media, a telephone call helps to build that feeling of personal connection between individuals. Being a regional news programme, we have strong relationships with our local council and emergency services and with some we'll chat and ask after the family even though we've never met in person. Many of our viewers also feel that sense of association with our newsroom because they know they are speaking to people who, like them, live and work in Yorkshire and Lincolnshire.

During the pandemic I found that people were picking up the phone more often to speak to us, their local newsroom. With so many people isolated at home, calling the newsroom was one way to feel a link with the outside world. They ranged from emotional calls from the recently bereaved, to angry calls from people wanting to report their neighbour for buying non-essential shopping. When I answered the phone in the newsroom it was always with a sense of anticipation. There could be anyone at the other end of the line, and what they had to say could potentially influence our reporting.

By April 30th we'd settled into our strange new way of working at ITV News Calendar. Arriving in the newsroom and scrubbing down our desks and equipment with antibacterial wipes had become part of our normal morning routine, along with checking in with the other ITV regions and scanning through the local papers and websites for any stories that might have broken overnight. But the kind of telephone calls we were receiving were still anything but routine.

Among the people who chose to call our newsdesk that day were colleagues of a Yorkshire Ambulance Service worker who had died from coronavirus. You could hear the shock in their voices as they spoke of their affection and respect for their friend. As it was a Thursday night, they were planning to invite other emergency service workers to assemble outside their ambulance station. They were going to take a few precious minutes to clap and pay tribute to their co-worker before they once again went out on the road, putting themselves at risk to help others. They wanted us to film their tribute.

Sometimes there is a perception that the media can be intrusive, feeding off people's grief and encroaching on situations where they are not wanted. But speaking to the individuals who called from the ambulance service, it was clear that they saw us, their local newsroom, as a means of ensuring that their late colleague's contribution to the fight against the pandemic did not go unnoticed by the rest of the world. It was an honour that they chose to call the ITV Calendar newsroom to share their thoughts and pay tribute to their friend.

Another call was from a local care home for young disabled people. The carers were buzzing with excitement because they'd arranged a surprise for residents in the form of a visit from a fire engine while they did their weekly clap for key workers. In previous weeks they'd invited a DJ to play a set, and they had lots of plans up their sleeves for coming Thursdays. It was one of many conversations that highlighted to me how there were still moments of great joy and fun to be had even in the middle of a crisis.

But for many of our viewers the pandemic exacerbated problems they were already facing. That day in April was like many others in that several people rang to tell us about the challenges they were dealing with. There was a social-housing tenant who called because they had an infestation of rats. In lockdown they were trapped at home with the vermin, unable to get answers about when someone could help them. Another person rang on their landline. They didn't have internet banking or a mobile phone and, as they were shielding at home, they couldn't visit their local post office to take out the cash they needed to pay for their vital supplies, nor could they look online for the latest coronavirus guidance. People who were falling through the cracks wanted to tell their stories to us, wanted us to give them a voice in a situation where they felt powerless.

That day was Captain Tom Moore's 100th birthday. A proud Yorkshireman, and a man people in Yorkshire are rightly proud of, his fundraising efforts moved several people to call our newsroom to express their admiration for everything he had achieved. They wanted to make sure their birthday wishes were passed on to "our Captain Tom". It was lovely to hear how his positive attitude and determination were inspiring people to adopt a similar approach to their own situations.

Answering the phone in the ITV Calendar newsroom during the pandemic felt like a responsibility but also an immense privilege. I must have spoken to hundreds of people, each one a unique and interesting experience. While communication moves ever more online, the conversations I had on the telephone during lockdown made me appreciate how that old-fashioned way of communication will always be at the heart of our news operation. It's good to talk!

A Musical Surprise

Rajiv Popat, Reporter, ITV News Central

Covid-survivor Barbara Briley is someone you might call a "fighter"; the 86-year-old pensioner has lived through the war, and has had open heart surgery, as well as two replacement knees and hips. Her family describe her as the bionic woman. But she wasn't expected to pull through a long stay in hospital with coronavirus, and amazed everyone when she made a full recovery.

I first met Barbara when she returned home for the first time in five weeks. She thanked NHS workers and her family for their support. When I asked what she had missed the most while in hospital, she told me "her cat and listening to André Rieu." The Dutch violinist is a classical music superstar, selling many millions of CDs and DVDs and filling giant venues around the world. Barbara is a huge fan and had already seen him in concert twice. She told me her ultimate dream would be to meet the musician she affectionately calls "her man".

As it happened, André Rieu was due to perform later in the year at the Motorpoint Arena in Nottingham and the team there saw our report on ITV News Central. They got in touch with André Rieu and he agreed to record a get-well message for his devoted fan. Our plan was to go back to see Barbara and surprise her with the video message. We needed a reason to film her again without giving the game away and her daughter Karen agreed to help. But she broke down in tears when she told me, "I can't tell you what this will mean to Mum. It won't just make her day, it'll make her year!"

On April 24th, my camera operator and I arrived at Barbara's house in Nottingham to set up our cameras in her garden. While we were discussing the logistics of filming, Barbara, eager to look her best, was busy getting her hair done, oblivious to the real reason we were there.

She thought it was to follow up from our first interview and find out how she was getting on, one week after returning home from hospital.

I'd been looking forward to meeting the feisty pensioner with a zest for life and a canny sense of humour once again. It was hot and sunny as Barbara emerged from her lounge, hair looking immaculate, ready for our socially distanced chat. I began the interview by asking how she'd been feeling and what the past week had been like. Barbara was expecting to look at the report from the previous week – that was when I turned to my laptop, told Barbara there was something I wanted to show her, and played the video message from André Rieu.

It was a beautiful message; personal, engaging and genuine. He started by saying: "Dear Barbara, you're eighty-six and what an amazing story that you've recovered from Covid-19, congratulations! What's your secret? To be honest, I know what it is. I've been told you love music, especially the waltz." I can still picture the look on her face. Complete and utter disbelief. Barbara's hands were over her mouth as she whispered and gasped, "ooh" and, "I can't believe it!" The entire message was around 45 seconds long and he ended it by sending her a personal invitation to join him at the Nottingham concert.

Barbara was quite literally lost for words. Just over a week earlier, she'd been lying in a hospital bed, fighting for her life. Now, she was happily sitting upright listening to her musical hero call her "Dear Barbara" and giving her a VIP invitation to see him in concert. During the interview, she told me "she couldn't get over what she'd just seen," and that her friends would be "green with envy." That video message will be treasured by Barbara.

The next time I meet her will be at the concert hall where she'll see "Her Man" up close and personal – the next episode in the touching tale of a woman who came close to losing everything but is now looking forward to waltzing the night away.

The Light That Means Hope

James Webster, Presenter, ITV News Channel TV

There should be a buzz in the air and knots in stomachs. For amateur actors, it's the night they've been preparing for; the opening night of one of the biggest productions on stage in Jersey this year. But tonight the seats in Jersey Opera House are unoccupied. There's no excited hubbub from the auditorium. The bars are empty. The refreshments stall is shut. *Ghost: The Musical* has been cancelled, and like every other arts venue around the British Isles, this theatre is closed. Just one lonely light bulb illuminates the stage.

It's 18 months since I moved to Jersey to present the local ITV News. To make new friends I decided to revisit my love of drama and discovered a vibrant amateur drama scene. With fewer professional touring shows than other parts of the UK, it's down to large-scale amateur productions to entertain audiences here instead.

For many of those involved it's so much more than just a hobby. It's their lives. Cast members might give up three or four nights a week to rehearsals. Others will spend entire weekends making scenery and props. None of them, hearing news reports in January of a strange new virus in China, could ever have imagined it would take all of that from them.

I had been rehearsing *Noises Off*, a calamity-filled farce, with a growing sense of futility. I didn't believe the show would make it onto the stage in April. In the end we didn't even have a "goodbye" moment. Lockdown intervened and we were left in the limbo of having scenery built and painted, a play half rehearsed. There was no doubt about it. This time, the show could not go on.

The same was true at theatres and venues up and down the country. This was an entire industry forcibly shut down with recovery likely to take a long time. Theatres will not be able to reopen the day that restrictions are eased. Shows are not staged that quickly. Cast members may have prior commitments. Productions will have to be re-rehearsed. Some may never reopen and social distancing could make it impossible to sell enough seats to cover costs.

And through all this it felt like there was more of a need for arts and culture than ever before. People in lockdown turned to the arts in so many unusual ways: celebrities performing from home, videos of people singing on balconies, previous theatre shows streamed online. It felt like many were craving entertainment and looking to the arts to help them cope with isolation. You could sense on social media that people were searching for entertainment as a mental escape from the current situation.

In the UK the government would be asked within weeks to step in with urgent funding following fears that venues such as Shakespeare's Globe could run out of money. London's theatres are estimated to generate £133 million in VAT for the Treasury each year, yet industry experts were warning the West End could stay closed until next year.

For our report on how the coronavirus crisis was affecting local drama groups we went to film inside Jersey Opera House. That's when we discovered a little-known theatrical tradition: that one solaritary light bulb burning on stage as it had done since the venue closed for lockdown.

Those of a more superstitious nature say that the "ghost light", as it's known, is to ward off the ghosts that are said to inhabit many old theatres when they are in darkness. The more practical explanation is that the bulb shows the edge of the stage so anyone entering the building doesn't accidentally fall. But there is another reason, as Chris Wink, Technical Manager at the Opera House, explained to us: "Our ghost light is burning brightly on stage, downstage centre as it should be. It means hope. It means that theatre will come back. It means that entertainment will be back on this stage and that's the most important thing. It's that hope."

Timeline

May

1 Health Secretary Matt Hancock says the 100,000-tests-a-day target by end of April was met

5 Trials of an NHS contact tracing app start on the Isle of Wight

7 Many newspapers wrongly focus on the possibility of lockdown easing from May 11th

8–10   VE Day, and bank holiday weekend

10 Prime Minister Boris Johnson announces a plan for easing the lockdown in England. The message is changed to "Stay Alert, Control the Virus, Save Lives". The devolved governments of Scotland, Wales and Northern Ireland say their message will not change

23–25   Bank holiday weekend

23 It is reported that Dominic Cummings, senior advisor to the Prime Minister, drove 250 miles to his parents' farm in Durham, while his wife showed virus symptoms, during lockdown

25 Dominic Cummings holds a press conference in the Downing Street rose garden

26 Protests over the death of George Floyd in Minneapolis begin and quickly spread in support of the Black Lives Matter movement, raising concerns about mass gatherings

28 The last weekly Clap for Carers

VE Day in Warwickshire

Charlotte Cross, Reporter, ITV News Central

Being a journalist is a tricky career path to choose. It's highly competitive, often difficult, and involves both long hours and abuse from those who regard you as the enemy – either for reporting things they would rather not be reported, or for not reporting things they believe ought to be. But it's also an immense privilege. Our viewers and our readers invite us into their lives during the day, and into their living rooms each evening; trusting us to give them not only a window onto the rest of the world, but an insight into corners of it they may never have otherwise encountered. Amidst the online abuse and the "fake news" accusations (oh, for that phrase to have never been invented!) it can be easy to forget quite what an honour it is. And then, sometimes, you're reminded in the most wonderful way.

It was May 8th – the 75th anniversary of VE Day. The sky was a glorious blue, the sun smiling down on a country in the midst of strict lockdown. In some areas, the sound of prosecco corks popping could be heard well before the clock struck midday. For weeks, we had seen the death toll climb ever higher and the impact on the economy was looking grim. I had personally reported on warnings over increasing instances of domestic abuse, and growing concerns over the disproportionate impact coronavirus was having on BAME communities.

But our producers had also been working hard to find uplifting stories to break up what could easily have been an endless stream of misery. When the early May bank holiday rolled around and communities seized the opportunity for a celebration, I was among those rostered to work for ITV News Central and was delighted to be dispatched to one of the many socially distanced street parties being staged across the region.

A glorious event it turned out to be too. Residents along this particular small cul-de-sac in Warwickshire had spent several days creating homemade bunting and decorations, each household setting up tables and chairs in their front gardens and driveways for an afternoon tea with their neighbours at a distance. Their excitement at being interviewed for the news was palpable. My arrival was heralded by the organisers via loudspeaker, and one of the neighbours asked me to pass on her thanks to the team for the "wonderful" work ITV News Central was doing. "It can't be easy," she said. "But we're really grateful." As well as keeping viewers updated on the situation across the Midlands, worthy of special mention were the "good news bits at the end", which, she said, always made her smile. This alone buoyed me for the morning's work, and once my camera operator for the day had set up, we began our business of interviewing some of those joining the celebrations, including a 97-year-old veteran who had marked the original VE Day in Coventry 75 years ago.

Truth be told, we spent far more time filming there than a two-minute report required. But the lockdown tales of how this small neighbourhood had pulled together and grown closer, helping those shielding and organising weekly driveway community bingo nights and various other activities, were so heartwarming it was difficult to tear ourselves away. We wanted to do them justice, ensuring the camera caught the fun and upbeat atmosphere even while people were confined within their own property boundaries.

When we finally, regretfully, decided it was time to leave, I made my way to the organiser's driveway once more to thank him for inviting us along. "Charlotte and Daniel are going now," he announced via the loudspeaker as we walked back down the street towards our cars. And out of nowhere, someone began clapping; within seconds, the whole street was clapping and cheering us as we bade our farewells. It took me completely aback; to call it "unexpected" feels like an understatement. I've been a journalist now for more than a decade, across newspapers, online and television – and not only was this a career first, I'm not sure I've ever been more surprised in my entire life. "We're journalists – we're used to being booed, not applauded," my colleague joked to one of those we passed. I'm glad I have him as a witness. It was so surreal, so wonderfully abnormal, that I'm sure others would suspect I'd fabricated it without a second source to corroborate the story. It didn't last long, but the sound rang in my ears as I took a moment to reflect; the sun warming my head and shoulders, the sharp sting of happy tears prickling behind my eyes.

It wasn't the first time I was pushed to the brink of tears during the pandemic, nor would it be the last; more often than not under circumstances far sadder and more troubling. But whenever I began to struggle on later days, I thought back to that occasion and took heart in the relationship our team had managed to build with our local communities from afar.

From bringing them the difficult latest developments at the top of the programme, down to the good news bits at the end.

Liberation Day in Guernsey

Gary Burgess, Reporter, ITV News Channel TV

It was early January and I just couldn't see the light at the end of the tunnel. My rational brain knew I was two months into three months of chemotherapy, that I was well past the halfway point, and that the end was on the horizon. But in that moment, I couldn't summon the imagination to know that the darkest hour was just before dawn. I couldn't, frankly, imagine getting through the day.

Last autumn, I'd been told my cancer had come back. Five little nasties growing around my trachea, oesophagus and lungs, almost exactly 20 years on from my original cancer diagnosis. Back then surgery and chemotherapy did the trick. Four years ago two rounds of further surgery had also worked. But this time it was considered much more serious.

I'm telling you this because as I sit here in lockdown in the beautiful Channel Island of Jersey, I have already been through months of enforced lockdown for a very different reason. I assumed it would set me up well for having my freedom suddenly taken away by the coronavirus crisis. But it's not quite been like that. I've personally found lockdown tough but being a journalist has helped a lot.

Jersey went into lockdown on March 30th. Across the water in Guernsey the approach was a little different. The lockdown and the closing of borders happened earlier there. But the effect of both islands' approaches has been broadly similar. There have been a couple of hundred positive cases identified and the hospitals have never been stretched.

I've been working from home while my immune system restores itself. It means my connection with the world has been through video calls – and I'd never even heard of Zoom before this pandemic! As well

214

as my regular live reports into our 6pm programme, where I bring viewers highlights from government press conferences, I've also been filming a series called *Gary's House Call*.

The idea is really simple. I make a video call to a different family somewhere in the Channel Islands to see how they're getting on. I then ask them to film some footage of their home life, whether that's working, schooling, cooking or playing, and then it's all knitted together into a lovely piece of television that's really helping to show the best of people at the toughest of times; how, throughout the lockdown, community spirit has been in abundance.

My favourite House Call happened on May 9th. Why do I remember that date so readily? It's Jersey and Guernsey's Liberation Day, our annual celebration of the day in 1945 that the islands were freed from Nazi occupation during the Second World War. The island of Sark was liberated a day later. Alderney, by the way, celebrates Homecoming Day in December as the whole population was evacuated and took many months to return.

So, on May 9th, I linked up with the Duport family in Guernsey. Debbie and Clive are grandparents, who had their children and grandchildren with them for Liberation Day. But that was just the start of it.

They rallied their entire estate to take to their front yards and gardens to create all the atmosphere and spirit of a normal Liberation Day, while keeping each household at least two metres away from each other at all times – carefully observing the letter and spirit of the lockdown laws.

They dressed in wartime costume, they played the classic songs (think Vera Lynn and Glenn Miller on a loop) and they flew union flags with pride, alongside the Guernsey flag and no shortage of colourful bunting to remind themselves of the hardships their predecessors faced for five brutal years and the joy they experienced when it all came to a sudden end.

They sang, they laughed, they even staged an estate-wide household treasure hunt by WhatsApp. Ingenuity and imagination proved lockdown didn't need to mean separation. They all shared a special moment, but in a way not seen in the 75 years the islands have been marking Liberation Day.

And that's the day that's stuck with me above all others. It's a reminder that the lockdown rules don't mean life grinding to a halt, don't mean people being completely separated from one another, and don't mean the things that mattered previously can't still be given the prominence they deserve.

As an ITV News journalist, it's my privilege on a daily basis to shine a light on the lives of islanders, on their hopes, their fears, their victories and their challenges, to help us all get a better understanding of the weird world we find ourselves in, and to bring people closer together through their television sets.

And while the experiences of those who lived through the oppression of the occupation is a world away from the lockdown caused by this pandemic, and while this lockdown is very different to the lockdown I experienced during the course of my chemotherapy, the common thread is hope.

Hope that better times will come, hope that we will see the best of people even in the toughest times, hope that those in charge will find a way for us all to resume some semblance of normality, soon.

In January, for me, that ability to see the light at the end of the tunnel had gone. But, eventually, it came. Right now, thanks to the connections I make on a daily basis through my journalism, that light may be a distant one, but it still shines bright.

Two Tales from Teesside

Rachel Bullock, Reporter, ITV News Tyne Tees

In Redcar there's a blast furnace that made steel for decades. It's as much a part of this seaside town as its racecourse and lemon top ice-creams. But after a bitter fight to try to save steelmaking here, this mighty old furnace has been cold now for five years. Its loss has left a sad legacy; steelmaking families severed from the industry that had defined them for generations. An identity swept away overnight, leaving behind proud, hard-working people in economic hardship.

It was in the shadow of this industrial giant that I met the family who, for me, defined an unforgettable reality of the coronavirus crisis. It was the week beginning May 11th. Days earlier, the Prime Minister had eased lockdown in England into phase two, signalling a little more freedom ahead; a light, albeit dim and fragile, was flickering.

The father of this family was pale and quiet; he'd just spent five hard weeks in hospital fighting the virus. His wife had cared for their seven children throughout. But I wasn't there to report on the father's survival against the odds. It was to report on a new scheme to loan laptops to children from disadvantaged backgrounds who would otherwise have no way of accessing online school work from home. A similar government project had been introduced, but delays meant children weren't getting the devices quickly enough and vital learning time was passing. So private companies stepped in, sweeping their cupboards of old devices and passing them on to families who needed them. This family was one of them.

Of the couple's seven children, aged from three to their early twenties, five of them were at school. "I was mainly worried about our Stephanie," their mother told me. Stephanie is 14, and desperately wants to become a lawyer. Meeting her, I could see no reason why not.

She was clearly very bright and, perhaps far more important than that, determined. Stephanie had carefully chosen GCSE subjects to support her way to a future law degree. But just five months into the course the schools were closed and her only way of keeping up was by accessing her work online. Her mother explained that money for a laptop was out of the question. Stephanie had tried to use her mother's phone, sharing with her brothers and sisters. "A total waste of time," she said.

We filmed Stephanie working on the new laptop as her little sister bounced around on a trampoline in the garden. Their mother looked on proudly, relieved that her daughter was finally getting help to work towards her dream. It was then that it struck me, the stark reality of lockdown laid bare in this small garden in Redcar. I'd reported *literally* the night before on how this virus doesn't discriminate. But of course it does. It had discriminated against this clever girl who, without school, would inevitably fall behind. A girl whose only chance during the many weeks of school closure was the charitable loan of a laptop. And she was one of the lucky ones.

Later from home I Skype-interviewed the leader of the partnership running the laptop loan scheme and listened as he reeled off demands. "Many more devices needed; businesses please pass on second hand laptops to us." I squirmed as he referred to the children of better-off parents now being able to unfairly get ahead, my own young daughters quietly working in another room on their iPads.

Often in journalism you get a glut of similar stories within a few weeks and this was one of those times. Soon after reporting on the family in Redcar I visited a school in Stockton; again in a deprived area. The story here was astonishing. Many of this school's children were entitled to free school meals, which they were missing because the school was closed. The head teacher was worried that some of them might be going hungry at home. And so Sue, their school cook of 25 years, had come into school every day for the previous nine weeks to make packed lunches. Volunteers then delivered the lunches to homes where they were needed, and Sue assured me that they were needed. She was making an average of 130 packed lunches every day. Sandwiches and a proper school pudding – white icing with pink sprinkles on yellowy soft, buttery sponge. "Because they like it?" I asked. "Because it fills them up," she replied. I asked her if she was tired because of such a demand on her time. "It's why I'm here," she told me.

Of course kindness and strength come in many forms. I really don't know if Sue considers herself extraordinarily kind, if Stephanie fully recognises her ambition and intelligence, or even if the partnership that provided that laptop will ever know what it meant to her family. I just know that both these stories here on Teesside provoked an admiration in me that I truly didn't expect to find during this crisis.

I'd anticipated reporting stories of people breaking lockdown laws, or medical breakthroughs, or people surviving against overwhelming odds. And while it certainly has included those stories, none have meant quite as much to me as the quiet, dignified strength that I've found in the most challenged areas of the patch where I work, live and love. Those with the least giving the most.

It brings to mind an interview with the British journalist who broke the story of the last defining moment in world history. In 1939 Clare Hollingworth saw German tanks rolling into Poland and reported that war had started. Many years later she was asked if she'd ever feared that Germany would win the war. "No," she said "because the Nazis didn't care about people."

This virus, our new invisible enemy, doesn't care about people either. So what a privilege it's been to report such acts of love and connection by people to defeat its awful impact. I've used two examples here, but so many more have gone and will go unseen by television cameras, unheard by our microphones. Please know that it's there, try to share some of it around and perhaps, perhaps, it will help us win.

The Fears of a Community in a Virus Hotspot

Ronke Phillips, Senior Correspondent, ITV News London

It was an assignment that felt personal. As a Black journalist I knew I would be telling the story from my heart.

We were seven weeks into the crisis, and it was already becoming clear that Covid-19 was hitting Black, Asian and minority ethnic communities harder than any other. Every day the newspapers and television bulletins were showing the names and photographs of the latest victims to die from the disease, and as I watched I was overwhelmed by the numbers from the BAME community.

Then the Office for National Statistics (ONS) confirmed what had been suspected. Black people were four times more likely to die from Covid-19 than white people.

When Newham was named as one of the London boroughs with the highest mortality rates from the virus, it was no shock. Newham has the most diverse population profile of any local authority in the country. 78 percent of residents are from ethnic minority communities.

I have been to Newham on countless occasions, but this time driving through the area felt truly different. There were fewer people on the streets than normal because of the lockdown, but what was almost palpable was the fear in the eyes of those who had ventured out.

"People are anxious," the mayor Rokhsana Fiaz told me. She was elected two years ago and has lived in the borough her entire life. "Every day we hear about a Covid death. Everyone seems to know a friend, a colleague, a relative, a loved one who has been infected or died. While the pandemic has spread widely across the UK, it has taken a huge toll on this part of east London and the ONS figures clearly amplify the disproportionate impact that Covid-19 has had on

Black and ethnic minority communities. Little has been done over the years and now is the time for money and resources to be poured into areas like this. Enough of the talk, we need action to save lives."

Interviewing people about the death of a loved one is never easy. Thousands have died in this pandemic. Our job as journalists is to ensure we don't treat the victims as statistics. They are wives, aunts, sisters, daughters, brothers, fathers, uncles. Each was loved and will be missed, and each has their own story.

Bob Kulothungan was still emotionally raw after losing his beloved wife, Louisa Rajakumari, to the disease. The couple had met 30 years ago in southern India. Bob would cycle past Louisa as she waited for the school bus and wooed her with poetry and roses from his mother's garden.

62-year-old Louisa was a teacher at Kingsford Community School in Beckton. She was one of six teachers at the school to contract Covid-19 and although she was taken to hospital, at first her symptoms didn't appear too serious.

Bob told me: "The last time I spoke to Louisa was on a video call. After that her condition deteriorated and they had to put her into an induced coma and onto a ventilator. Her breathing got worse and on the second day after her admission the consultant called and told me it wasn't looking good because almost 80 percent of her lung cells had been affected by the Covid."

Louisa died on April 17th. "I still miss her voice and even her nagging. She would always ask me if I really needed to have that second beer," Bob says bravely. The family allowed Louisa's funeral to be live-streamed on social media and thousands of people from the school and community joined to pay their respects.

Louisa's death came almost a decade after Newham was in the news as the main host borough for the 2012 Olympic Games. The legacy promised was better jobs, housing and quality of life. Parts of the borough have been regenerated and house prices have rocketed for some but the reality for many has not changed.

The borough's deprivation and diversity made it particularly vulnerable to Covid-19. More than half the children live in poverty. The borough has one of the highest rates of households living in temporary accommodation in England. Newham has long been in the top ten local authorities in the country with the highest levels of health deprivation.

So the council knew from the start it was facing a health emergency. The vulnerable would need shielding. Pensioners, families and youngsters would be desperate for support. From the outset, more than 20,000 residents at risk were identified.

At Curwen Primary School in Plaistow I watched as an army of volunteer staff, furloughed from their council jobs, packed food and hygiene products into parcels for those in need. Already they had delivered 10,000 tins of soup, 4,000 litres of milk, and over 3 tonnes of potatoes.

These volunteers told me about the families they were helping: parents whose weekly budget could not stretch to feeding hungry children now at home all day; pensioners who couldn't get out and didn't have friends or relatives to shop for them; others who had chronic medical needs. Each one was in desperate need.

"If it wasn't for us and these food parcels, people would go hungry," they said.

Dr Muhammed Naqvi is the lead GP for Newham. His practice is in a highly populated area of Forest Gate and looks after 16,000 patients. "Deprivation, overcrowding and all the other issues that come with poverty are the reality in an area like this. Newham is also the worst place in the UK for air pollution. We have lots of patients who have cardiovascular and respiratory problems as well as diabetes. It would be far too simplistic to say any one of these is the main reason behind the high death rate, but as soon as we realised a lot of people in the borough could become infected we introduced measures to try and keep them safe. We worked with the council to identify those most in need and asked some people who hadn't even been contacted by the government to shield at home."

David Lammy, the MP for Tottenham, also with a high death rate during the pandemic, called for more research. He told me: "There are definitely going to be multiple factors that affect why we're seeing such high numbers in Black communities dying. What we have to communicate quickly to communities is what those factors are. What are the risk factors? How do we protect our loved ones?"

My television news report on Newham was also posted on the ITV London website. It drew many comments, particularly from the Black community who were concerned after hearing rumours of a lifting of the lockdown. They were the ones who would be returning to their front-line jobs and felt their vulnerability. How could they protect themselves and their loved ones, they asked? The online comments mirrored the faces I had seen that morning. They were frightened.

Discrimination on the Frontline

Roohi Hasan, Producer, ITV News

I became a journalist to try to tell untold stories and shine a light on injustices both at home and abroad. What I didn't realise is sometimes those stories come to light when you aren't chasing them.

The coronavirus crisis was brought home to me in the early weeks when I started waking to news almost daily of someone I knew dying, always from Asian and Muslim communities. I interviewed an Asian doctor friend of mine at one of the worst-hit hospitals in the country. He described the situation inside as "carnage" and told me he hadn't seen anything like it in his career.

It appeared that the virus had a disproportionate impact on Black, Asian and minority ethnic communities. And then it was apparent that the majority of those dying within the NHS were from those same communities and I wanted to know why. I thought the best way to find out was to ask NHS workers from those communities why they thought more of their BAME colleagues were dying than their white counterparts.

After discussions with Black, Asian and minority ethnic medics, I wrote and distributed a survey through large medical organisations such as the General Medical Council, as well as leading medical groups representing those communities. I was hoping for perhaps 200 responses but in fact we received over 2,000 replies from health workers of different ethnicities and roles within the NHS. That made it the biggest survey of its kind.

One theme was evident from the start: our respondents, medics and healthcare workers from Black, Asian and minority ethnic communities, told us that "systemic discrimination" on the basis of race on the frontline may have been a factor in the disproportionate number of their colleagues dying after contracting the virus.

Comments revealed that staff felt fearful in the most at-risk front-line roles, while others felt unfairly deployed and at an increased risk of infection, with many feeling unheard, and some driven to leave their jobs.

Perhaps most shocking, 50 percent of respondents felt discriminatory behaviour had played a role in the high death toll, with one in five claiming to have experienced it personally.

There is "systemic discrimination at the frontline – BAME staff being disproportionately allocated to Covid wards," said one.

Comments like this were common: "All BAME nurses allocated to red wards and my white colleagues are constantly in green wards."

"Snowy white mountain tops. Many of the white doctors are in management positions leaving more BAME on the coal face."

"It feels as if we have been assigned to the role of foot soldiers without adequate support or protection."

It was clear that many welcomed the opportunity of a confidential platform to talk about what they were seeing, experiencing, feeling and fearing; a platform they did not feel they had at work: "Not feeling heard, or ignored"; "My concerns and views have been aggressively dismissed."

As a journalist reading these comments, I realised we had uncovered an important story. As a fellow human it was sad to read experience after experience of such palpable fear, especially as a person from an immigrant background myself.

85 percent of respondents said they were more scared as a result of the disproportionate deaths of Black and Asian minority ethnic medics. One worker described their work as "absolute hell" and said they were "extremely fearful". Another respondent said those medics had been going to work "knowing they are on the firing line."

One person wrote: "We have been so scared . . . personal death has hit us hard while doing a job we love. Some of us have an entire family of front-line workers."

We continued to follow the story and, over the course of our regular reporting, built trust with BAME medical organisations, as well as individual doctors and nurses, who were grateful for our work, which, they felt, was thorough and sensitive.

A few weeks after our survey, a Public Health England review appeared to corroborate our findings. It said: "Stakeholders pointed to racism and discrimination experienced by communities and more specifically by BAME key workers as a root cause affecting health, and exposure risk, and disease progression risk."

But Black, Asian and minority ethnic group leaders expressed "upset" and "confusion" at the review, telling me they felt it was a "lost opportunity for addressing the unfairness and disproportionality" of deaths. One said: "The toothless report has turned out to be a damp squib. Another nail in the coffin for equality and transparency."

The overwhelming hope of those I spoke to was that tangible progress in righting the wrongs of what they see as discrimination within the NHS could be made as a result of the coronavirus crisis. I am humbled and honoured that so many dozens of Britain's Black and Asian minorities, people I have never met, trusted me with their concerns. It helped us do what we do best at ITV News, tell stories with real people's experiences at their heart.

Don't We Control Wales As Well?

Adrian Masters, Political Editor, ITV News Cymru Wales

It was a very frustrated motorist in the Brecon Beacons who was trying to understand what the police officer was patiently explaining to him. The man had driven for over an hour from the west of England in order to swim in the ice-cold pools at Ystradfellte and enjoy the picturesque waterfalls. He even had his wetsuit, as he showed to the officer and the ITV Wales camera operated by Tim Ward. He and my colleague Hannah Thomas had been watching Dyfed Powys Police attempt to enforce Wales' lockdown rules on the first weekend of significant difference from the rules in England.

There was no malice in the young man, no anti-Welsh arrogance. He just didn't know that things were different on this side of the border. As he put it to the officer, "So even though Boris says you can go where you want, do what you want . . .?"

"Yes, that's England."

"But don't we control Wales as well? Because it doesn't say that bit on the news, that you cannot drive here. And then to end up getting a fine! You should be like, mate, and we should be like – oh right, let's go home. Wasted two and a half hours."

It certainly was a wasted two and a half hours for him and, yes, he was fined but I'm fairly sure he wasn't the only person to have asked similar questions. There have been a number of times when I've imagined hearing the words "Don't we control Wales as well?" echoing in all sorts of offices and Zoom meetings.

A couple of weeks earlier there'd been incredulity at the idea that the governments of Wales, Scotland and Northern Ireland would take significantly different approaches towards lockdown restrictions to that of the UK Government for rules in England. After all, the four governments had gone into lockdown on March 23rd together and, barring a few gripes and very minor differences, had renewed the same lockdown rules on April 16th.

The four-nation approach to taking decisions had been praised by many, criticised by some and had surprised others, including me. I've been reporting for far too many years on the differences of devolution and have seen the whole range of tensions it can bring. I've become used to being exasperated when politicians and some in the UK media get it wrong either wilfully or by mistake. I've seen how politicians on all sides can exaggerate devolution differences to suit their own agendas.

So I took it as a sign of how serious this situation was that four governments led by five different political parties were able to put aside their differences in order to try to combat the coronavirus pandemic. Money flowed from London to Cardiff – more than £2bn extra at the time of writing – with few of the squabbles that usually involves. Welsh ministers moved quickly to match schemes being announced in England with little of the usual reluctance they show at following suit.

When I was still attending socially-distanced press conferences at the Welsh Government building in the centre of Cardiff in person, I was surprised to see uniformed military personnel standing around and chatting. Perhaps unsettling to see in peacetime, but also visible proof of the four-nation approach. Welsh ministers had requested and received the help of the military in working out the logistics of delivering personal protective equipment and, later, in trying to sort out some of the problems getting tests delivered.

I don't want to overstate the differences. It's true, as many have said, that cooperation has never been as close. What's more, differences between the nations aren't necessarily a problem, even if they do cause some temporary confusion and frustration. After all, we're used to navigating different parking rules in different towns and cities on different days. And there was always going to be divergence between the nations as the lockdowns ended.

What shouldn't and needn't have happened was for there to be such a stumble at such an important time: during the build-up to the second lockdown review that the governments were legally obliged to conduct on May 7th. Miscommunications and missed opportunities in the week or so before and after that date left both governments looking as if they weren't talking or listening to each other. And it led to a long bank holiday weekend of unnecessary confusion for the public. What surprised me was that the warning signs were there. From my privileged point of view I could see it unfolding in slow motion even if some of those involved couldn't or wouldn't admit that it was happening.

By Friday May 1st it had become clear to me that the four governments weren't communicating well. First Minister Mark Drakeford said in a radio interview that "a plan that comes like Moses coming down from the mountain is not going to work." It's difficult sometimes to decode the First Minister's softly spoken aphorisms but someone who knows him well helped me by messaging to say: "They won't push him around Adrian. He's a lovely man but he has a core of steel as they're about to discover."

The UK Government was also frustrated. I was told there was a feeling that ministers and officials from Wales, Scotland and Northern Ireland seemed to have little recognition of the economic harms prolonged lockdown could cause, dismissing them as Tories wanting to reopen golf courses.

Following a weekend of briefing and counter briefing, on Monday May 4th I was saying online and on air, "don't expect lockdown to end on Thursday." There'd been a consistent note of caution in briefings from the Prime Minister's official spokesman as well as in Welsh and Scottish Government press conferences.

Even at this stage senior figures in all four governments weren't overly worried about potential differences because they thought, with some justification, that by the end of the week, they'd all settle on pretty much the same cautious changes.

But there wasn't much conversation, and there wasn't much time. As late as Tuesday the 5th there was a phone call between the First Minister, Chancellor of the Duchy of Lancaster Michael Gove and the Welsh Secretary, Simon Hart.

Newspaper headlines such as "Hurrah! Lockdown freedom beckons" on Thursday May 7th could have been the product of briefings or wishful thinking. Certainly official briefings from Number 10 continued to downplay any changes due in the Prime Minister's planned statement.

The first of two Welsh cabinet meetings ended around lunchtime and after it a spokesperson said crossly: "Some reporting in today's newspapers is confusing and risks sending mixed messages to people across the UK. The First Minister of Wales will announce the outcome of the Cabinet's decision in due course. Our message for this bank holiday remains; Stay at Home, Protect the NHS, Save Lives."

That afternoon the Prime Minister spoke to the First Ministers for the first time since he returned to work. But to head off accusations of lack of engagement, the Wales Office pointed out that it was one of a series of ministerial and official phone calls. The official account of the call from Number 10 acknowledged for the first time that the Prime Minister expected there to be differences of approach: "He reiterated his commitment to continuing our UK-wide approach to tackling coronavirus, even if different parts of the UK begin to move at slightly different speeds. Those decisions will be made based on the science for each nation."

Having waited to hear what Boris Johnson had to say, Welsh ministers held their second cabinet that evening. They made it clear they would not do anything that would risk the "R" rate escalating. There'd be no "Hurrah! Lockdown freedom beckons" headlines in Wales.

While they were talking, I spoke to the Welsh Secretary Simon Hart via Zoom from his home in Pembrokeshire. "I hesitate to say this," he told me. "But I think the PM's announcement over the weekend is going to be a very cautious one. Nobody wants to rush this. Nobody wants to risk triggering a second spike. Nobody wants to go through all of this horrendous agony again."

But he also made what seemed to me the first acknowledgement from the UK Government that ministers in London (or wherever they were locked down) may not have been in lockstep with ministers in Cardiff.

"I'm hoping we can operate alongside the Welsh Government and take the Welsh Government with us as far as it is possible to do so," he said. "I think it would be a pity if we can't because I think it will lead to some confusion and potentially some sort of economic consequences to that too."

It was a bank holiday on Friday May 8th, but that didn't mean a rest for anyone in Welsh politics.

Michael Gove called the First Minister to talk about the imminent announcements. Then at 12.30pm the First Minister made his announcement. Lockdown would continue for another three weeks. No change to the rules. No easing of lockdown.

And certainly no new message. On the morning of Sunday May 10th, it was being widely reported that the UK Government would be changing its message to "Stay Alert. Control the Virus. Save Lives." Not in Wales and Scotland. A Welsh Government source who was eating a croissant from a Cardiff Tesco Extra told me between mouthfuls that it was "not a UK slogan. Ours remains 'Stay Home, Save Lives.'"

After a meeting of his cabinet, Boris Johnson chaired a meeting of COBRA, in which the First Ministers took part. But it was the first since April 16th and they'd made their announcements.

In the end the differences were relatively minor. When he made his statement at 7pm Boris Johnson was as cautious as the First Ministers had been, even with the changed message.

But a week or so of misjudgements and misunderstandings on both sides had nearly brought the four-nation approach to an end. And it would happen again. In July the UK Government announced its plans for "air bridges" but without first gaining the support of the devolved governments, who would have to implement changes to the quarantine rules. It sparked another unnecessary argument over something all four governments were actually prepared to agree on.

But behind such high-profile fallings-out, officials continued to talk and the Chief Medical Officers of all four nations continued to work closely together to agree the UK's alert level.

Let's be positive. Maybe the crisis has brought the devolved UK to a more realistic and sustainable position. One in which differences are acknowledged and dealt with rather than ignored. That might be healthier in the long term for the way the governments manage their dysfunctional relationships.

How To Stay Open When You're Closed

Elodie Harper, Education Correspondent, ITV News Anglia

When camera operator Tony Aldous and I arrive at Mile Cross Primary School on May 18th, the head teacher Stuart Allen takes our temperatures before we can enter the building. The last time we were here, just two months ago on the eve of lockdown, he shook our hands. A snapshot of how life has changed due to coronavirus.

Once the niceties of infection control are out of the way, Tony and I catch up with Stuart and have a look around the building. Mile Cross is a large primary school with 465 pupils on its roll. The main entrance leads straight into a spacious atrium. Today it is full of piles of large brown envelopes many loaded up on trolleys. There is an envelope for every pupil, full of workbooks. Staff know many of their children have no access to a computer; giving out printed work ensures homeschooling is possible for every family.

It is a very different scene to the one Tony and I saw in March, when the atrium was full of children hurrying on their journeys from class to class. We spent several days here, filming the rhythms of daily school life and, in particular, focusing on the exceptional level of pastoral care provided to pupils and their families. From breakfast for all children on arrival, to the dedicated one-to-one counselling offered to children and parents who need it, this is a school that believes in order to educate a child, you have to support all their needs.

And those needs are considerable. Mile Cross in Norwich is ranked as one of the most deprived areas in the UK. According to the Office for Standards in Education (Ofsted), which rates the school outstanding in all areas, almost two-thirds of children here are eligible for the pupil premium, the government funding available for schools to spend on children who face significant disadvantage.

232

What's clear to us this May Monday is that the school is still striving to meet those needs in spite of being closed to the majority of its pupils. A steady stream of parents drop by the school office throughout the day. The reception area has a table set with breakfast food – giant cans of baked beans, cereal boxes, bagels – to pick up for free along with the weekly work packs. Hovering at the end of a two-metre microphone pole, and then standing two metres away from each other, Tony and I chat to parents. It's a blazingly hot day. The record sunshine this spring has been a striking feature of lockdown. There's little chance to enjoy it, but filming outdoors is safer for everyone.

First we meet Dora Price, here to collect food to feed her seven children. Three of them attend the school. Life right now is hard for Dora, made harder due to one of her children having disabilities. She talks me through her daily routine: setting seven pairs of clothes out at night, laying the table for everyone's breakfast before bedtime, then two to three hours of homeschooling in the morning, lunch, exercise in the park. It is psychologically and financially draining. The school is a lifeline for her, taking some of the pressure off providing meals. "They've been doing food parcels," she tells me. "I've been collecting food from the school, they give me any help I need with the kids, they give me packages, they help me in every way." Dora is desperate for the school to reopen, to take the pressure off homeschooling, but says she trusts the staff to decide when that should be.

Around 11.30am the first table of food is joined by another, piled with pre-packed lunches. More parents arrive. Stuart tells us that on Thursdays and Fridays the school also helps provide fresh produce, meat and vegetables. He says some families have not had to pay for a single meal during the lockdown.

Jonathan Fitt is here after a shift at Asda, clutching an armful of library books for his three young daughters who run around excitedly, swinging from the school railings. A key worker, Jonathan puts in long hours at the supermarket from 4am to 12pm. Tony and I met him the last time we were here. Back then, Jonathan's daughter Ebony had just started extra sessions for her speech and language. Those classes stopped with lockdown, and the children have not taken up their key worker places because the family fall into the at-risk category for Covid-19. "Until it's 100 percent safe I'm not going to send the girls back," Jonathan tells us. "Because my wife has health issues and one daughter has health issues and I don't think it's safe to send them."

This dilemma about safety is of acute concern to the school. According to the Office for National Statistics, the risk from Covid-19 is twice as high in the most deprived areas of England and Wales than it is in the most affluent. Mile Cross falls into the two worst categories for risk of premature death due to poor physical and mental health. The negative impact of school closures on the most disadvantaged children has been widely reported, but the greater risks to the health of those same children's communities that reopening carries is less often discussed. For Mile Cross Primary, this raises the stakes on both sides of the debate about when to reopen the whole school.

For now, the senior leadership team here has decided to weigh the risks in favour of staff and families' health. The school will not open to more pupils on June 1st, the date set by the government. Stuart Allen is visibly emotional when I ask him what the impact will be on his pupils' education. "Every single day that goes by that children are not in school, it's like a dagger in the heart. I know that. I've been working at Mile Cross for twenty years now so I know full well what every single day missed means to those children and I will argue with anyone in the land that what we are trying to provide while they are at home, the support they are getting, is second to none."

But for all the school's efforts, staff cannot take away the pain of pupils missing their friends or losing out on a childhood rite of passage. While Tony and I are filming we catch up with Amy Davis and her dad, Steve, who is a teaching assistant here. Amy is in Year Six and this should be her last term of primary school. It is poignant watching Amy in her school playground, the only child in that huge open space, helping her dad water the plants.

Amy misses her friends and misses her teachers. Even more so because she fears she won't ever be coming back. The next time she is in class it will most likely be in an unfamiliar secondary school, with unfamiliar students. "I feel disappointed because when lockdown started I had just come back from a residential trip so I didn't have time to say goodbye to anyone," she tells me. "So I don't know if I will be back in time to say goodbye, and it's really sad."

Amy is not the only pupil we see. Others turn up at the school with their parents to collect work and say a brief hello. And of course, vulnerable children, or those with key-worker parents, are still being taught here. There are so few of them, classes are mainly held outside to make sure everyone keeps their distance. Tony films a class lining up to collect their lunch, spaced two metres apart, each walking the length of the dining hall alone. Staff say remaining open, even though they are closed, is a key part of what they are trying to do. I interview Ruth Pomeroy, who is one of nine emotional literacy support assistants at the school. "We are here for them, we haven't gone away," she says. "So any parent can come in and any child."

Ruth is currently counselling children over the phone rather than face to face, and has even increased the number of children she is supporting. She knows however, that this is not as effective as being present for a child in person. "It's not the same," she says. "In school it's lovely to have them there, see their faces, make things together, do some baking. But a telephone call is a close second. We've still got that contact with those children because they can tell us what they are doing and how they are coping."

I am very aware, while filming at Mile Cross Primary, that the school's struggle to provide emotional, financial and academic support to families is an everyday dilemma that has been magnified a hundredfold due to Covid-19. In the eight years I have been an education correspondent for ITV News Anglia, teachers have been telling me repeatedly that what they are expected to provide is no longer just an education. I've reported on "holiday hunger", schools providing breakfast, buying children stationery, teachers using their own pay to make sure their pupils get what they need. Now it feels like everyone is having to recognise the weight that schools carry.

Our economy's reliance on schools has also been exposed in the most immediate way to every single family with children in Britain, including mine. I'm only able to work for ITV on May 18th because my son's father has taken a day's leave. The whole time we are filming,

I am conscious of this fact. Every week of my working life is like that now, alternating annual leave with my ex-partner to look after our son on the days we cannot work from home. Although I had never thought of it this way before, I realise it's my child's teachers who partly enable me to have a job.

There have been many promises about a different world when this pandemic is over. New ways of doing things, a better quality of life for working people. I wonder if there will also be a new deal for schools like Mile Cross Primary in recognition of what they do. I hope so.

Italy as the Unlock Begins

Emma Murphy, Senior Correspondent, ITV News

Travel in the time of corona is certainly a changed experience. On May 19th I was on my way to northern Italy to report on how the epicentre of the country's coronavirus crisis was managing to unlock and return to some sort of normal.

At Heathrow, pretty much everything was closed – no airport snacks or shopping now. And after weeks of lockdown and warnings about social distancing it felt slightly disconcerting. For all the signs reminding passengers to stay two metres apart, the flow of people through the terminal made that seem more theory than practice. It was better on board the plane. The airlines still flying were doing as much as possible to keep a distance between passengers. So for the relatively short flight to Milan I found myself on board a 777 Jumbo, normally used to cross the Atlantic, taking full advantage of the nine seats in each row to keep socially distant.

At Milan's Malpensa airport the Covid-19 warnings were everywhere, unsurprising given the dreadful toll the virus has taken on this country. There were temperature checks and an awful lot of paperwork.

But on the streets it felt like the life we used to lead. After weeks of very severe lockdown Italians, wearing mandatory masks, are getting out and about again. Some restaurants were open though the regulations were strict; the tables a metre apart, often a temperature check at the door and some hand-spray. Some were trying to use technology to reduce physical contact, though the result was hit and miss. I was offered laminated cards with QR codes to scan for the menu. It seemed like a great idea until I realised the cards were being passed around to everyone just as the menus would have been. Though a

237

little faltering at times there was clearly relief that life was finding a path back towards normality after the dreadfulness of the past months.

I travelled on to Venice. Rarely had this place of beauty looked so beautiful – bereft of visitors, the city's true splendour clear to see. But the 30 million visitors who normally clog the canals and alleys are the lifeblood of this city. They bring in billions and tourism is the only real source of employment.

I arrived in an empty water bus, along the empty Grand Canal. No gondolas, no other boats and no sound, save the tolling of a bell every now and again. Most of the shops were still shut and to those which had opened I was something of a rare breed. "Where are you from, how did you get here?" one shopkeeper asked before speaking the words he probably never thought he'd say and I certainly didn't think I'd ever hear. "We don't have tourists here in Venice anymore. You've surprised us." Whoever thought that day would come?

I'd clearly surprised the hotel too. Despite booking the day before, it was all locked up. The arrival of visitors from beyond Italy's shores was clearly viewed as a booking error rather than a genuine booking.

The last time I visited Venice, the queue to get into L'Arlecchino decorative mask shop was almost as long as the queue for ice-cream. Now the beautifully ornate plaster masks stare down on an empty store. Marilisa Dal Cason, the owner, told me how the beaked doctor masks from the days of the plague used to be a bestseller. Now, in a world of masks, in a pandemic not unlike a plague, she didn't think anyone would want to buy these anymore. And she's not sure how long her beloved shop can survive without the tourist euros.

Even the Roman Catholic Church was having to assess its reliance on foreign visitors. St Mark's Basilica used to be filled with worshippers and visitors from around the world, but when lockdown came only those in the local parish could visit for private prayer. But so few people actually live in the city, on some days only eight people turned up. "This city was dying because we had so many tourists," Father Angelo Pagan told me. "Now it's dying because we have none."

Throughout the visit, the only language to be heard on the streets was Italian – for now Venice is for the Venetians. It was a moment of history, a moment few Venetians ever thought they would witness.

And it may yet prove to be the moment Venice reassesses its relationship with mass tourism. This pandemic has provided a pause and a chance for Venice to reimagine its future – the quieter streets a reminder of a lost past.

After Venice, I travelled on across Europe to see the impact of coronavirus and the slow unlock in Portugal, France, Belgium, Spain as those countries also started their journey back to a version of normal. With borders closed there was a strange yet beautiful emptiness. As in Venice there were profound fears for the future. But also a hope that after the dreadfulness of isolation and distance the joy of family, friends and togetherness will be cherished even more.

The job I do takes me to many places in times of crisis. It is a privilege and this trip has been no different. Usually, returning home feels like a return to normality. Not this time. It was almost the opposite. As I write the crisis in the UK is worse than anywhere I visited. These are changed days for sure.

Fury and Failure on the Frontline in Brazil

Juliet Bremner, Correspondent, ITV News

It was an extraordinary and overwhelming sight; arriving at Vila Formosa Cemetery on the eastern side of Sao Paulo, we realised for the first time the full impact the virus was having on Brazil. In sharp contrast to the rich red earth, men dressed in white protective suits, the kind I would have previously associated with nuclear disasters, carried coffins. Small family groups followed in their wake. Dozens of them making their way between row upon row of newly dug graves awaiting the bodies that would surely follow in the coming days and weeks. Although this was shocking it wasn't until we saw the footage captured by our drone that we realised just how appalling this disaster was for Brazil. It showed graves stretching to the horizon.

At the end of May the UK was just emerging from the worst days of the pandemic. But South America's largest country, with a population of over 211 million, was in the deadly grip of Covid-19. Officially Brazil was recording over 1,000 deaths a day although scientists believed the figure could be far higher. Worse still, the World Health Organization was warning the peak was probably another month away. Yet flamboyant President Jair Bolsonaro appeared to think the threat to the economy was more serious than the threat to the nation's health. As the death rate soared, Bolsonaro, an ardent admirer of American President Donald Trump, was urging people to get back to business as usual.

To my surprise, when camera operator Rob Turner, producer Emma Burrows and I landed in the sprawling metropolis of Sao Paulo, our first impression was one of disturbing normality. Many cars were still on the road and plenty of people were walking along the pavements, strikingly many more of them wearing face masks than people in London. The first signs that we'd entered a country in crisis came when we checked into an almost deserted hotel. Temperature checks and face masks were mandatory.

Back at the cemetery Natali Kuiaba was placing flowers on the grave of her 44-year-old brother. She told me that nurses had refused to come into the house to treat him because he was coughing and had a fever. He died several days later with no mention of the virus on his death certificate. But his family have few doubts about what killed him and lay the blame squarely at the door of their disbelieving President, who had notoriously compared the virus to a little cough. Natali gestured towards the expanse of graves, saying bitterly, "all these graves because of his 'little cough'."

The family of nurse Cidinha Duarte went further, accusing the President and the authorities of murder. We were invited into their cramped apartment, where it was impossible to keep a safe distance. Instead, we put on our face masks and opened the patio doors before sitting down to hear how their mother had died. Cidinha was 63 and suffered from diabetes and high blood pressure, which she knew made her vulnerable. Originally she was allowed to stay away from her work in a Sao Paulo hospital but, according to her daughter Andreza and son Alexandre, the authorities forced her to return as the number of infected patients spiralled. Inevitably, as they see it, their mother caught Covid-19 and it claimed her life. Andreza alleged there had been complete disregard and disrespect for her mother, adding angrily, "I see that as murder."

Compounding their misery, Cidinha had brought the virus home, infecting eight members of her family, including her son. Alexandre only narrowly escaped with his life. He spent 32 days unconscious, kept alive by a ventilator. When we met him he was still struggling for breath. He looked like a weak, broken old man but in fact was only 39, the father of a two-year-old son. In a rebuke to Bolsonaro and all those who failed to realise how deadly the virus could be Alexandre told me: "This is no joke. Today people think Covid-19 is a fantasy but it is not, just look at me."

It was a sentiment echoed by the exhausted doctors and nurses in a recently built field hospital where we spent a morning. Nothing was a joke here. The hospital was constructed in six days on a former car park, a proud achievement, but inside the conditions were pretty grim. First we went to the "Red Zone", full of the sickest patients, and were immediately confronted by desperate attempts to save the life of a 43-year-old man. His oxygen levels had become dangerously low and the doctor had no choice but to intubate him. There was frenzied activity as tubes were inserted and injections administered.

We watched as Dr Bernardo Guimaraes, the head of intensive care, manually pumped a device that pushed extra air into the patient's lungs. Gradually, the monitor started to climb until he said the man now had a chance of survival. This was one small success but Dr Guimaraes remained frightened that they were losing the wider Covid war. He told me: "Every day it's becoming more frightening, we are very worried that the hospitals will collapse."

The "corona combat hospital" was built to take the overflow from Sao Paulo's public hospitals but already Dr Guimaraes believed they were at "breaking point". He estimated they had less than three weeks' supply of the drug needed to sedate patients before they could be put on ventilators.

As we filmed in the makeshift hospital, I was worried about the lack of protective clothing the medics wore. Actually it made me feel quite awkward as we seemed to be far better equipped than them. Dr Guimaraes brushed this aside, explaining it was a pragmatic choice allowing staff to take the regular coffee and smoking breaks that are part of Brazilian culture, and kept spirits up.

Far more distressing for the medical team, it emerged, was the lack of a clear message from the government, which might have helped to bring the virus under control. "They have to do something now," pleaded Dr Anna Camargo, a dermatologist, who like everyone else in the field hospital had volunteered to work there. "The politicians have to do more, they can't close their eyes and say it is just a little cold – it is not."

Our 45-minute flight to Rio de Janeiro perfectly illustrated this lack of national guidance. We found ourselves crammed onto a plane with every seat booked, passengers queueing along the aisle and reaching over one another to put luggage in the overhead lockers. It felt dangerous and we quickly reached for our face masks.

The atmosphere in Rio was far more disciplined. We found the city famed for its party vibe closed. No tourists, no restaurants, no bars and perhaps most surreal, no access to the beach. Police patrols ensured no one could walk along the famous Copacabana, which was one vast empty stretch of golden sand.

There had been a dramatic split between Bolsonaro's national government and the Governor of Rio State, Wilson Witzel. Former allies, they are now bitter foes. Witzel wanted to keep Rio locked down until the number of infections began to drop but the President was adamant that caution should be put aside and the tourists invited back.

We woke on our first morning in Rio to see crowds of Bolsonaro supporters on the promenade that runs alongside the beach noisily demanding an end to lockdown. But what really stuck in my mind was the response from those keen on a more cautious approach; families leaning from the balconies of their apartments, loudly banging pots and pans.

The voice of the favelas that cling to the hillsides surrounding Rio was harder to hear. Vidigal is one of these iconic shanty towns that are home to around a fifth of Rio's population. It boasts a spectacular view but that's no safeguard against the new enemy, a virus that flourishes in these cramped, often unhygienic, conditions.

In recent years Vidigal has become the tourists' favela of choice; they are taken on guided tours to a stunning viewing platform overlooking Ipanema beach. But favelas remain crime ridden communities controlled by gangs and on the day we visited Vidigal a young man of perhaps 16 or 17 stood guard at this high point, a gun slung across his shoulder. Our guide explained the weapon made the teenager seem powerful to the other kids. I wondered if anyone had told him that it would offer no protection against the new killer stalking these narrow streets.

We were told that five deaths had been recorded in Vidigal but the more I spoke to people living there the more I doubted it. Everyone appeared to know someone who had died; it wasn't scientific but seemed to point to a far higher casualty rate.

Ambulances, like many of the civic services, don't want to venture into the favelas, making it difficult to take the sick to hospital. Speaking to us from behind the iron bars on her veranda, Elisabete explained how she watched helplessly as the elderly man living next door had become progressively sicker. For three days she begged the ambulance crews to come but they refused, saying Vidigal was "high risk". By the time they arrived, it was too late.

I left Brazil with the impression that the official number of people infected or dying only hinted at the true story. Bolsonaro even tried to stop the daily recording of deaths, claiming that the left-wing media was using the data to spread fear and lies.

When we arrived in Brazil the official death toll had just passed 30,000 and six weeks later as I write it has nearly doubled to 60,000, making Brazil one of the worst-affected countries in the world.

And at the cemetery in Sao Paulo times are so desperate they are digging up the bones of people buried in the past and storing them. They are making room for the new Covid dead.

A Time For Heroes

Paul Davies OBE, Senior Correspondent, ITV News

At 8pm on Thursday May 28th the sound of clapping and assorted kitchen utensils being enthusiastically knocked together once again rang out from the streets of cities, towns and villages across Britain. It had become a ritual for people to briefly leave their lockdowned homes at the same time each week to join their neighbours in saying thank you to NHS workers and all the others taking risks on our behalf in the battle against the virus.

But after two months, it had been decided that this would be the last Thursday night expression of the nation's gratitude, and ITV News was appropriately covering the event through the eyes and words of some of those who had experienced life and death on the frontline.

We saw Ralf and Brenda Deocampo, both nurses at London's Charing Cross Hospital, joining in with their neighbours when the clapping started. The couple are originally from the Philippines, like many NHS workers who became victims of the pandemic. Ralph explained what this public show of support had come to mean. "It has helped so much in the bad times. It makes us feel valued and appreciated, that we are not on our own in this fight."

Grace Dudley, who contracted the virus and then survived it, stood applauding alongside her family and neighbours before telling a deeply personal story. Just three days after she was finally discharged from Queens Hospital, Romford, the virus claimed the life of her father.

"We were told on a Thursday that it wasn't looking good for him and he wasn't going to make it. When 8pm hit we were all in a complete state but we all came out of our houses and clapped for the work they did and that they continue to do."

Those Thursday nights will remain one of the strongest memories of a uniquely strange and disturbing time that affected every community and every home in Britain. It was a threat that claimed tens of thousands of victims but it also created many thousands of heroes. For the first few weeks the job of pulling together images of people from all four countries of the United Kingdom clapping the NHS for ITV's News at Ten had fallen to me. From the start it was immediately clear that this would be one of those rare moments of coming together.

That last Thursday night I was happy to let those most intimately affected tell their own story. I stood in the street with my own family applauding the carers and remembering those whose dedication had ultimately cost their lives.

This autumn I will complete 50 years working as a journalist. Most of that half century has been spent covering national and international news. I can honestly say this story in so many ways has been the biggest with the most impact. Globally the number of lives lost to the virus exceeds the death toll from any of the multiple conflicts I have reported on. In my lifetime no manmade or natural disaster has effectively brought Britain and many of our European neighbours to a standstill. No other catastrophe has crippled the economy as this one has or required government intervention on this scale. So many businesses have haemorraged jobs, it is likely to be years before there is a full recovery.

There have been other invisible killers of course, all terrifying in their own way. I recall a night in the Saudi Arabian desert during the first Gulf War when the dreaded cry of "Gas, gas, gas" had British soldiers, and the handful of journalists with them, scrambling in the dark for masks and protective equipment. We were being warned that Saddam Hussein's forces had fired missiles carrying chemical weapons and nerve agents in our direction. Fortunately it turned out to be a false alarm.

Reporting on the outbreak of deadly Ebola in Africa was for some of us a dress rehearsal for the coronavirus. While other colleagues, not me thankfully, have told the world about the leak of radiation from damaged nuclear plants while worrying about their own proximity to the leak and what problems it could be storing up in their own bodies.

A threat you can't see takes on a new level of fear but the examples I have just listed were easier to deal with for one key reason: you had to travel to other parts of the world to report on those stories and, at the end of your assignment, however tough, you would travel back to the safety of home.

Coronavirus was different. Having hitched a lift halfway round the world from China, it threatened us where we live and where we work. There was no going home to escape because it could follow you there. It also introduced that unthinkable possibility, that those of us in the few jobs that continued to function at the height of the crisis could unwittingly carry the killer back to our homes where our families were obediently following all the lockdown rules.

So we adapted to new ways of working to reduce the risk. In came masks and gloves and extendable microphone poles to conduct interviews at a distance. Out went filming in other people's homes and the cosy practice of travelling to assignments with our camera crew colleagues and huddling over a laptop with an editor as we pieced together the latest report.

It had its frustrations and sometimes the high production standards we expect had to be compromised, but it meant we could fulfil our role at a time when the public needed it most. The increased audience figures demonstrated that.

I would also stress that the difficulties the news organisations encountered in covering this epic story were as nothing compared to the life and death struggle that was being fought every day in our hospitals and care homes. Collectively we were aware of that and humbled. It became a heartbreaking but essential part of our job, telling the stories of medical staff and patients lost to this foul virus. We met many of their families, grief stricken but bravely determined to voice their pride. Over the weeks there were many cruel stories of loss along with the uplifting cases of survival against the odds. I was also lucky enough to meet the remarkable Captain Tom Moore as he raised millions for the NHS, even joining him on his 100th birthday.

Standing outside my home on that last Thursday night of country-wide applause, I thought about all of them and the thousands of men and women whose names we haven't heard but who continue doing life-saving work every day. At times of crisis the world needs heroes and this pandemic has reminded us we have so many of them.

Measuring Up for a Safe Commute

Martin Stew, Reporter, ITV News London

Did you know your arm span is almost exactly the same as your height? Try it. Being six foot three means if I stretch my arms out, the distance from the fingers on one hand across to the other is just shy of two metres.

I was thinking about this as I rode on a deserted rush hour Northern line tube train eight weeks into lockdown. My arms could stretch across four seats, meaning another socially distanced passenger would have to be at least that far away. In a pre-Covid world I would have had to fold myself onto that train. A sweaty act of origami with unfortunate shorter passengers pressed into my armpit. How then is social distancing possible on a post-pandemic commute?

The answer, of course, is that it's not. To work out just how impossible it is I enlisted the help of Cambridge academic and mathematician Matthew Scroggs. Together we sketched a rough chalk outline of a tube train on the floor of a car park. The internal measurements of one carriage are 2 metres by 17. We tried several different configurations but found simply having passengers at the corner of two-metre squares was the most efficient. Best case scenario: 18 passengers compared to a normal capacity of around 135. To make matters worse, for any one of them to get off, the whole carriage would have to move in a coordinated loop to stay a safe distance apart.

Using those numbers Matthew calculated the train would be completely full by the second stop on the line if demand returned to normal. Even if you capped the number of people who could get on at each station the queue outside Tooting Broadway would be 4,000 people long at 8am. Assuming they each stood two metres apart the line would stretch five miles – about as far as Vauxhall Bridge.

That's obviously not sustainable, so how can you make it work? As far as I can see there are only four things you can change: how many passengers are using the service, when they're travelling, how far apart they can stand and the number of trains you run.

Controlling the number of people using the tube and when they do so are the most powerful tools at Transport for London (TfL)'s disposal. During lockdown, rush hours moved to 7am and 4pm – a reflection of the fact that construction workers made up a large bulk of the workforce. Spreading rush hour traffic throughout the day would make a huge impact but needs employers to get on board with flexible working hours.

Increasing capacity is tough. TfL can't add more trains as they were already running every two minutes and train length is limited by platform length. That leaves finding a way to get more passengers on each carriage.

One way of achieving that is by following the example of the Metro in Paris, where mask wearing was made mandatory weeks before London. By setting social distancing at one metre not two you can triple the number of passengers on each carriage. However, even with that increase, nearly 500 passengers would be unable to board each train. No wonder the government policy (as I write this) is to walk or cycle where possible.

So will a post Covid-19 commute be different forever – or is this just a temporary blip? In the aftermath of the 7/7 (July 7th 2005) terror attacks the number of people using the tube dropped by 60 percent. Within five months it was back to normal levels but two things did change permanently. Firstly, the Thames Clipper ferry services saw their passenger numbers rise by 80 percent – an increase they continued to build on until the start of lockdown. They now face exactly the same capacity challenges as buses and tubes.

Secondly, the number of cyclists shot up. The number of bike journeys in 2005 was 62 percent higher than 2004 and although it did fall back the following year, the drop-off was only nine percent. To encourage a similar spike in bike use as a result of the Covid crisis, the government created a £250 million Emergency Active Travel Fund. Pavements have been temporarily widened for walking, and bike lanes have been bolstered. Cyclists will also be able to apply for £50 vouchers to get their bikes serviced.

Early results (during the sunniest spring since records began) have been positive but will London's peloton of new fair-weather cyclists brave the changes in season? Many office showers have been turned off for hygiene reasons, making a summer commute a sweaty prospect. Winter wind and rain will test the resolve of all but the hardiest cyclists.

Environmental campaigners would love the change to stick. At the peak of lockdown, the city's air improved so much that the levels of toxic nitrogen dioxide were between 20 and 24 percent lower than the same time in 2019. But what happens when offices reopen and the Home Counties commuters want to return to the City? Not everyone lives close enough to get to work under their own steam. Those who can avoid public transport are being urged to do so, leaving only one option: getting back behind the wheel.

TfL's modelling shows the number of cars entering central London could double from 100,000 to 200,000 a day. Those drivers are being squeezed from every direction. Physically there's less space for cars on the roads since more space has been created for cyclists and pedestrians. Financially the Congestion Charge has been increased to £15 a day as a condition of the government's £1.6 billion bailout of TfL. More congestion equals slower journeys and extra pollution.

Even if drivers do pay to subsidise public transport it's not going to be anywhere near enough. In the last decade a third of all journeys in London were by train, tube or bus. In April and May income from fares fell 90 percent, leading Mayor Sadiq Khan to warn of a £500 million black hole in TfL finances. If commuters don't start buying tickets again soon there could be no service left for them to come back to.

Stay two metres apart. The width of my arms. It was a straightforward instruction at a time when life was anything but. The consequences for the capital and its commuters will last far longer than coronavirus.

Timeline

June

1 Children in reception, Year One and Year Six in England are allowed to return to school

9 Education Secretary Gavin Williamson tells MPs that not all primary school pupils in England will return before the summer break

10 The Organisation for Economic Cooperation and Development predicts that Britain's economy will suffer the most of any developed country following the crisis

13 "Support bubbles" are introduced in England, allowing single-adult households to stay overnight at another home

15 Non-essential shops reopen in England, as do zoos, safari parks and places of worship for private prayer. Face masks must be worn on public transport

17 The Premier League restarts behind closed doors

18 The government announces it will work with Apple and Google on a contact tracing app

23 The Prime Minister announces in the last daily briefing that pubs, cinemas and restaurants will reopen in England from 4 July

26 Boris Johnson warns of a potential "serious spike" in infection as thousands flock to beaches during a heatwave

An Unexpected Olive Branch

John Irvine, Senior International Correspondent, ITV News

Just like people, places can have underlying vulnerabilities and Gaza looked like particularly fertile ground for the coronavirus. The strip is a living breathing tragedy and given its battered history, logic insisted that Covid-19 must impose a new layer of suffering.

Gaza has always been in a bind. Wedged between Israel, Egypt and the Mediterranean, it is 25 miles long and 7.5 miles across at its widest point. It's a congested home to almost two million people, many of whom are poor. And yet cases of Covid-19 have been rare. As luck would have it Gaza has been spared by the isolation imposed on it by Israel and Egypt. A blockade that limits the movement of people across the border has also kept coronavirus at bay. Ironically, strict frontier controls in place for years have served Gaza well on this one.

As recently as early March militant groups in Gaza and the Israeli Defence Forces were exchanging fire. Rockets were being launched from the strip on an almost daily basis and the Israelis were responding with air strikes and artillery. Word got out that Israeli infantry units were carrying out exercises in preparation for another invasion of Gaza. Seasoned observers predicted the start of what would have been the fourth war since the Islamist group Hamas seized control of Gaza in 2007. Having covered the last one in 2014, I knew it was a grim prospect.

But then a new, unexpected and common enemy appeared on the horizon. Coronavirus altered one aspect of the Israel–Gaza relationship and would lead to very different cross-border exchanges – raw materials from Israel into Gaza; millions of pieces of personal protective equipment from Gaza into Israel. Early on in the crisis, Israel, like most other countries, found itself woefully short of masks and overalls for hospital staff. The situation was serious enough for the government here to instruct the country's foreign intelligence service – the Mossad – to help search for and secure supplies. There were a few plane-loads that came in from China and elsewhere, but it wasn't enough.

It wasn't immediately apparent to anyone that the answer lay in neighbouring Gaza, which the Israeli Army had been preparing to invade. Then, out of the blue and flying in the face of history and convention, coronavirus became an olive branch of sorts that would provide a boost to one important sector of Gaza's battered economy – the garment industry.

Tailors in Gaza began working with Israeli companies to export masks, overalls, shoes and gloves. The Israelis sent in samples and specifications and Gaza's skilled tailors did all that was asked of them.

The garment sector used to be one of Gaza's most prosperous, but business deteriorated significantly after Israel imposed the blockade 13 years ago. Nearly 90 percent of the factories, which employed about 35,000 workers, were forced to close. Then, last year, Israel allowed Gaza to export limited amounts of clothing and textiles to the West Bank and Israel as part and parcel of a truce agreement with Hamas. More than 5,000 tailors were able to return to work. Back in operation, more than 150 factories were in a position to respond when the clamour went up for PPE.

Israeli companies gave their business to the Gazan apparel sector for a number of reasons: close proximity; a common currency; speed of production and the quality of workmanship. Critics and sceptics argue that given individual tailors earned little more than the equivalent of £10 a day, it was also exploitative. Whatever the reasons, Gaza's tailors were glad of the work and had no qualms about making protective clothing and face masks for erstwhile enemies.

"This is a humanitarian issue and there is no difference between Jews and Arabs," said Mohammed as he sat working on his sewing machine. "I don't have a problem that what I make is going to Israel," said a colleague seated nearby.

Reflecting on the unexpected turn of events, one of the Gazan factory owners told us: "They are our political enemies, but this is a humanitarian issue and they are our neighbours as well as our enemies. We shouldn't think about politics at a time like this and we want to make jobs for our workers. I have to help the Israelis and maybe it will shame them. I believe this will lead to a re-think by both sides. We (the people of Gaza) want to eat and they want safety and security. There must be a solution to our problems. I am hopeful that things will get better because of this."

His optimism may prove far fetched. And there are many reasons to fear that Israel and Gaza's rapprochment over the common cause of PPE may be all too brief. Nonetheless, what happened when corona-virus came along makes for an uplifting chapter in this age-old story. A virus that has wrought havoc around the world ended up doing some good in this troubled corner.

Given that their long-running conflict has cost so many lives, it's ironic that Israelis and Gazans found common cause in the business of saving lives. For both sides the coronavirus proved novel indeed – they discovered they needed each other.

What is Long Covid?

Emily Morgan, Health Editor, ITV News

"I had to deal with heart attack-like symptoms and breathing problems at home. For a few weeks they would come in waves that got closer together and more intense until I was having them every half hour, day and night. I'd wake up through the night with difficulty breathing, crushing chest pain, utterly exhausted, despairing of how I'd make it through to morning."

This was not the testimony of a woman with Covid-19. She'd had the disease, but the horrific symptoms she was detailing here were the ones she still had months later. Catherine Skinner came down with Covid-19 two weeks before lockdown. She had the usual symptoms, a cough and night sweats. It got progressively worse and she ended up in an accident and emergency unit but luckily was sent home to recover. Four months on, she was still "recovering" and her life was on hold. She had brain fog, abdominal pain, diarrhoea, a throat that felt like she had "inhaled caustic chemicals", pins and needles, dehydration, low blood pressure, plunging body temperature, hives, her face swelling up at night . . . the list went on and on and at its worst, she says, she was developing a new and disturbing symptom every day.

I am writing about Catherine because, as we started to ease out of lockdown, it was clear that she was not unique; she had what is now being called "long Covid" and thousands of others like her were starting to share similar stories. I'd like to tell you precisely what long Covid is, but no one really knows. As I write, the term is being used to describe illness in people who've either recovered from Covid-19 but still have lasting effects, or have had the usual symptoms for far longer than would be expected.

By June there were reams of anecdotal evidence emerging online from patients relieved to hear that others were complaining of the same debilitating long-term effects. Many had doubted themselves, fearing they were suffering some sort of psychological breakdown. So they felt vindicated, proof, they said, that they were not going mad or becoming delusional. The stories were not just from those who we knew had suffered badly from Covid-19; middle-aged men or those from Black, Asian and minority ethnic backgrounds. It was the young, it was women, it was a whole new demographic who had initially only suffered relatively mild versions of the disease. We appeared to be entering a whole new ball game.

The difficulty was, and still is, that aside from anecdotal evidence very little research on this issue has been done. I have asked professors of infectious diseases to explain it to me, to tell me what was causing it, how best to treat patients and whether it would affect them for the rest of their lives. The answers? There were none. One such scientist from the Liverpool School of Tropical Medicine, Professor Paul Garner, spoke from a unique position; he studies infectious diseases and had suffered from long Covid for seven weeks. He likened the long-term effects of Covid-19 to the tropical viral infection dengue fever. Dengue symptoms are usually mild but in a small percentage of cases can be severe or life-threatening. And persistent effects of dengue tend to come and go, as they do with Covid-19. That's a worrying prospect given the huge numbers of people who've contracted the virus.

There is some early research that suggests about 1 in 20 Covid patients experience long-term symptoms. And researchers in Italy, which remains a few weeks ahead of us, are warning that the long-term effects of the virus could be far worse than initially anticipated. Psychosis, strokes, spinal infections and insomnia are all being detected in former Covid patients. Doctors there have voiced fears that some patients may never overcome their illness.

As Health Editor, I have tried to make sense of coronavirus for ITV News viewers. To report its trajectory through our nation, to inform our viewers what it can do to the body, how it can flood the lungs with fluid until patients feel they are drowning and now, how it is cutting otherwise healthy people down until they are begging their GP to take them seriously.

At the beginning of July a major UK study into the long-term impact of coronavirus on patients was announced. Led by the National Institute for Health Research and Leicester Biomedical Research Centre, it's the largest study of its kind in the world and was given emergency funding to ensure its future. That research is desperately needed and is the crucial next step in answering the elusive question – how do we combat this brutal disease?

Over the past six months, I have interviewed dozens of doctors and scientists who say this is the most unpredictable, unconventional and weird virus they have seen. I would love to be able to report "we have solved this" but it's hard to imagine that day coming soon.

A Postscript from China

Debi Edward, Asia Correspondent, ITV News

A mask, a temperature check and a health code app. Life in Beijing now revolves around these three things. Without a face covering, an average temperature and proof from my mobile phone that I haven't been in any virus-risk areas, I can't even grab a coffee in the café across the road.

An outbreak at a food market in the capital had reset the clock. Once again travel was put on hold and the restrictions recently lifted were re-imposed. We had almost been at the point of schools, even swimming pools, reopening when cases emerged at the Xinfadi Wholesale market. It supplies a majority of Beijing restaurants and shops with their meat, fish, fruit and vegetables.

If there was any criticism of the authorities back in January for not reacting quickly enough, this time they showed they had learned their lesson. Millions of people were forced back into quarantine and they and anyone they'd had, or might have had, contact with were tested. It was a systematic and tough response. But within three weeks the outbreak had been contained.

Since the end of January, we have lived with the constraints and precautions of a pandemic in our midst, but since March virus cases had all but gone in Beijing and were rapidly diminishing across China. The new outbreak centred on this market brought back, to me at least, a concern about getting the virus and a realisation that the warnings about it not going away any time soon were true.

Living abroad you are separated from family for many months at a time. It's a choice you've made but that doesn't make it easy. To be forced apart by the virus, and not be able to get home when my parents in Scotland fell ill with it, was the hardest thing I've had to face since moving to China. I wasn't unique in this heartache and hardship; sadly, millions of other families were going through the same, or worse, in every continent around the world. Cold comfort.

The Chinese Government wants its people to move on and forget. To not ask questions, to look at the devastating toll the virus has taken elsewhere and be grateful that China was spared the same fate. The public here is meant to overlook the fact that early warnings from doctors in Wuhan were ignored. They are supposed to forgive the authorities for those days and weeks they deliberated and delayed divulging important information; details that could have saved lives and prevented a pandemic.

I have been privileged to speak to some of those brave enough to challenge the Chinese Government's narrative. Despite them being warned not to talk to us, and being pursued by the police, we have managed to tell the stories of some of those who lost family members in Wuhan. Some are daring to demand justice; I fear their efforts and risks will be in vain.

Each of them disputed China's official death toll and was in no doubt that in the weeks before the lockdown officials knew they were dealing with something serious but failed to act, allowing the virus to spread. Reflecting on what might have been can lead you down a futile path but it's hard not to ask if the Chinese Government could have prevented this pandemic. If they had acted sooner might they have contained Covid-19? There is evidence to suggest that it was in those crucial days, those first three weeks of January, that the virus established its grip not just on Wuhan, but the world.

Some suggest we were due another pandemic, that this was a disaster waiting to happen. Whether you believe that, or that China could have done more, one thing is certain – 2020 has altered how we live. It is impossible to comprehend the scale of loss suffered in such a short period of time and hard to move on from the lives taken, the jobs lost, the time stolen. Let history judge what this year might have been. There will be investigations into the why, what, where and when. But until we get those answers, when the lockdowns are over and the virus has abated, l hope the disaster that has driven us apart will bring us together.

Soho's Super Saturday: Time To Reflect

Chris Choi, Consumer Editor, ITV News

The storm clouds were gathering. July 4th was grey, damp and windy. I was in London's Soho, one of the UK's most iconic drinking districts. On the day pubs and restaurants were allowed to reopen in England, they were waking up enthusiastically. By mid-afternoon large groups were gathering. There was loud laughter and alcohol served in plastic containers for consumption on the street – delivered via apps and paid for digitally. As friends came together, there was lots of hugging. A hen party in matching outfits was giggling through the crowds. Old Compton Street had been temporarily pedestrianised and a police observation tower built. Early in the evening most people were social distancing, but after a few hours and a lot of drink many were bunching closely together. As revellers shouted against the rising background noise, things got louder and more clumsy. Pictures of Soho's "Super Saturday" would be flashed around the world and fill front pages.

This landmark day in the nation's coronavirus journey put me in a reflective mood, remembering the people I met and the stories I had heard as ITV News' Consumer Editor when I set out to find and hear some of the more hidden voices of the crisis.

Like the children I filmed at an inner-city community project in Brixton, south London. I was there to see the kind of work that had become vulnerable because of a sharp drop in charity income caused by lockdown. A six-year-old girl used the word "pandemic" with the familiarity you'd expect her to have for toys and games. An eight-year-old told me she never had nightmares before this, but now has them all the time. The girl who told me she was afraid when her mum went to work in a care home was shy as she expressed her fears. Each of the girls painted something to show me how the pandemic had affected them. They all featured trees, suns and people – things they all missed during lockdown.

When I met Sharon Chater she was in a wheelchair on her front doorstep. I had been investigating gaps in the provision of food for people who were unable to go out. Sharon has multiple sclerosis and was told to remain at home for three months because of her vulnerability to this deadly virus. Sharon lived with her son who, like her, was isolating due to an underlying condition. As panic-buying gripped much of the nation, the upsurge in demand for online groceries left Sharon unable to get a delivery slot. She started to cry as she spoke to me about her almost empty food cupboard. She told me of her many failed attempts to get a slot. In the end the only option had been for Sharon's son, who has asthma, to go to the supermarket. By breaking isolation there was a risk of bringing coronavirus into their home.

Sharon's were the first tears I saw as a result of this scourge. She made me realise that in this sophisticated modern society, it had taken only days of pandemic to create genuine fears of hunger. But meeting Sharon also showed me how communities were pulling together. We looked to find her some support and contacted a neighbourhood scheme. Volunteers quickly delivered groceries and people in the area began to leave food on her doorstep. A few days after my report was broadcast, a small package was delivered to my desk in the ITV newsroom. Inside was a handwritten note: "I don't have much to spare but please will you send this box of biscuits to the lady you interviewed."

I won't forget a walk in a park with Mandy Mahoney. I had been researching how the coronavirus crisis was affecting people already coping with serious illness. Mandy has incurable cancer and when I met her she had spent 100 days without leaving her home, apart from hospital appointments. Only recently had her consultant told her she could go out for rigorously distanced walks. Mandy told me she doesn't know how long she has left to live, which makes every day precious. Staying at home alone is on nobody's bucket list. Many of the medical treatment trials that could have brought fresh options for cancer patients have been suspended. Even routine treatments have been disrupted and every trip to hospital has become a calculated risk for people most vulnerable to coronavirus. Many cancer therapies affect the immune system, leaving patients extremely vulnerable to infection.

Yet Mandy was wonderfully positive and quick to share a smile or even to laugh about her situation. She told me she rarely cries in public, but behind closed doors she often weeps. She is in a buddy system organised by the Macmillan cancer charity and she provides phone support to others. Night-time is the hardest, she told me, it's when isolation and fear can seem to swallow people up and they need to talk to somebody who understands what they are going through. She spends hours providing this companionship to people struggling to get through the relentless grind of isolation. For Mandy this long pitiless haul has been as hard as the first time she was told she had cancer.

People often think that a journalist's job is to write or to broadcast. Of course the real job is to hear – to properly listen to the stories people have to tell. In Devon I met a funeral celebrant who knew the importance of letting other people speak. I was looking into how coronavirus had robbed people of life's very final comforts. Funerals could only happen with minimal attendance and Jo Brewer explained that meant nobody could hug the widow at a recent service. Although funeral directors had been told not to touch any attendees, one had instinctively gone to hold the widow as she collapsed in grief at the coffin. As a celebrant, Jo's job had become more important than ever. She had to explain to the bereaved that restrictions meant most family members couldn't be at the service. That didn't mean that goodbyes had to be undignified or impersonal. She would learn all about the person who had died and make sure their story was lovingly told.

I was moved by the heartbreak of all this, but didn't know at the time just how significant Jo's words would become for me. Just two months later, on June 1st, I lost my amazing little sister Nicola. I too had to arrange a funeral restricted to only eight people with strict instructions not to touch the coffin. Even so, it was full of love and Nicola's story was joyously told. I had taken Jo's advice and got a good celebrant.

All the drinkers in Soho's slippery streets on July 4th had stories of how this viral monster has hit them. The last few months have changed

265

us all and devastated many. Soon the national job of listening will begin, with inquiries and investigations into how things were handled. Not everyone agrees on government performance, but everyone is entitled to accurate information. As news reporters that's been our job through all this. When times are bad, news teams like ours become their best. It's also when our viewers most need us. As lockdown eases and people socialise in pubs, what I saw in Soho on July 4th said it all. Enjoy life and value those you love and loved. The sky is still very grey, but people are daring to hope that the storm clouds may be passing.

Shining a Light on the Decision-Makers

Robert Peston, Political Editor, ITV News

The greatest challenge in covering coronavirus, and in writing about it now, is that it is so hard to obtain distance from a story that affects all of us so directly and powerfully. Even by my obsessive standards, I've not been able to switch off from it.

It was personal too, as it was for most British people, because immediately after my show at around midnight on March 18th, my partner, the journalist Charlotte Edwardes, went down with Covid-19 symptoms, and we went into full-scale quarantine at home. She had it fairly badly, and I thought I too had mild symptoms. But who knows? I kept doing broadcasts for the news and the *Peston* show, and writing blogs, in between dribbling a deflated football up and down the garden in an eccentric attempt to keep relatively fit. At almost the same time, my cousin, the newspaper photographer Alan Davidson, died in hospital of an unspecified infection. The doctors did not think he had Covid-19, but we can't be certain. However my late wife Siân Busby's uncle Peter did die of, or with, Covid-19. And one of our friends has been seriously and possibly permanently incapacitated by the terrible illness.

Once lockdown began, work and home became a 24/7 Covid-19 reporting hub. My journalism and most of my broadcasting took place in our living room or (my preferred office, where I write now) on our bed. In this instance working from home meant working all the time, because there was so much to find out, by ringing and texting doctors, scientists, ministers, MPs and assorted experts, or reading the astonishing amount of first-take global research on the pathology and potential treatments. This was the story of our age. Any time I took a break in my effort to understand what was happening I felt uneasy.

One upsetting part of the work was hearing from traumatised doctors who were witnessing death on a scale none of them had ever expected to experience in their careers. They were having to send home spouses and children of patients, telling them that most likely dad or mum, husband or wife, would die without them in the room or holding his or her hand. But probably more stressful were the emails I received from hundreds of people who were terrified of losing their livelihoods, or were frightened of being in lockdown alone, or whose loved ones were dying or had died. I tried to respond to all, other than those who were abusive (there was the predictably relentless torrent of personal abuse on social media).

What some viewers told me informed my journalism, especially about the government's slowness to increase testing capacity, or helped me shape the questions I asked at those bizarre 5pm televised Zoom press conferences held by the Prime Minister and his colleagues. There was no glossing this terrible story as being about other people. It was about all of us. One especially harrowing message was from the family of Damian Holland, who died at home age 56 in late April after repeatedly ringing NHS 111 and being told he was not ill enough to be taken into hospital. All this happened when Boris Johnson was, by his own account, having his life saved by the doctors and nurses of St Thomas's Hospital in London. And this disjunction between what happened to the PM and to Damian Holland prompted ITV News to highlight what is known as happy or silent hypoxia. This is when the oxygen levels of a sufferer fall to mortally dangerous levels, but without the ill person experiencing conspicuous breathing difficulties. I wrote about Damian in my blog and we got his story on air, in a short film by our Health Editor Emily Morgan, and almost immediately the Health Secretary Matt Hancock ordered a review into how NHS 111 conducts triage over the telephone and the criteria used for admitting a sufferer to hospital.

I was constantly sending messages to ministers and officials about people falling through the safety net they thought they were constructing. When I received an email from a desperate and vulnerable man who was threatening suicide because he had run out of cash, had no food and had spent fruitless hours on the phone to the Universal

Credit helpline, I contacted the Work and Pensions Secretary of State, Thérèse Coffey, who arranged for an official to call him. He got his money. These were the victories that mattered, even though they were not journalism in a conventional sense.

So many of the rules of the job had to be changed, for a while at least. In the face of what looked like a systematic government failure to take the right evasive action at the right time – too slow to lock down, too little personal protective clothing and equipment for those working in high-risk settings, too little testing, too little safeguarding of the vulnerable in care homes – the normal response for a political interviewer like me would have been to adopt a prosecutorial approach at those televised press conferences or on my show. But the scale of the crisis somehow made it wrong to accuse. Instead I tried to ask constructive questions about, for example, the shortage of PPE but even then some viewers accused me of doing a "gotcha". It was also frustrating that so many questions seemed to fall into the black holes of a government with other priorities.

From an early stage, I was obsessed with why we were testing so many fewer people than countries with a lower mortality rate like Germany, or why we weren't being asked to wear face coverings, or whether too many sick people were at large in the community because only those with a high fever or persistent cough were being asked to quarantine. For example, on April 3rd, I asked the Health Secretary Matt Hancock and the Deputy Chief Medical Officer Jonathan Van-Tam whether loss of taste and smell – or "anosmia" – should be seen as a tell-tale symptom. Professor Van-Tam said the government's experts on the New and Emerging Respiratory Virus Threats Advisory Group had been asked their advice and concluded that it would not be helpful to add anosmia to the simple list of symptoms that trigger quarantine. And that seemed to be that. Although six weeks later the quarantine criteria were finally changed.

There was an even longer delay, of three months, between my putting questions on whether face coverings should be worn in social settings and the government making it mandatory to wear them in shops. And the lag was weeks rather than months between questions about whether the two-metre social-distance rule was causing too much economic damage, and the adoption of a more flexible rule. To be clear, I am not arguing I got everything right. Far from it. I cringe at some of my naïve lines of enquiry. Professor Van-Tam rightly ticked me off when I appeared to be asking – which I didn't think I was, my question came out wonky – whether self-administered pin-prick blood tests could be a useful tool for assessing whether someone was presently infected.

But too often ministers and officials seemed to pooh-pooh the experience and practice of other countries. There was a depressing British exceptionalism on display. I respected the scientists most when they admitted how little they really knew, which the Chief Scientific Adviser Sir Patrick Vallance and the Chief Medical Officer Chris Whitty conceded from time to time, and was disappointed at how rarely this led the government to take a precautionary approach to policy making (even if there was doubt about the exact efficacy of wearing face coverings, there would have been no cost in mandating they should be worn in certain settings).

All of which is to say that the imperative of being calm and impartial, which has been my compass all my career, from the *Financial Times*, to the BBC and to ITV, has been tricky. Being gripped and interested has, however, been a piece of cake right from the start, partly because of where it all started, namely China. For 20 years I made it a priority to understand the causes and implications of the rise and rise of China. In 2013 I filmed a documentary in Wuhan called *How China Fooled the World*, about whether the Chinese boom was about to go bust. So as soon as coronavirus caused turmoil in this huge city of 11 million people, largely unknown in the West but connected to us via the scheduled flights I had taken there, I paid more than normal attention, though I was not sure where it would take us.

At the time, in January, I had been looking forward to a relatively quiet 2020, after four of the busiest years of my professional life that had encompassed a historic vote to leave the European Union, two changes of prime minister, two general elections, and the mayhem of negotiations to leave the EU and associated parliamentary battles. Covering a government led by Boris Johnson was probably never going to be boring, but after his decisive general election victory in

December 2019, politics would surely feel a bit more stable and normal.

I was disabused at a dinner on February 11th, where I had a long conversation with a senior minister about the implications of Covid-19 for the UK. That night I emailed a summary of this conversation to my senior ITV and ITV News colleagues, to help them shape our coverage of what was already a big international story. This is what this minister told me, as relayed in my contemporaneous email: "If there is a pandemic, the peak will be March, April, May . . . the risk is 60 percent of the population getting it. With a mortality rate of perhaps just over one percent, we are looking at not far off 500,000 deaths."

What the minister already knew, and told me, was that this illness was far more lethal for the elderly than for younger people. And he also, reassuringly, explained how anyone returning to the UK from Wuhan would be compelled to quarantine in government requisitioned facilities. There was an impression given of a serious and credible plan to keep the virus from our shores. But at the same time there was a frank admission that in a world of global travel, and when Chinese people were probably already infecting citizens in many other countries, there was a significant risk of epidemic or pandemic in the UK. What was also striking was the way that this minister and the government as a whole was deferring to the Chief Medical Officer, Chris Whitty.

Latterly, the Prime Minister and his colleagues have stressed that when they say they have been "following the science", they take responsibility for their policies and exercise discretion. Back in February however I was left in no doubt that Chris Whitty – whether he liked it or chose it or not – was in effect in charge. "Following the science" meant acting on the recommendations of Whitty and the Scientific Advisory Group for Emergencies (SAGE), on which Whitty sat and which was chaired by the Chief Scientific Adviser, Sir Patrick Vallance. "We are guided in everything by Chris Whitty," was what the minister said that night.

This should not really come as a surprise. There was no one at the apex of the Cabinet with any serious background in science or medicine. And what compounded the uncertainties was that this was a brand new illness that was poorly understood. This lack of expertise was also, to be frank, a problem for me in doing my day job. Back in 2007, when I was business editor of the BBC and was shouting from the rooftops that banks had taken crazy risks, that they were going bust and that we'd all end up poorer, I had the confidence to challenge the complacency of ministers, regulators and bankers because I had spent many years as a specialist financial reporter acquiring a deep knowledge of banking and markets. But in February and early March 2020, it would have been an act of supreme hubris for me to claim I had the background to challenge the analysis of Whitty, Vallance and the other SAGE scientists. In those early days, when they gave private briefings to groups of political and science journalists, we were there to learn and probe, but few of us were expert enough to argue they were not doing what they should to keep us safe.

Hindsight, even at this near distance, raises important questions about whether we should have been less trusting. Having reviewed the minutes of SAGE's meetings in February, what stands out, and will eventually be the focus of an expected public inquiry, is that more or less from the start among the scientists and ministers there was a fatalism that the best to be achieved was to slow the spread of the virus, so that the peak of infection would not overwhelm the NHS. The policy of trying to suppress it almost totally, as happened in parts of Asia, was rejected, seemingly without serious debate. The official policy, as recorded in the minutes of a SAGE meeting on February 25th, was that "interventions should seek to contain, delay and reduce the peak incidence of cases, in that order". There was no consideration given to the Chinese, Korean, Taiwanese and Singaporean strategies of attempting to eliminate the virus altogether through mass testing and isolation of infected and potentially infected individuals. Partly that was because the UK started the crisis with limited public-sector testing facilities and very little capacity in Public Health England to trace potential sufferers. Partly, I fear, it was because of a misplaced conviction that British experts knew better than the Asians. All the talk in SAGE in February and early March was of abandoning testing and tracing outside of hospitals once the virus was surging in the community. There was no discussion of a headlong wartime-style charge over just a few weeks to expand testing and tracing capacity – though this is precisely what happened two months later.

The conviction of the government's experts, including Whitty and Vallance, was that the virus would do what the virus would do. We had no natural immunity and a vaccine was probably years away. The risk of suppressing it too fast and too soon was that it would rear its vicious head with a vengeance just a few months later, probably in the depths of winter when the NHS would be least able to cope. Or so they feared. Better then for more of us to become ill and recover, probably with some kind of immunity, sooner rather than later (though obviously the old and more vulnerable would always have to be shielded).

After a conversation I had with a senior member of the government on March 12th, there was an almighty public outcry after I disclosed in an instantly written blog that "the strategy of the British government in minimising the impact of Covid-19 is to allow the virus to pass through the entire population so that we acquire 'herd immunity', but at a much delayed speed so that . . . the health service is not overwhelmed". The idea that we had such limited control of our Covid-19 destiny was anathema to most, and 11 days later was rejected by the Prime Minister too, when he adopted near total lockdown.

What of Dominic Cummings, Boris Johnson's most powerful aide, whose influence over the Prime Minister and government has become the stuff of legend and myth? He was otherwise engaged for much of February, as was Boris Johnson, but from early March he understood the gravity of the challenge ahead. On March 2nd I broadcast that the economic shock from, and costs of, Covid-19 were likely to be greater than the 2008 banking crisis. And for what it's worth the easiest part of this story, given my background, was forecasting quite what a catastrophe it would be for our prosperity. By then Cummings had recognised this was likely to be the momentous struggle, far more than Brexit, that would define the government, though the government still pressed ahead with a budget that was largely irrelevant to containing the looming disaster. If anything defined the lack of government understanding of the virus it was that the Prime Minister, Cummings, the then most senior civil servant, the Cabinet Secretary, Sir Mark Sedwill, and the Health Secretary Matt Hancock all became ill with it. Social distancing was a concept they understood but didn't practise until too late either for themselves or, some would say, for the country.

Cummings later acknowledged there were "a lot of things I could have done better in general in dealing with the whole crisis . . . a lot of things I could have done better over the last few months." He went out of his way to plead that he was a relatively early proponent of comprehensive lockdown, and it is certainly true he got there significantly before the Prime Minister. His mea culpa was made on May 25th in the garden of 10 Downing Street, when he hosted the most surreal press conference I've ever attended. His admission of error did not extend to his decision on the night of March 27th to drive his wife and child hundreds of miles from his home in London to a cottage on his father's farm in Durham, in apparent defiance of lockdown rules. Nor did it extend to the subsequent 30-mile drive to Barnard Castle, when recovered from Covid-19, to test, he said, whether he could drive safely in that his "eyesight seemed to have been affected by the disease". I asked him whether his night-time flight had undermined the credibility of the social distancing and lockdown rules urged on us by the government to keep us safe. His defence was, characteristically, that it was not his actions, which he insisted were allowed in his circumstances, that had damaged confidence in the rules but media coverage of them. This precept, that the government is never wrong, it's just wilfully misunderstood by the press and television journalists, may turn out to be the defining conceit of Boris Johnson's government.

The corollary of course is that the journalism of ITV and ITV News, our commitment to impartiality, objectivity, holding power to account, matters more than ever. In 36 years in journalism, divided almost half and half between print and television, I've never sought a quiet life. Right now I could do with a break. But for all of us, there is no sleep until a vaccine is available. And for ITV News and our competitors, this is the story that will not only define the prosperity, solidarity, confidence and wellbeing of the nation, but will, I hope and trust, reinforce our licence, our mandate, our mission to shine the brightest light on the decision-makers that shape our lives.

Acknowledgements

Thanks go to all those who work for ITV News. Teamwork is at the heart of everything we do and this book is no exception. The dedication, skill and commitment of everyone in our international, national and regional newsrooms and bureaus made covering the stories in this book possible.

We are immensely grateful to all the people who helped ITV News cover the opening months of the pandemic. They included many medical staff, carers, key workers, scientific experts, public officials and members of the public both in the UK and around the world who offered information to our news teams or shared their own stories. We are grateful to all those who've given their time, knowledge, expertise and insight to help us fairly and accurately report the story of the pandemic.

Finally, we would like to thank all of ITV News' viewers and online users; the millions of people who trusted us to do our best to report the biggest story of our time accurately, impartially and fairly. We are grateful for the trust they placed in us.